Political Science

ILLUSTRATED SEARCH STRATEGY AND SOURCES

WITH AN INTRODUCTION TO LEGAL RESEARCH FOR UNDERGRADUATES

(LIBRARY RESEARCH GUIDE SERIES, NO. 12)

by

Roger C. Lowery
Professor of Political Science
University of North Carolina at Wilmington

Sue A. Cody
Head of Reference Services
University of North Carolina at Wilmington

The Pierian Press
Ann Arbor, Michigan
1993

Internet Addresses

Roger C. Lowery
LOWERY@VXC.UNCWIL.EDU

Sue A. Cody
CODYS@VXC.UNCWIL.EDU

ISBN: 0-87650-290-7

The Pierian Press
Box 1808
5000 Washtenaw
Ann Arbor, MI 48106-1808
1-800-678-2435

TABLE OF CONTENTS

PREFACE

Do You Need This Book?

This book is for you if:

- You are a college student (undergraduate or graduate) majoring in political science faced with research that requires information from library sources.

- You are a college student in any major that requires the use of government documents; legal sources; specialized reference sources of biographical, statistical, and factual information; or computerized bibliographic databases.

- You are a professor whose students often need to locate information on politics and government.

- You are a librarian often asked for advice by faculty or students on which public affairs information sources to use. This guide can also be used as a collection development tool to build a basic reference collection in politics and government.

Caveat Lector (Let the Reader Beware)

- Innovations in information technology are accelerating. Practically every week, enhancements are made to finding aids. Each year, new approaches to information storage and retrieval are announced. For example, innovations in computer networking provide increasing access to library information sources from remote locations, such as your classroom or even your residence.

- Because of these rapid innovations, this guide cannot be completely up-to-date. Although the basic search strategies remain essentially stable, the finding aids that you apply those search strategies to are often evolving. The conventional, print-format finding aids in college libraries are rapidly being replaced by more powerful, computerized versions. This guide does cover both print and computerized formats and their search strategies at the present level of evolution.

- Ask a reference librarian which new information technologies are available to you.

ACKNOWLEDGMENTS

We are indebted to the entire reference staff of Randall Library at UNC-Wilmington—especially Arlene Hanerfeld, who reviewed the government documents chapter. Gene Huguelet, the director of Randall Library, also lent his encouragement. We are also grateful for the support of the faculty of the political science department, with a particular note of thanks to the former chair, Jim Dixon, who proofread and offered useful comments on the manuscript. Special thanks are due our editor, Tom Kirk, for his patience and guidance.

CREDITS FOR FIGURES

Without the cooperation of the many publishers cited below, this book could not have been the illustrated guide we set out to create. These publishers have granted us permission to reproduce excerpts from their copyrighted works. To make this list of figures complete, the uncopyrighted materials used in illustrations are also cited.

Figure 1-1: Derivational Dictionaries: *Safire's Political Dictionary* and *American Political Terms: An Historical Dictionary*. Reprinted by permission.

From *Safire's Political Dictionary* by William Safire. Copyright © 1968, 1972, 1978 by William Safire. Reprinted by permission of Random House, Inc.

Reprinted from *American Political Terms: An Historical Dictionary* by Hans Sperber and Travis Trittschuh by permission of the Wayne State University Press. Copyright © 1962. All rights reserved.

Figure 1-2: An Analytical Dictionary: *American Political Dictionary*, Seventh edition by Jack C. Plano and Milton Greenburg. Copyright © 1985 by Holt, Rinehart and Winston, Inc. Reprinted by permission of the publisher.

Figure 1-3: *Encyclopaedia of the Social Sciences*. Reprinted with permission of Macmillan Publishing Company from *Encyclopaedia of the Social Sciences*, Vol. XIV by Edwin R.A. Seligman. Copyright © 1934, and renewed 1962, by Macmillan Publishing Company.

Figure 1-4: *International Encyclopedia of the Social Sciences*. Reprinted with permission of Macmillan Publishing Company, a Division of Macmillan, Inc., from *International Encyclopedia of the Social Sciences*, Vol. 17 (Index), David L. Sills, Editor. Copyright © 1968 by Crowell Collier and Macmillan, Inc.

Figure 1-5: *International Encyclopedia of the Social Sciences*. Reprinted with permission of Macmillan Publishing Company, a Division of Macmillan, Inc., from *International Encyclopedia of the Social Sciences*, Vol. 7, David L. Sills, Editor. Copyright © 1968 by Crowell Collier and Macmillan, Inc.

Figure 1-6: *International Encyclopedia of the Social Sciences*. Reprinted with permission of Macmillan Publishing Company, a Division of Macmillan, Inc., from *International Encyclopedia of the Social Sciences*, Vol. 7, David L. Sills, Editor. Copyright © 1968 by Crowell Collier and Macmillan, Inc.

Figure 1-7: *Social Science Encyclopedia*, edited by Adam Kuper and Jessica Kuper. Copyright © 1985 by Routledge, Inc. Reprinted by permission.

Figure 1-8: *Contemporary International Politics*, by Robert D. Cantor. Copyright © 1986 by West Educational Publishing. Reprinted by permission.

Figure 1-9: Index to *Global Terrorism: A Historical Bibliography*, edited by Suzanne Robitaille Ontiveros. Copyright © 1986 by ABC-Clio. Reprinted by permission.

Figure 1-10: *Global Terrorism: A Historical Bibliography*, edited by Suzanne Robitaille Ontiveros. Copyright © 1986 by ABC-Clio. Reprinted by permission.

Figure 1-11: *International Terrorism: An Annotated Bibliography and Research Guide*, by Augustus R. Norton. Copyright © 1980. Reprinted by permission of the author.

Figure 1-12: *International Terrorism: A Bibliography*, by Amos Lakos. Copyright © 1986. Reprinted by permission of Westview Press, Boulder, Colorado.

Figure 1-13: *Encyclopedia of Terrorism and Political Violence*, by John Thackrah. Copyright © 1987 by Routledge, Inc. Reprinted by permission.

Figure 2-1: LS/2000 Online Catalog and Card Catalog Records for *Punishing International Terrorists*, by John Francis Murphy. Reprinted by permission of Ameritech Information Systems and OCLC Online Computer Library Center, Inc.

Figure 2-2: Index to *Punishing International Terrorists*, by John Francis Murphy. Copyright © 1985 by Rowman and Littlefield Publishers. Reprinted by permission of the publisher.

Figure 2-3: LS/2000 Online Catalog and Card Catalog Records for *Winning Back the Sky*, by David G. Hubbard. Reprinted by permission of Ameritech Information Systems and OCLC Online Computer Library Center, Inc.

Figure 2-4: Johnny Hart, "B.C." comic strip. Los Angeles: Creators Syndicate, 1971. By permission of Johnny Hart and Creators Syndicate, Inc.

Figure 2-5: *Library of Congress Subject Headings*, 14th ed., 1991. Washington, DC: Library of Congress.

Figure 2-6: *Library of Congress Subject Headings*, 14th ed., 1991. Washington, DC: Library of Congress.

Figure 2-7: *Library of Congress Subject Headings*, 14th ed., 1991. Washington, DC: Library of Congress.

Figure 2-8: LS/2000 Online Catalog Subject Search. Reprinted by permission of Ameritech Information Systems.

Figure 2-9: LS/2000 Online Catalog and Card Catalog Records for *Kidnap, Hijack, and Extortion*, by Richard Clutterbuck. Reprinted by permission of Ameritech Information Systems and OCLC Online Computer Library Center, Inc.

Figure 2-10: LS/2000 Online Catalog Search by Call Number. Reprinted by permission of Ameritech Information Systems.

Figure 2-11: *Book Review Digest*, page 780, 1986 Cumulation. Copyright © 1986 by The H.W. Wilson Company. Material reproduced with permission of the publisher.

Figure 2-12: *Book Review Index 1986 Cumulation*, edited by Barbara Beach. Copyright © 1987 by Gale Research Inc. Reproduced by permission of the publisher.

Figure 2-13: *Essay and General Literature Index*, page 1634, 1985-1989 Cumulation. Copyright © 1989 by The H.W. Wilson Company. Material reproduced with permission of the publisher.

Figure 2-14: *Essay and General Literature Index*, page 2022, 1985-1989 Cumulation. Copyright © 1989 by The H.W. Wilson Company. Material reproduced with permission of the publisher.

Figure 3-1: *Public Affairs Information Service Bulletin*, 1987 Cumulation. Copyright © 1987 by Public Affairs Information Service, Inc. Reprinted by permission.

Figure 3-2: *PAIS International in Print*, May-August 1991 Cumulation. Copyright © 1991 by Public Affairs Information Service, Inc. Reprinted by permission.

Figure 3-3: *General Periodicals Index—Academic Libraries Edition*™. Copyright © 1992 by Information Access Company. Reprinted by permission.

Figure 3-4: Key Word Search of *General Periodicals Index—Academic Libraries Edition*™. Copyright © 1992 by Information Access Company. Reprinted by permission.

Figure 3-5: *Social Sciences Index*, page 23, Volume 2, 1975-1976. Copyright © 1976 by The H.W. Wilson Company. Material reproduced with permission of the publisher.

Figure 3-6: *United States Political Science Documents*, Volume 12 (1986), Part 1: Indexes. Copyright © 1987 by NASA Industrial Applications Center, University of Pittsburgh. Reprinted by permission.

Figure 3-7: *United States Political Science Documents*, Volume 12 (1986), Part 2: Document Descriptions. Copyright © 1987 by NASA Industrial Applications Center, University of Pittsburgh. Reprinted by permission.

Figure 3-8: *Social Sciences Citation Index*™, 1987, Volume 1. Reprinted with the permission of the Institute for Scientific Information™ (ISI™). Copyright © 1992.

Figure 3-9: *Social Sciences Citation Index*™, 1987, Volume 4. Reprinted with the permission of the Institute for Scientific Information™ (ISI™). Copyright © 1992.

Figure 3-10: *Social Sciences Citation Index*™, 1986, Volume 6. Reprinted with the permission of the Institute for Scientific Information™ (ISI™). Copyright © 1992.

Figure 3-11: *Social Sciences Citation Index*™, 1986, Volume 4. Reprinted with the permission of the Institute for Scientific Information™ (ISI™). Copyright © 1992.

Figure 3-12: *Readers' Guide to Periodical Literature*, page 45, Volume 45, 1985. Copyright © 1985 by The H.W. Wilson Company. Material reproduced with permission of the publisher.

Figure 3-13: *New York Times Index*, 1986. Copyright © 1986 by the New York Times Company. Reprinted by permission.

Figure 3-14: *New York Times Index*, 1986. Copyright © 1986 by the New York Times Company. Reprinted by permission.

Figure 3-15: *National Newspaper Index*™. Copyright © 1992 by Information Access Company. Reprinted by permission.

Figure 3-16: *NewsBank Index*. Copyright © 1991 by NewsBank, Inc. Reprinted by permission.

Figure 4-1: *Monthly Catalog of United States Government Publications*, Cumulative Subject Index, 1987. Washington, DC: Government Printing Office.

Figure 4-2: *Monthly Catalog of United States Government Publications*, Main Entry Section, 1987. Washington, DC: Government Printing Office.

Figure 5-11: *Congressional Quarterly Weekly Report*, Cumulative Index for 1989 and May 6, 1989 issue, page 1035. Copyright © 1989 by Congressional Quarterly Inc. Reprinted by permission.

Figure 5-12: *Congressional Quarterly Weekly Report*, October 22, 1988, Table of Contents. Copyright © 1988 by Congressional Quarterly Inc. Reprinted by permission.

Figure 5-13: *Code of Federal Regulations*, 1991 Index. Washington, DC: Government Printing Office.

Figure 5-14: *Code of Federal Regulations*, Title 14, Federal Aviation Administration, DOT. Washington, DC: Government Printing Office.

Figure 5-15: *Federal Register Index*, January-December 1989. Washington, DC: Government Printing Office.

Figure 5-16: *Federal Register Index*, January-December 1989. Washington, DC: Government Printing Office.

Figure 5-17: *Federal Register*, Volume 54, No. 4, January 6, 1989. Washington, DC: Government Printing Office.

Figure 5-18: *Weekly Compilation of Presidential Documents*, 1989. Washington, DC: Government Printing Office.

Figure 5-19: *Federal Regulatory Directory*, 5th ed. Copyright © 1986 by Congressional Quarterly Inc. Reprinted by permission.

Figure 5-20: *Government Agencies*, edited by Donald R. Whitnah. Copyright © 1983 by Donald R. Whitnah and published in 1983 by Greenwood Press. Reprinted by permission of Greenwood Publishing Group, Inc., Westport, CT.

Figure 5-21: Slip Opinion for "Lauro Lines S.R.L. v. Chasser et al." Washington, DC: Government Printing Office.

Figure 5-22: Mullenix, Linda S. 1989. "Is a Trial Court's Decision Not to Enforce a Forum Selection Clause Immediately Appealable?" *Preview of United States Supreme Court Cases*. 1988-89 Term: 388-390. Copyright © 1988 by the American Bar Association. Reprinted by permission.

Figure 5-23: *United States Supreme Court Reports Digest, Lawyers Edition*, Volume 16D, General Index, 1990. Reprinted by permission of Lawyers Cooperative Publishing, a division of Thomson Legal Publishing, Inc.

Figure 5-24: *United States Supreme Court Reports Digest, Lawyers Edition*, Volume 1, 1984. Reprinted by permission of Lawyers Cooperative Publishing, a division of Thomson Legal Publishing, Inc.

Figure 5-25: *American Jurisprudence 2d*, General Index, 1991. Reprinted by permission of Lawyers Cooperative Publishing, a division of Thomson Legal Publishing, Inc.

Figure 5-26: *American Jurisprudence 2d*, Volume 8, 1980. Reprinted by permission of Lawyers Cooperative Publishing, a division of Thomson Legal Publishing, Inc.

Figure 5-27: *United States Treaties and Other International Agreements*, Volume 20, Part 3, 1969. Washington, DC: Government Printing Office.

Figure 5-28: *Treaties in Force*, 1990. Washington, DC: Government Printing Office.

Figure 6-1: *Biography Index*, page 615, 1986-1988, Volume 15. Copyright © 1988 by The H.W. Wilson Company. Material reproduced with permission of the publisher.

Figure 6-2: *Biobase Master Cumulation*, 1990. Copyright © 1990 by Gale Research Inc. Reproduced by permission of the publisher.

Figure 6-3: *Biobase Master Cumulation Bibliographic Key*, 1990. Copyright © 1990 by Gale Research Inc. Reproduced by permission of the publisher.

Figure 6-4: *Biography Almanac*, Volume 1, 3d edition, edited by Susan L. Stetler. Copyright © 1987 by Gale Research Inc. Reproduced by permission of the publisher.

Figure 6-5: *Current Biography Yearbook 1973*. Copyright © 1973, 1974 by The H.W. Wilson Company. Material reproduced with permission of the publisher.

Figure 6-6: *International Who's Who*, 47th ed. 1983. Copyright © 1983 by Europa Publications, Ltd. Reprinted by permission.

Figure 6-7: *General Periodicals Index—Academic Libraries Edition*™. Copyright © 1992 by Information Access Company. Reprinted by permission.

Figure 6-8: *Data Map*, Subject Index. Reprinted from *Data Map 1989*, by Allison Ondrasik. Copyright © 1989 by The Oryx Press, 4041 N. Central at Indian School Rd., Phoenix, AZ 85012. Reprinted with permission.

Figure 6-9: *Data Map*, Listing of Tables. Reprinted from *Data Map 1989*, by Allison Ondrasik. Copyright © 1989 by The Oryx Press, 4041 N. Central at Indian School Rd., Phoenix, AZ 85012. Reprinted with permission.

INTRODUCTION

LIBRARY RESEARCH: WHY, WHEN, WHAT, AND HOW

WHY YOU NEED TO LEARN TO USE THE LIBRARY

When you look back over your schooling prior to entering college, you will probably agree that a great deal of your time was spent memorizing and absorbing information that the teacher and textbook authors collected and organized for you. In college, while you still are required to memorize a large amount of information, there is a new emphasis on learning to find and analyze theories and observations on your own. Success in college (as well as in all post-graduate careers or endeavors) requires the skills necessary to collect and interpret ideas and evidence. A veritable gold mine of information, empirical and analytical, is available in your college library. Once you have learned to efficiently search out and utilize that information, you are well on your way to success in educational as well as vocational pursuits.

WHEN TO USE THE LIBRARY

In your political science course work, you will often be given class assignments that require library research. The need for library research is most obvious with term paper assignments. However, you may have already discovered that many other forms of classwork and homework either require or benefit from searching out information in the library. Day-to-day reading assignments in your textbook or in reserved reading materials can often leave you with questions you want answered. Perhaps, for example, the subject of airline hijacking as a terrorist tactic has come up in your classwork or homework and you want to find out more about specific incidents or countermeasures to prevent future hijackings. Busy faculty are often unavailable to give you such information. The ability to find those answers on your own is often part of the assignment.

WHAT TO LOOK FOR IN THE LIBRARY

As you proceed through your undergraduate courses, your library searches will take different forms. With a term paper or other major research project (perhaps one analyzing government policies intended to prevent terrorist hijacking of commercial airliners), your library search efforts will be lengthy and broad in scope. However, many times you will head to the library for a much shorter search effort, much more narrowly focused on only one or a few information sources (such as the facts of a specific airliner hijacking incident). In both cases, you will be using the same sets of library research skills.

As the study of politics has adopted more of the tools and methods of the natural and physical sciences, greater emphasis has been placed upon the collection and analysis of empirical data. Most undergraduate programs in political science now introduce the student to at least elementary levels of quantitative methods of research. As the political science discipline has integrated scientific methods with other traditional methods of analysis, undergraduate course assignments now send students to the library in search of data as well as books and articles. Returning to our terrorism example, perhaps you are asked to find out which airport has been most frequently used by terrorists to board airliners that were then hijacked.

HOW TO LOOK FOR INFORMATION IN THE LIBRARY

When faced with any task that requires library research, your success in using the library depends upon two sets of skills: 1) the *searching skills* to use the appropriate *finding aids* (catalogs, indexes, bibliographies, etc.) to quickly find the most up-to-date *sources* (books, periodical and newspaper articles, government documents, reference works, etc.) of relevant information, and 2) the *analytical skills* to thoroughly utilize and evaluate those sources once you have used finding aids to locate them. The purpose of this guide is to teach you these searching and analytical skills and to introduce you to the reference sources most commonly used in political science. It is also important for you to become acquainted with the manner in which your library is arranged. Many libraries organize their holdings in more than one of the following separate collections—the main book or *monograph* collection, the *reference* collection, the *index* collection, the *periodicals* collection, and the *government documents* collection.

THE ORGANIZATION OF THIS GUIDEBOOK

The following chapters are intended to introduce you to most of the library search strategies and basic sources which undergraduate political science students will need to know. By using the sample topic, prevention of aircraft hijacking, you will be shown the searching and analytical skills and the basic information sources available on many different aspects of that topic. We will demonstrate how to research broad historical, analytical, or theoretical topics as well as how to find quite specific factual, biographical, or statistical information.

The first chapter will illustrate how to use the library to choose—and narrow to a workable size—a topic for a major term project. You will also be shown why it is useful to consider several alternate approaches to the study of the same topic. Other chapters will illustrate how to use the library to locate more specific information relevant either to a term project or to shorter research tasks.

The order in which we have arranged the chapters of this book is not the only sequence to use in researching political science topics. Hence, you may want to read Chapter 7, "Computer Database Searching", immediately after Chapter 3, "Using Periodical and Newspaper Articles". You may also find it useful to read Chapter 6, "Locating General Information", before you read either Chapter 4, "Locating U.S. Government Documents", or Chapter 5, "Legal Research". While we often refer from one chapter to another, we have attempted to make each chapter understandable even when read out of sequence.

CHAPTER 1

GETTING STARTED ON A TERM PROJECT: CHOOSING AND NARROWING YOUR TOPIC

This first chapter focuses upon the library skills and sources most useful to the student faced with beginning a major term project, a written or oral report that requires the collection and analysis of a relatively large amount of general information. Later chapters take up the other library skills and sources needed to thoroughly research your term project or to locate information needed for shorter or specialized research tasks.

CHOOSING AN INTERESTING TOPIC (TO GET YOU MOTIVATED)

Being genuinely interested in your research topic is important in several ways. Such interest will motivate your efforts (both research and writing are work for most people—students and professionals). An interesting research problem will seem more challenging and rewarding than burdensome and tedious. If you are lucky enough to be allowed to choose your own topic, make the most of the opportunity. If your topic has been assigned to you and doesn't seem particularly interesting, withhold final judgment until you have had a chance to learn more about the subject. As you have no doubt already found with many people you have known, so it is with academic research topics, initial appearances can be very deceiving. A topic that motivates you, good search skills, and useful sources are the three main ingredients for successful library research.

We selected international terrorism as a sample topic for this library research guide because we think it will be both interesting and motivating to most undergraduate students of political science. Political terrorism is a difficult and significant problem with high stakes and a broad impact. Research into the causes, nature, and consequences of terrorism presents an intellectually challenging task. Controversies about terrorism are complex and timely, often involving long-term grievances that will not be quickly or easily solved. Thus, there already exists a large body of information on the topic, and it will undoubtedly continue to grow. The topic is broad in scope. Terrorism is subject to both traditional and quantitative forms of analysis using information drawn from both U.S. and international sources.

Narrowing Your Topic
(To Make It Manageable)

Because media coverage of terrorist-related events has been so prominent in recent years, you may already be aware of some of the most basic questions and controversies concerning international terrorism. What motivates a terrorist? What forms of terrorism characterize the past, present, and future? What can be done to prevent terrorism? Just one of these questions could be used as a starting point for your topic. Because so much is written about terrorism, you will need to narrow the scope of your project even further. You may wish to pick a particular terrorist incident to analyze, or select a type of terrorist activity and investigate its prevention.

It is important to keep your mind open to these alternatives for three reasons. First, considering alternative approaches allows you to more confidently select an interesting topic and narrow it to a workable size. Second, in the process of considering alternative approaches, you will probably discover more useful sources of information than you might otherwise. Third, a major purpose of both the introduction and conclusion in your finished term paper or research report is to place your specific findings within the broader context of that subject.

In the remainder of this book, we have narrowed the broad topic of political terrorism to the more specific question of what government policies have been adopted to reduce the incidence of aircraft hijacking. Researching this narrowed topic, we will see that, in recent years, the development of new anti-hijacking policies has contributed to a significant decline in the number of aircraft hijacked by political terrorists. However, we will also find that many terrorists simply switched to aircraft bombings as their tactic of choice once anti-hijacking policies were improved.

Documenting Your Sources
(To Allow You to Locate and Cite Your References)

An all-too-common frustration in doing library research is to find a piece of information that you need but later to forget in what source you found it. The habit of documenting every source in which you find information will save you from this time-consuming frustration. There are two sets of notes that you need to record to thoroughly document your library sources. One will record the information required to locate the publication in the library. The second will record the information needed to complete a bibliographic reference for your source.

First, you need to record information that is required to locate the publication containing your information. Hence, you must have the call number for each book and government document in order to locate it in the stacks. You will also need call numbers for periodicals if your library shelves periodicals by call number. Regardless, you will need volume number, issue date, and page numbers to locate articles within periodicals.

Second, you need to have a record of the additional information that will give you a complete *bibliographic reference* for each source. Such a reference includes three parts: author, title, and *facts of publication*. For books, the facts of publication are the place, publisher, and year of publication. For magazine articles, the facts of publication are the magazine title, starting and ending pages, and issue date. For journal articles,[1] the facts of publication are the journal title, volume number, starting and ending pages, and year of publication. For the order in which this information is listed in a formal bibliographic reference, you need to consult a style manual. In political science, the *Style Manual for Political Science* (reprinted in Appendix II) is the accepted standard. The *Style Manual for Political Science* will also describe and illustrate the correct bibliographic reference format for many other types of publications—including government documents, newspaper articles, chapters in books, etc.

LOCATING AUTHORITATIVE SUMMARIES
(TO GIVE YOU AN OVERVIEW OF YOUR TOPIC'S ISSUES AND VOCABULARY)

When you had a term paper to do in high school, probably the first place you looked for information was an encyclopedia. Why? Because it gave you an overview of your topic, with a lot of information packed into a relatively brief article. For the same reason, you are wise to start your college term project research with a search for similar kinds of **authoritative summaries**. They will give you an overview of your topic's basic questions, issues, or dimensions as well as definitions of the vocabulary used to describe and explain them. Your college library offers authoritative summaries of political science topics in at least four kinds of sources: dictionaries, encyclopedias, textbooks, and subject bibliographies.

Political Science Dictionaries

You have often used general dictionaries of two sorts, the standard desk types like *Webster's New World Dictionary of American English* (3d college ed., 1988), and the larger unabridged types like *Webster's Third New International Dictionary* (1981). If you have not already, you should now become familiar with some of the specialized dictionaries that focus on politics and government. Besides defining political terms and phrases not always found in general dictionaries, these specialized political science dictionaries can also provide more information about the origin and change over time in the usage of political terms as well as their historical and contemporary significance.

A few, very useful political science dictionaries emphasize **etymology**, that is, the origin of a word or phrase and how its meaning has evolved. Figure 1-1 illustrates two good examples of these **derivational dictionaries**: *Safire's Political Dictionary* (1978), which focuses on the origin of political "catchwords" and slogans, and *American Political Terms: An Historical Dictionary* (1962). Notice that Safire traces the probable origin of the term, "terrorism", to the "reign of terror" following the French Revolution in the late 1700s. Both dictionaries say the first American use of the term was during the fighting in Kansas in the late 1850s. Of course, the thorough researcher is still well advised to consult the general, twenty-volume *Oxford English Dictionary* (2d ed., 1989).

---

[1]See the beginning of Chapter 3 for an explanation of the common differences that will help you determine whether a periodical is a magazine or journal.

Figure 1-1: Derivational Dictionaries: *Safire's Political Dictionary* **and**
American Political Terms: An Historical Dictionary

next season—he will find a new spark that will enable him once again to tell it like it is."

on: .... would render the

TENNIS SHOES, *see* **LITTLE OLD LADIES IN TENNIS SHOES.**

TERRORISM   persuasion by fear; the intimidation of society by a small group, using as its weapon that society's repugnance at the murder of innocents.

Terrorisme may have originated with the Jacobins of the French Revolution. *Le Néologiste Français* (published in 1796) claimed that the extremists had coined the term about themselves and used it proudly, but soon after the "reign of terror," the word was a term of abuse with a con-...... ...... In 1795 Brit-

holidays; in the eleventh century, the *assassins* roamed Persia and Syria, killing political leaders systematically, always with a dagger as a part ....act: in the nineteenth .... may be advisable in some exception... cases; consistent conciliation of terrorism on the other hand is bound to claim a higher toll in human life in the long run than resisting it . . . societies facing a determined terrorist onslaught will opt for a hard-line policy in any case." The unanswerable question that faces all students of terrorism: What to do when a terrorist group builds or acquires a nuclear weapon, and the means of its delivery?

The American use of the word was traced by Sperber and Trittschuh to an *Atlantic Monthly* in 1858: "Every form of terrorism [in Kansas], to .... alike instinctively

---

terrapin (system)   452

1931 *Wash. Merry-Go-Round* 105–6. Half an hour later, he [H. L. Stimson] appeared on the White House tennis court. . . . Next morning the newspapers published a detailed account of the importance which Mr. Stimson attached to his membership in the "Tennis Cabinet."

terrapin (system).
   Goodrich (in *Recollections,* 578n.) gives the historical background of the term:
When the Non-intercourse act [1809]—the last of the so-called "Restrictive Measures," and which by way of ridicule had been nick-named the "Terrapin System," was repealed—Dwight wrote the following. . . .
   .... ons of democratic woel

may be behind the use of the turtle as representing the East in a cartoon of 1829. (See Murrell, *Hist. Am. Graphic Humor* I.67, 112.)

terrorism.◄——

   Terrorism has not been found before 1858 in American sources, but it is no doubt much older. (The *OED* has *reign of terrorism* from 1795.)
1858 *At. Mon.* I.113/1. Every form of terrorism (in Kansas), to which tyrants all alike instinctively resort to disarm resistance to their will, was launched at the property, the lives, and the happiness of the defenceless settlers.
1868 *Harper's W.* 5 Sept. 563/2. Political Terrorism [head of article treating with .... win Southern elec-

Figure 1-2: An Analytical Dictionary: *American Political Dictionary*

Terrorism Actions undertaken by governments, individuals, or groups using violence or threats of violence for political purposes. Internatinal terrorism has included aircraft hijackings, political kidnappings, assassinations, bombing, arson, sabotage, and the holding of hostages. Most terrorism is practice by groups representing extremist political parties or positions. Typically, terrorism of the Left is aimed at promoting revolution against the established order, and terrorism of the Right is used to preserve and protect a privileged group or class.

Significance Terrorism has been used increasingly in recent years by Third World movements seeking to gain political and economic independence and to call attention to their cause. Terrorism has also been used to maintain positions of power, once secured. Citizens and officials of the United States, including diplomatic personnel, military officials, airline personnel, corportion executives, and tourists, have increasingly become the victims of terrorism. The United States government has been directly affected by terrorist actions. For example, American diplomatic and military hostages were seized by Iranian militants in 1980 and held for 444 days, with the connivance of the Iranian revolutionary government, before being released. Terrorism is difficult to combat, since innocent lives are often in jeopardy, and the terrorists appear willing to sacrifice their own. Basically, the problem of dealing with terrorists resolves itself into the following question: Should counterviolence be used against terrorists, or should an effort be made to placate them through political compromises? Although most countries have agreed through the United Nations not to give sanctuary to terrorists and hijackers, the problem continues. The use of military force by national armies to achieve political objectives constitutes a form of terrorism used especially in the Middle East in recent years.

Third World Those nations, constituting a majority of the interna-
_____ that are—with the exception of the oil-exporting coun-
_____ and underdeveloped in contrast with
_____ Most Third World
_____

Most political science dictionaries resemble one-volume encyclopedias with fairly lengthy, interpretative articles that provide theoretical and historical analysis. Figure 1-2 illustrates a widely-used example of these *analytical dictionaries*: the *American Political Dictionary* (8th ed., 1989). Notice that in addition to a definition and examples, this type of dictionary also provides a discussion of the political significance of the terms covered; in this case a summary of the goals and tactics of terrorists as well as the problems facing governments attempting to engage in counter-terrorist activities. For examples of terrorist tactics, note the sentence, "International terrorism has included aircraft hijackings,

Figure 1-3: *Encyclopaedia of the Social Sciences*

TERRITORIES, UNITED STATES. *See* POPULAR SOVEREIGNTY; SLAVERY.

TERRORISM is a term used to describe the method or the theory behind the method whereby an organized group or party seeks to achieve its avowed aims chiefly through the systematic use of violence. Terroristic acts are directed against persons who as individuals, agents or representatives of authority interfere with the ˌˌˌˌˌˌmation of the objectives of such a group. ˌˌ ˌˌˌˌˌˌˌrtv and machinery or the gained a footˌˌˌ. ˌ ˌˌˌˌ ˌˌ ˌˌˌ he re- nomena may be described as iˌˌˌˌ intimidation rather than of terrorism.

Intimidation differs from terrorism in that the intimidator, unlike the terrorist, merely threatens injury or material harm in order to arouse fear of severe punishment for non-compliance with his demands. The intimidator will resort only to the degree of violence needed to insure collection of tribute or to force certain persons to abstain from committing overt or covert acts. Having committed a crime or engaged in criminal practises, usually through hired underlings, a racketeer or an employing company whose anti-union labor "protective" machinery has been apprehended in unlawful acts will seek the protection of the law through influential politicians, purchasable attorneys and accommodating judges. The attitude of the political terrorist is entirely different. He imposes the punishment meted out by his organization upon those who are considered guilty or who are held to interfere with the revolutionary program; thus he serves notice that his organization will be satisfied with nothing short of removal of the undesired social or governmental system and of the persons be- ᵀˡˌ terrorist does not threaten; death or ˌˌ ˌˌ rogram of action, ˌˌˌˡ is

two ˌˌ ment may also caˌˌ ˌˌ Terrorism as a method is always chaˌˌˌˌ by the fact that it seeks to arouse not only the reigning government or the nation in control but also the mass of the people to a realization that constituted authority is no longer safely intrenched and unchallenged. The publicity value of the terroristic act is a cardinal point in the strategy of terrorism. If terror fails to elicit a wide response in circles outside of those at whom it is directly aimed, it is futile as a weapon in a social conflict. The logic of terroristic activity cannot fully be understood without a proper evaluation of the revealing nature of the terroristic act.

Terrorism differs in several important aspects from such phenomena as mob violence, mass insurrection and governmental terror. Terror practised by a government in office appears as law enforcement and is directed against the opposition, while terrorism in its proper sense ˌˌ ˌˌˌ defiance of law and is the means boˌˌˌ ˌˌˌ ˌˌ to demoralize a will to revolution requˌˌˌ ˌ ˌ ˌˌˌ ˌower the heroism of isolated individuals or ˌˌˌ small, well organized groups. The art of revolution must be sustained by the interested will of a large proportion of the population and by concerted mass operations.

J. B. S. HARDMAN

See: REVOLUTION AND COUNTER-REVOLUTION; ASSASSINATION; INTIMIDATION; VIOLENCE; RUSSIAN REVOLUTION; FRENCH REVOLUTION; BOLSHEVISM; SYNDICALISM; ANARCHISM.

Consult: Diehl, Karl, *Über Sozialismus, Kommunismus und Anarchismus* (4th ed. Jena 1922) ch. vi; Hunter, Robert, *Violence and the Labor Movement* (New York 1914) pt. i; Masaryk, T. G., *Russland und Europa,* 2 ˌˌˡˌ (Jena 1913), tr. by E. and C. Paul as *The Spirit of* ˌ ˌˌˌˌ) vol. ii, p. 95–114, 362–72; ˌˌˡˌˌˌˌ-revolutsionerov ˌ ˌˌˌˌrad

political kidnappings, assassinations, bombing, arson, sabotage, and the holding of hostages".

Additional examples of analytical dictionaries are provided by a series published by ABC-Clio, Inc., which offers separate titles on international relations, Latin America, Soviet and East European politics, the Middle East, and African politics, as well as political analysis and presidential-congressional politics. These and other dictionaries are listed in Appendix I ("Bibliography of Sources and Finding Aids").

Together, the derivational and analytical political science dictionaries are a good place to start locating authoritative summaries of your topic. These brief articles will introduce you to important dimensions of your topic, and are particularly useful in familiarizing you with its specialized vocabulary. You are now ready to turn to

Figure 1-4: *International Encyclopedia of the Social Sciences, Index Volume*

INDEX

Guilt 235

ethnomedicine 10:91
functional analysis 6:35
generations, political 6:92
    ~~hy~~ social 6:137, 139, 140
~~~~ ~~~~ ~176
interaction, socia~ ~~
interaction and personality 7:45b, 462
interaction process analysis 7:467
interest groups 7:486
internment and custody 8:146
interpersonal influence 4:182
Islamic countries 11:93
Japanese society 8:245
labor relations: developing countries 8:515
    ~~~564
politicai ~~~~.
political organization 1z:1~.
political science 12:290, 291
Quetelet, Adolphe 13:249, 253
race relations: social-psychological aspects 13:281
rank-size relations 13:323
reason analysis 13:339
reference groups 13:353

region 13:379
religion, sociology of 13:412
reward systems in industry 7:250
role: sociological aspects 13:553
Sapir, Edward 14:11
~~lf concept 14:155, 157
    ~~~254, 257
social ~~~~~
social institutions 14:41u
social movements 14:439, 449
social psychology 14:464
social structure 14:485, 489
society 14:585
sociological thought 15:26, 31
sociology of work 7:232
sociometry 15:53
speech community 9:384
stereotypes 15:260
    ~~ation, social 15:330
~~~~~
Growth of American ~~~~
    fertility control 5:384
Growth of Philosophic Radicalism, The (Halévy) 6:308
Growth of the Mind, The (Koffka) 8:436

Grundherr
    feudalism 5:395
Grundzüge der Psychologie (Ebbinghaus) 4:327
Guaranteed annual wage
    collective bargaining 8:497
Guardianship
    psychiatry, forensic 12:630
    ~~,
    paternalism 11:4~~
Guérard, Albert L.
    creativity 3:442
Guérard, Benjamin
    manorial economy 9:562
Guerrilla warfare 7:503, 499
    military law 10:318
Guerry, André M.
    social research 15:46
Guetzkow, Harold
    international relations 8:64
    ~~~~ international
~~~~
Angyal, Anaras ~
    brainwashing 2:140, 141
    gambling 6:57
    Klein, Melanie 8:417

[CAPITAL LETTERS indicate main articles or headings; SMALL CAPITALS indicate articles grouped under main headings; **boldface** indicates volume numbers.]

encyclopedia articles, which are longer authoritative summaries providing a broader historical and theoretical perspective on your topic.

Social and Political Science Encyclopedias

Social and political science encyclopedias are specialized encyclopedias whose articles focus on social and political science topics. Because encyclopedias vary in subject scope, it is a good idea to check with the reference librarian when choosing a specialized encyclopedia. The articles in encyclopedias often include select bibliographies that allow you to begin to collect a working list of sources of further information. Also useful are cross-references to related articles in that particular encyclopedia. We will look at the specialized encyclopedias chronologically because they have tended to be superseded, rather than revised. As we shall see, even the older, and somewhat outdated, encyclopedias contain articles that are quite useful in gauging the various dimensions of complex topics with long histories such as terrorism.

First published in the 1930s and reprinted several times since, the fifteen-volume *Encyclopaedia of the Social Sciences* (1930-35) includes a very useful article that offers

Figure 1-5: *International Encyclopedia of the Social Sciences*

INTERNAL WARFARE: Guerrilla Warfare   505

gence agents, and food providers. In fact, guerrilla wars, and particularly revolutionary guerrilla wars, are frequently referred to as "people's wars," although, of course, never by the opposing ruling power.

The nature of guerrilla conflict, with its inherent sociopolitical subtleties, has thus far precluded the systematic application of modern social science methodology. Generally, however, available data imply that, at the outset of many modern guerrilla wars, the populace may be found to be divided into three distinct opinion groups: a minority (perhaps 20 per cent) are disposed to favor the guerrillas; a majority (perhaps 60 per cent) are completely neutral; and another minority (again 20 per cent) are actively opposed to the objectives of the guerrillas. Both the guerrillas and the ruling power compete for the support of the 60 per cent. The guerrillas' efforts are facilitated by the fact that the bulk of the population will refrain from participating actively on either side and will remain passively neutral until confident of the eventual outcome. The political apathy of the majority favors the guerrillas because the ruling power cannot enact adequate defensive or offensive measures without intelligence provided by the segment of the populace that is aware of guerrilla movements. The guerrilla force increases its support percentage and keeps the majority passively apathetic by the advocacy of an acceptable political doctrine or the identification with a popular "cause," by the use of terrorism, and by demonstrations of military victories. And these functions are all amplified and reinforced by an extensive propaganda program.

Guerrilla wars have often occurred in nations in which societal grievances are manifested by a desire for social and political change, resulting in conflict and disorganization. These grievances are often considered primary causes of revolutionary wars. The severity of conditions causing the grievances can be actual or imagined. Societal grievances can be nationalistic, e.g., foreign occupation, _____ political, e.g., a corrupt _____

sympathy, as well as the neutrality, of the civil populace.

Guerrilla methods

Specific and common acts of terrorism by guerrilla, as well as ruling-power, forces are murder (assassination), kidnaping, and property destruction. Although there have been a few cases in history in which guerrillas have attempted to garner popular support or neutrality primarily by pure nonselective terrorism, guerrillas have generally attempted to keep this tactic at a minimum. Terrorism is an obvious indication of weakness, and it has proved to have short-term effectiveness. In the long run its use usually alienates essential popular support.

Guerrilla terrorism is generally "selective," that is, the targets are representatives of the ruling power, such as local government officials, uncooperative and influential village chiefs, town mayors, local police and other security forces, school teachers, and ruling-power informers. The populace itself is not immune to experiencing terrorism. Complete villages are sometimes burned to the ground. Psychologically, and in this case practically, selective violence is patterned to influence the perceivers of the violence. The assassination of one individual is intended to influence many. The burning of one village is intended to influence the attitudes and behavior of the populations of many villages.

However, guerrillas usually will not implement terrorism—selective or nonselective—until they have established a firm foothold within the population. Also, guerrillas will attempt to justify, through various psychological operations techniques, the necessity of any particular act of terrorism.

In guerrilla warfare, favorable political propaganda is at least as important as success in combat and the destruction of enemy resources. The goal of the guerrillas' psychological operations program is to solidify public and international opinion in favor of their objectives. Although specific guerrilla _____ for carrying out a psycholog- _____ are

information relevant to several approaches—biographical, normative, tactical, and historical (see Figure 1-3). Beginning with a definition much like those given by the various political dictionaries, it then proceeds to distinguish terrorism from numerous similar but distinct phenomena: intimidation, mob violence, and mass insurrection. Prophetically, the 1930s article emphasizes the importance of propaganda and publicity to the terrorist's goals. The remainder of the article traces the use of revolutionary terrorism against various national regimes in the late 19th and early 20th centuries, including anarchists in the U.S., Irish nationalists against the British, and various

Figure 1-6: *International Encyclopedia of the Social Sciences*

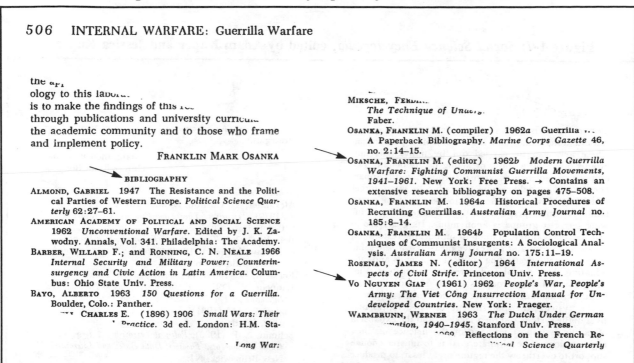

506 INTERNAL WARFARE: Guerrilla Warfare

the ap...
ology to this labor...
is to make the findings of this re...
through publications and university curricu...
the academic community and to those who frame
and implement policy.

FRANKLIN MARK OSANKA

BIBLIOGRAPHY

ALMOND, GABRIEL 1947 The Resistance and the Political Parties of Western Europe. *Political Science Quarterly* 62:27–61.

AMERICAN ACADEMY OF POLITICAL AND SOCIAL SCIENCE 1962 *Unconventional Warfare.* Edited by J. K. Zawodny. Annals, Vol. 341. Philadelphia: The Academy.

BARBER, WILLARD F.; and RONNING, C. N. NEALE 1966 *Internal Security and Military Power: Counterinsurgency and Civic Action in Latin America.* Columbus: Ohio State Univ. Press.

BAYO, ALBERTO 1963 *150 Questions for a Guerrilla.* Boulder, Colo.: Panther.

~~~ CHARLES E. (1896) 1906 *Small Wars: Their* *Practice.* 3d ed. London: H.M. Sta-

Long War:

MIKSCHE, FERD... *The Technique of Unde,...* Faber.

OSANKA, FRANKLIN M. (compiler) 1962a Guerrilla ... A Paperback Bibliography. *Marine Corps Gazette* 46, no. 2:14–15.

OSANKA, FRANKLIN M. (editor) 1962b *Modern Guerrilla Warfare: Fighting Communist Guerrilla Movements, 1941–1961.* New York: Free Press. → Contains an extensive research bibliography on pages 475–508.

OSANKA, FRANKLIN M. 1964a Historical Procedures of Recruiting Guerrillas. *Australian Army Journal* no. 185:8–14.

OSANKA, FRANKLIN M. 1964b Population Control Techniques of Communist Insurgents: A Sociological Analysis. *Australian Army Journal* no. 175:11–19.

ROSENAU, JAMES N. (editor) 1964 *International Aspects of Civil Strife.* Princeton Univ. Press.

VO NGUYEN GIAP (1961) 1962 *People's War, People's Army: The Viet Công Insurrection Manual for Undeveloped Countries.* New York: Praeger.

WARMBRUNN, WERNER 1963 *The Dutch Under German* *...ation, 1940–1945.* Stanford Univ. Press.

... Reflections on the French Re- *...al Science Quarterly*

revolutionary parties in Russia both before and after the overthrow of the Czarist regime. The article concludes with a select bibliography and cross-references.

The seventeen-volume *International Encyclopedia of the Social Sciences* (1968) was published as an entirely new effort at summarizing the methods and content of the social sciences. Surprisingly, it failed to include an article on terrorism in the index. However, this encyclopedia does include information on terrorism. To find it, you must look under those related terms that you discovered in your dictionary searches. For example, Figure 1-4 shows the index entries for "guerrilla warfare". When you turn to Volume 7, page 503, you will find a four-page article with a thirty-item bibliography. The section on "Guerrilla methods" (see Figure 1-5) discusses the types, targets, and timing of terrorist acts commonly used by guerrilla or insurgency forces. The article's bibliography, although dated, does include references to books and journal articles, including a guerrilla manual and an *anthology* with a twenty-three page bibliography (see Figure 1-6). Anthologies, also known as readers, are collections of representative essays or articles on a particular topic. The essays or articles are usually authored by separate writers and compiled by an editor.

Happily, a one-volume publication, the *Social Science Encyclopedia* (1985), does offer a more up-to-date overview of terrorism from several perspectives—tactical, normative, and policy evaluation (see Figure 1-7). It notes that with modern terrorism, "The amount of violence is often disproportionate, apparently random, deliberately symbolic: to hit a target which would convey a message to the rest of the population". It goes on to argue that the resort to terrorist measures by a regime or by those seeking to overthrow it follows from a common weakness—lack of broad-based support. This

Figure 1-7: *Social Science Encyclopedia*, **edited by Adam Kuper and Jessica Kuper**

Terrorism

Terrorism consists of a series of acts intended to spread intimidation, panic, and destruction in a population. These acts can be carried out by individuals and groups opposing a state, or acting on its behalf. The amount of violence is often disproportionate, apparently random, deliberately symbolic: to hit a target which would convey a message to the rest of the population. Violence perpetrated by the state or by right-wing terrorist groups is anonymous. Its goals are to shift sectors of public opinion to support the restoration of law and order and repressive measures, at the same time physically destroying political opponents and intimidating their actual and potential supporters. Violence from left-wing groups is usually 'signed'. Its goals are the awakening of public opinion to the injustices of the 'system', the 'punishment' of hated representatives of the system and their lackeys, and the expansion of political support for, and/or the defence of, their organizations. The ultimate goal is to muster enough support to overthrow the regime or, at least, to produce a revolutionary situation. An intermediate stage might be the unmasking of the 'fascist face' of the regime and the revelation to the population of its repressive reality.

Terrorism by the state or against it must be considered rational behaviour within the context of alternative options. It is suggestive of the lack of vast support both for the state and for terrorist organizations. Otherwise, both would utilize different political means. It is indeed a short cut to the problem of the

ments to pursue their goals and implement their strategies.

Gianfranco Pasquino
University of Bologna

Further Reading
Alexander, Y., Carlton, D. and Wilkinson, P. (eds) (1979), *Terrorism: Theory and Practice*, Boulder, Colorado.
Bell, R. (1975), *Transnational Terrorism*, Washington.
Crenshaw, M. (ed.) (1983), *Terrorism, Legitimacy and Power*, Middletown, Conn.
Eckstein, H. (1963), *Internal War*, New York.
Laqueur, W. (1977), *Terrorism: A Study of National and International Political Violence*, Boston.
Lodge, J. (ed.) (1981), *Terrorism: A Challenge to the State*, London.
Schmid, A. P. (1983), *Political Terrorism: A Research Guide to Concepts, Theories, Data Bases and Literature*, New Brunswick, NJ.
Stohl, M. (ed.) (1979), *The Politics of Terrorism*, New York.
Wardlaw, G. (1982), *Political Terrorism: Theory, Tactics, and Countermeasures*, Cambridge.
See also: *force*.

article also concludes with a select bibliography and a cross-reference to the term, "force". Another recent publication, the four-volume *Encyclopedia of Sociology* (1992), offers a very detailed, authoritative essay on terrorism.

Finally, you may even find a very specialized encyclopedia devoted solely to your topic. The one-volume *Encyclopedia of Terrorism and Political Violence* (1987) is just such a work. Although there is no separate article about hijacking, the index entry for hijacking sends you to the article, "Threats to persons and property".

Textbooks and Reserve Books

Your course textbook may provide a useful, authoritative summary of your topic. For example, our topic of international terrorism is discussed in many of the textbooks used in introductory courses on comparative politics and international relations. Figure 1-8 displays a line graph tracing the increasing frequency of serious international terrorist incidents between 1968 and 1983. This data is part of a four-page authoritative summary of information about terrorism that is offered in Robert Cantor's *Contemporary International Politics* (1986).

Figure 1-8: *Contemporary International Politics*, by Robert D. Cantor

the IRA has some degree of legitimacy as a revolutionary movement seeking to end British rule. Opposition by acts of terror is one of the most effective means of weakening a central government and hastening its collapse. This type of strategy was widely used by the Viet Cong in the years before North Vietnamese aid reached a level of armaments that permitted more conventional warfare. It is difficult to separate an attack by insurgents on government installations from terrorist activities, but there is one important difference. Terrorist activities usually occur beyond the borders of the nation spawning the effort, while acts of violence within the nation of the propagators are usually classed as insurgent activities.

The use of terrorism as a weapon of national governments or political groups seeking control of a government is a growing phenomenon. As-

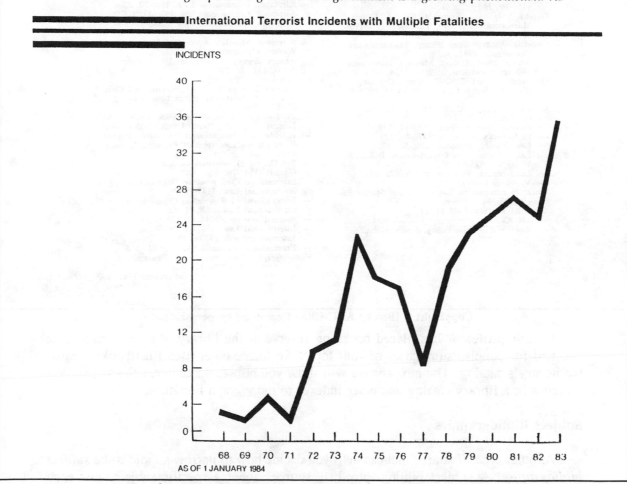

International Terrorist Incidents with Multiple Fatalities

INCIDENTS

AS OF 1 JANUARY 1984

Figure 1-9: Index to *Global Terrorism: A Historical Bibliography*

Hostages *123*

—. Churchill, Winston. Foreign policy. Palestine. World War II. 1937-47. *306*
—. Colonialism. Northern Ireland. 1850-1980. *110*
—. Cyprus (Liopetrios). EOKA (organization). 1958. *396*
—. Democracy. Irish Republican Army. 1969-78. *142*
—. Egypt. Nationalism. Secret societies. 1870-1924. *339*
—. Foreign Relations. Ireland. Political Attitudes. 1921. *198*
—. Guerrilla Warfare. Irish Republican Army. Northern Ireland. 1970's. *153*
—. Ireland. Northern Ireland. Sunningdale Conference. 1973. *196*
—. Irish Republican Army. Military training. Northern Ireland. 1969-70's. *157*
—. Irish Republican Army. Northern Ireland. Novels. Stereotypes. 1975-79. *257*
—. National Front. Racism. 1970's. *141*
—. National Front. Voting and Voting Behavior. 1979. *181*
—. Northern Ireland. Politics. Violence. 1690-1972. *239*
—. Northern Ireland. Social Problems (review article). Violence. 1918-78. *183*
—. Palestine. Zionism. 1939-48. *308*
—. Police. 1970-79. *172*
—. Political Systems. Reporters and Reporting. 1970's. *245*
Greece. Assassination. Papadopoulos, George. ca 1956-76. *186*
Greeks. Bulgarians. Exarchate Church. Letters. Macedonia (Megarovo, Turnovo). 1870-1904. *129*
Grenada. Assassination. Bishop, Maurice. Cuba. Documents. 1983. *555*
—. Assassination. Bishop, Maurice. Intervention. Military operations. Politics. USA. 1980-83. *526*
Grzesinski, Albert C. Civil service. Germany (Prussia). Social Democratic Party. 1926-30. *169*
Guatemala. Araña, Carlos Manuel. Political instability. 1971. *512*
—. Assassination. Politics. 1954-81. *539*
—. El Salvador. Violence. 1970-79. *531*
—. Government. Violence. 1966-80. *491*
—. Labor Unions and Organizations. Politics. Violence. 1973-82. *518*
—. Land tenure. Violence. 1940's-70's. *515*
—. Violence. 1966-72. *498*
Guerrilla movements. Latin America. Middle East. 1970-75. *94*
Guerrilla warfare. 1945-74. *21*
—. 19c-20c. *70*
—. Apartheid. Public Policy. South Africa.

Gurakuqi, Luigj. Albania. Nationalism. Politics. 1911-25. *232*
Guyana. Assassination. Democracy. Rodney, Walter. Violence. 1800-1980. *538*
—. Assassination. People's National Congress. Revolution. Rodney, Walter. 1966-81. *505*
—. Intellectuals. Political Leadership. Rodney, Walter. 1960's-80. *503*
—. Rodney, Walter. Working People's Alliance. 1953-79. *543*

H

Haase, Hugo. Assassination. Germany. Revolution. Social Democratic Party. 1894-1919. *188*
Habsburg Empire. Assassination. Francis Ferdinand. Stürgkh, Karl. World War I. 1914-18. *125*
Haganah. Irgun. Israel. Labor movement. Political Factions. Stern Gang. Zionism (Revisionism). 1930's-82. *320*
Haiti. Duvalier family. Government, resistance to. Political repression. USA. 1957-74. *508*
Hijacking. Airplanes. Cuba. Deportation. International law. Refugees. USA. 1983. *520*
—. Airplanes. Economic Conditions. USA. 1961-76. *572*
—. Airplanes. International Civil Aviation Organization. 1963-80. *37*
—. Airplanes. International law. 1930-73. *1*
—. Airplanes. International Law. 1950-70. *32*
—. Airplanes. International law. 1970-73. *109*
—. Airplanes. International Law. USA. 1971-74. *561*
—. Airplanes. Montreal Agreement. Victims. Warsaw Convention. 1929-73. *89*
—. Atomic Energy Commission (US). Nuclear Arms. 1970-74. *57*
—. Behavior. 1970's. *100*
—. Canada. Foreign Relations. International Civil Aviation Organization. International Law. 1959-72. *560*
—. Civil aviation, international. USA. 1960-76. *557*
—. Dissent. Sosnovski, Vasili. USSR. 1958-77. *427*
—. Entebbe raid. International law. Israel. Popular Front for the Liberation of Palestine. Uganda. 1976. *4*
—. Entebbe (raid). International law. Israel. Uganda. 1961-76. *3*
—. International Civil Aviation Organization. International Law. 1947-71. *2*
—. International Civil Aviation Organization. International Law. 1948-71. *38*
—. International law. 1944-70. *120*
—. International Law. 1961-73. *36*
—. International law. 1970's. *105*
—. Prevention programs. USA. 1968-71. *565*
Historiography. Dimitrov, Georgi. Fascism. 1930's-70's. *82*
Political protest. 1943. *250*

If your professor has placed books on reserve at the library, they also should be checked for concise summaries of your topic. To locate other useful textbooks, search the library's catalog. The next chapter will show you how to do author, title, and subject searches in a library catalog and other indexes to monograph literature.

Subject Bibliographies

Another type of source that can help you decide how to narrow a topic is the ***subject bibliography***. A subject bibliography lists sources about a specific subject. For each source listed, information such as author, title, place of publication, publisher, and date

Figure 1-10: *Global Terrorism: A Historical Bibliography*

will be given to help you locate a copy of the material. If the bibliography is ***annotated***, it will also include a summary, either descriptive or evaluative, providing more information about the content and potential usefulness of the source. Bibliographies range from the more selective to the more comprehensive. The introduction to the work should specify the criteria for selection of entries. The bibliography will usually be restricted by one or more of the following: subject scope, publication date, document type, language, or author's evaluation of a source's value. Having a subject bibliography available is obviously convenient for information gathering, but it may also be valuable in the first stages of narrowing the topic.

Subject bibliographies can be found in the library catalog under the subject heading which best describes the book's scope, with the sub-heading BIBLIOGRAPHY. For example, a bibliography on international relations may contain a section on terrorism. Therefore, it is wise to ask a reference librarian for suggestions about subject bibliographies, since there may be some bibliographies of broader or related topics that contain portions helpful to you.

Another finding aid for subject bibliographies that may be available in your library is *Bibliographic Index*. Issued in April and August with an annual cumulation in

Figure 1-11:
*International Terrorism:
An Annotated Bibliography
and Research Guide,* by
Augustus R. Norton

---

4.   SKYJACKING

1.   Aggarwala, Narinder; Fenello, Michael J.; and
     Fitzgerald, Gerald F. "Air Hijacking, An
     International Perspective." International
     Conciliation, No. 585 (November 1971):
     7-27.

     Includes treatments of political aspects
     of hijacking, and technical prevention and
     legal suppression of hijacking. An appendix
     listing the ratification states of the Tokyo,
     Hague, and Montreal Conventions is now some-
     what dated; however, the overview of attempts
     to control hijacking through treatymaking is
     useful still.

2.   Agrawala, S.K. Aircraft Hijacking and Interna-
     tional Law. Dobbs Ferry, NY: Oceana,
     1973.

3.   Arey, James A. The Sky Pirates. New York:
     Charles Scribner's Sons, 1971.

4.   Baldwin, David A. "Bargaining with Airline Hi-
     jackers." The 50% Solution: How to Bar-
     gain Successfully with Hijackers, Strikers,
     Bosses, Oil Magnates, Arabs, Russians, and
     Other Worldly Opponents in this Modern
     World, edited by I. William Zartman. Gar-
     den City, NY: Anchor Press/Doubleday,
     1976, 404-429.

5.   Barrie, G.N. "Crimes Committed Aboard Air-
     craft." South African Law Journal, 83
     (1968): 203-208.

December, this subject index lists bibliographies with fifty or more citations that have been published separately or as parts of books, pamphlets, or periodical articles. Almost 3000 periodicals are scanned for bibliographies by the editors of this index.

Bibliographies are commonly arranged in one of two ways. Either the articles are arranged in chapters on different specific topics within the bibliography's subject scope, or the sources are listed alphabetically by author and accompanied by a subject index. The first method is the most convenient one for narrowing a topic since it breaks the subject up into organized parts. The table of contents serves as an outline for the discussion of the subject. You could pick just one part of that outline for your term project. Turn to that chapter of the bibliography for the list of sources and you already have some specific materials to look for in your library.

Because terrorism is such an important problem worldwide, there are several bibliographies devoted specifically to this subject. An example of a selective bibliography is *Global Terrorism: A Historical Bibliography* (1986). The introduction notes that 598 abstracts and citations of journal articles were selected out of thousands that were

Figure 1-12:
International Terrorism:
A Bibliography, by
Amos Lakos

<u>C. COUNTER MEASURES - AIRCRAFT HIJACKINGS</u>

<u>1. Books</u>

2182. Hubbard, David G. <u>Winning Back the Sky: A Tactical Analysis of Terrorism</u>. Dallas, TX.: Saybrook Publishing, 1986. 140p.

2183. Moore, Kenneth C. <u>Airport, Aircraft and Airline Security</u>. Los Angeles, CA.: Security World Publishing, 1976. 374p.

2184. Rich, Elisabeth. <u>Flying Scared: Why We Are Being Skyjacked and How to Put a Stop to It</u>. New York: Stein & Day, 1972. 194p.

<u>2. Journal Articles</u>

2185. "Air Guards to Ride Shotgun." <u>Senior Scholastic</u>, 97 (September 28, 1970), 9-10.

2186. Air Law Group. "Hijackings: Why Governments Must Act." <u>Aeronautical Journal</u>, 74 (February 1970), 143-145.

2187. "Airport Security Searches and the Fourth Amendment." <u>Columbia Law Review</u>, 61 (1971), 1039-1058.

2188. "Anti-Hijacking Moves Accelerate in Wake of Pilot's Work Stoppage." <u>Aviation Week and Space Technology</u>, 97 (July 3, 1972), 7, 29-30.

2189. Ashwood, Thomas M. "The Airline Response to Terrorism." In: Y. Alexander and R. A. Kilmarx, eds. <u>Political Terrorism and Business: The Threat and Response</u>. New York: Praeger, 1979. pp. 129-139.

2190. Baldwin, David A. "Bargaining with Airline Hijackers." In: I. W. Zartman, ed. <u>The 50% Solution: How to Bargain Successfully with Hijackers, Strikers, Bosses, Oil Magnates, Arabs, Russians, and Other Worldly Opponents in the Modern World</u>. Garden City, NY.: Doubleday, 1976. pp. 404-429.

2191. Bell, Robert G. "The U.S. Response to Terrorism Against International Civil Aviation." <u>Orbis</u>, 19 (Winter 1976), 1326-1343.

Terrorism Against

examined. The table of contents shows that the arrangement of entries is by geographic area. You can find an article on your narrowed topic by using the subject index. Figure 1-9 shows an index entry for "Hijacking. Prevention programs. USA. 1968-71". Upon looking up that entry number, 565, shown in Figure 1-10, we find a 1971 journal article on the technical aspects of preventing aircraft hijacking.

A more comprehensive bibliography on terrorism is *International Terrorism: An Annotated Bibliography and Research Guide* (1980). It includes both books and journal articles, fiction and nonfiction, numbering over twelve hundred entries. The table of contents groups materials both by geographic area and topic. Figure 1-11 shows the first page of the "skyjacking" section. The first and last entries are citations to journal articles. Entries number 2 and 3 are references to books. And, entry number 4 cites a separately-authored chapter in an edited book.

A newer, and even more comprehensive bibliography about terrorism is *International Terrorism: A Bibliography* (1986). Although restricted to English language materials

Figure 1-13:
Encyclopedia of Terrorism and Political Violence, by John Thackrah

Abu Nidal It was reported in June 1984 that Mr Sabri Khalil al Banna, [the leader of the Revolutionary Council of Fatah (a Palestinian splinter organisation which was commonly referred to as the Abu Nidal group after Mr al Banna's code name)], had left Damascus for Baghdad for treatment of a heart ailment, and that the group's activities had been curtailed. Mr al Banna had been expelled from Baghdad in November 1983, and his readmission to Iraq was seen as being conditional on the cessation of the group's operations. Mr al Banna was again expelled from Iraq in November 1984, and relocated the headquarters of the group in Damascus.

The Abu Nidal group had claimed responsibility for the attempted assassination in June 1982 of Mr Shlomo Argov, the then Israeli ambassador to the UK, and also for the assassination of the moderate Palestinian leader, Dr Issam Ali Sartawi, in April 1983. The group had also been associated with terrorist activity in France and had recently supported the Syrian-backed rebellion by units of the PLO opposed to Mr Yassir Arafat.

In almost simultaneous actions in December 1985 by Arab gunmen at the international airports at Rome and Vienna, 20 people were killed, including four of the seven gunmen involved. Responsibility for the incidents was widely attributed to the Palestinian Abu Nidal group, acting with the support of Libya. The four gunmen who participated in the Rome operation had statements on them signed by the 'Palestinian ～～～ ⌐ ～～rilla Cells also claimed responsibility, stating ～～～ suicide

published since the late 1960s, this source identifies over fifty-five hundred books, journal articles, reports, government documents, and films. Chapter VI, "Counter Measures to Terrorism", contains a subdivision specifically for aircraft hijackings. This section is further divided by type of document. Notice that the heading, "Journal Articles", also contains articles or chapters in books (see Figure 1-12). Entry number 2188 cites an article in the magazine *Aviation Week and Space Technology*. Entry number 2189, on the other hand, identifies an article about the prevention of airline hijacking in a book on the broader topic of terrorism and business. When using a bibliography, you may have difficulty in determining whether the source is a book, a section in a book, an article in a periodical, or a government document. In that case, consult a reference librarian for assistance.

CHOOSING BETWEEN BASIC APPROACHES TO THE ANALYSIS OF YOUR TOPIC

Grasping the larger conceptual and historical context of your topic is an important starting point for two reasons. It allows you to begin to see alternative ways to narrow your topic to a more manageable size that will fit your time and talents. Having the broad view also ensures that, when you do focus your research and writing, you will be able to relate that narrow research to a larger conceptual and historical context. The next paragraph illustrates how authoritative summaries can help you to identify alternative approaches to the study of prevention of airline hijacking by terrorists. These same five approaches can be applied to many other topics as well.

First, a *tactical approach*: what strategies do terrorists use to achieve their goals and what countermeasures are used to thwart them? Why do terrorists target airlines so often rather than other forms of hostage-taking and attacks on property? Should counterviolence be used against terrorists and their sponsors, or should their grievances be recognized and their demands negotiated? As *The American Political Dictionary* notes, "Terrorism is difficult to combat, since innocent lives are often in jeopardy, and the terrorists appear willing to sacrifice their own". Second, a *normative approach*: what are the goals of the political actors that you are studying? What short- or long-term concessions do airline hijackers expect to force by their actions? Do they have other intentions beyond their stated demands? Third, a *historical approach*: is your topic a modern phenomenon? Can it be traced back through history? With our sample topic, we could ask: where did airline hijacking originate and how have preventative measures been successful in reducing the incidence of hijacking. Fourth, a *legal approach*: what laws have governments and international organizations considered that bear upon your topic? How successful have these national laws and international agreements been? *The International Relations Dictionary* (1988) points out that "Efforts have been made by the international community to condemn terrorist activities through the United Nations, but the majority of the world's leaders retain sympathy for guerrilla warfare and terrorism used for pursuit of political objectives with which they agree". Fifth, a *biographical approach*: who is it that you are studying? *The African Political Dictionary* (1983) clarifies that "Terrorists may be individuals, but they are most likely to be organizations or even governments". In the case of our topic, a major personality behind numerous aircraft hijackings allegedly has been Sabri Khalil al Banna, known as Abu Nidal. Figure 1-13 illustrates biographical material on Abu Nidal and the group named for him found in the *Encyclopedia of Terrorism and Political Violence* (1987).

These five approaches are not the only alternatives; there are others, as well. For example, the *case-study* approach focuses upon a single incident or example of a process or phenomenon, and the *geopolitical* approach attempts to explain and predict political events in terms of the physical environment.

WHEN IN DOUBT, ASK A REFERENCE LIBRARIAN

Almost every college or university library has a *reference librarian*. They have been specially trained in graduate degree programs to help library users locate and understand reference sources. Most libraries have a well-marked reference or information desk where you can seek assistance. Thus, when you have difficulty finding or using a source, find a reference librarian and state your problem in a brief and clear manner.

SUMMARY

1. Choose a topic that is both interesting and manageable given your time and talents.

2. Begin your library search by reading authoritative summaries of your topic. Such discussions can be found in dictionaries, encyclopedias, and textbooks. They will give you an overview of your topic's issues and vocabulary. Continue your library search by locating subject bibliographies on your topic.

3. Consider more than one approach to the study of your topic. Alternate approaches that we illustrate are: tactical, normative, historical, legal, or biographical. There are others, such as: case-study and geopolitical.

4. If you run into problems with your library search, ask your reference librarian for assistance.

CHAPTER 2

LOCATING BOOKS

When you need information for an assignment or to satisfy an interest, books are an obvious choice. You may not need to read an entire book, but you will need the skills to locate information contained in your library's book collection.

Your library's catalog, whether on cards or in a computer *database*, is the guide to that particular library's holdings of books and (depending of the policy of the library) its other materials such as audiovisual resources, government documents, and periodicals. There may be collections of materials in your library which are *not* in the catalog. Government documents, microforms, or periodicals may not be in your library's catalog at all. Ask a reference librarian about the types of materials included in the catalog and about the availability of other collections that may be useful in your research.

Also, remember that this is a catalog, not a detailed index to subjects covered within publications. For example, Figure 2-1 shows the catalog entry for the book, *Punishing International Terrorists*. Notice that the only subject heading under which it is listed is "Terrorism" and not "Aircraft hijacking". However, the book's index reveals that hijackers and hijacking are discussed in several locations throughout the book (see Figure 2-2). This example illustrates the need to examine sources broader in scope than your narrow topic to extract relevant information.

Almost all catalogs list materials by author, title, and subject. You can search for materials in the catalog by using any one of these three *access points*. Some computer *online* catalogs now available in many libraries allow other access points, such as keywords. Chapter 7, "Computer Database Searching", provides principles and illustrations of searching computerized finding aids. The search options available to the user of library online catalogs may vary significantly from one library to the next. Therefore, you should become familiar with the particular search options available at your library.

In the preceding chapter, we searched authoritative summaries and subject bibliographies to identify key works on the prevention of airline hijacking. One such work is a book by David G. Hubbard titled, *Winning Back the Sky: A Tactical Analysis of Terrorism*. To see if your library owns this book, you can search the catalog by the author's name or by the title. When searching for the author, look for the last name first (e.g., Hubbard, David G.). Consult with a reference librarian on how to deal with first names and initials. Figure 2-3 illustrates both the catalog card and the online catalog

Figure 2-1: LS/2000 Online Catalog and Card Catalog Records for
Punishing International Terrorists, by John Francis Murphy

```
JX5420  .M88 1985
     AUTHOR:        Murphy, John Francis, 1937-
     TITLE:         Punishing international terrorists :  the legal
                    framework for policy initiatives /  by John F. Murphy.
     PUBLISHER:     Totowa, N.J. : Rowman & Allanheld, c1985.
     PHYSICAL DESC: x, 142 p. : ill. ; 25 cm.

     SUBJECTS:      Terrorism

LOCATION          CALL#/VOL/NO/COPY                    STATUS

GENERAL COLL      JX5420 .M88 1985 c.1                 Available


(END) Press RETURN to continue or /ES to start a new search:
```

```
        JX5420
        .M88      Murphy, John Francis, 1937-
        1985         Punishing international terrorists :
                  the legal framework for policy
                  initiatives / by John F. Murphy. --
                  Totowa, N.J. : Rowman & Allanheld,
                  c1985.
                     x, 142 p. : ill. ; 25 cm.
                  Includes bibliographies and index.
                  276805    $24.95
                  ISBN 0-8476-7449-5




              1. Terrorism.   I. Title


    NcWU   21 FEB 86 DH            NXWWsl      85-15845
```

Reprinted by permission of Ameritech Information Systems and
OCLC Online Computer Library Center, Inc.

screen for this particular book. Remember, when searching for titles that begin with articles—such as A, An, or The—those titles will be alphabetized by the second word. Also, be aware that, unlike authors' names, editors' names may or may not be searchable in your library's catalog; hence it is sometimes more efficient to search by title for edited books.

Most of your searches for information will be to find out about a subject. You may not know of a specific author or book title. Because of the variety of terms that may be used to describe a concept, subject searching can also be the trickiest way to search for information (see Figure 2-4). In an effort to systematically use the same subject heading every time for books on the same subject, libraries use an *authority list* of terms.

Figure 2-2:
Index to *Punishing*
International
*Terrorists***, by**
John Francis Murphy

Copyright © 1985 by
Rowman and Littlefield
Publishers. Reprinted
by permission of
the publisher.

USING THE RIGHT WORDS
LIBRARY OF CONGRESS SUBJECT HEADINGS

Most college and university libraries use the *Library of Congress Subject Headings* (**LCSH**). This list provides an entire network of headings with **cross-references** to related terms to help you find the headings that most precisely define the concept for which you are searching. These headings also serve as a standard for several indexes, such as *Monthly Catalog of United States Government Publications* and *General Periodicals Index*.

The LCSH reduces the number of synonyms to look under for a comprehensive search of a topic. For instance, looking under "Sky hijacking" in the LCSH directs you to use the phrase "hijacking of aircraft" instead of skyjacking (see Figure 2-5). Going on to the correct heading, "hijacking of aircraft" (see Figure 2-6), you will find additional searching guidelines: *UF, BT, RT*, and *NT*. UF means "use for" or use this heading (Hijacking of aircraft) instead of other possible terms, such as Air piracy, Airlines—Hijacking, Seizure of aircraft in transit, Sky hijacking, or Skyjacking. Remember, it was by looking under "Skyjacking" that we located the heading "Hijacking of aircraft". BT stands for "broader terms"; in this case "Crimes aboard aircraft" would be used for books dealing with various crimes committed aboard aircraft. RT refers you

Figure 2-3: LS/2000 Online Catalog and Card Catalog Records
for *Winning Back the Sky*, by David G. Hubbard

```
HE9779  .H83 1986
      AUTHOR:        ⟶ Hubbard, David G., 1920-
      TITLE:           Winning back the sky :  a tactical analysis of
                       terrorism /  David G. Hubbard.
      PUBLISHER:       San Francisco : Saybrook ; New York, NY : Distributed
                       by W.W. Norton, c1986.
      PHYSICAL DESC: xvi, 140 p. ; 22 cm.

      SUBJECTS:        Hijacking of aircraft - Prevention.
                       Criminal psychology
                       Terrorism - Prevention.


LOCATION          CALL#/VOL/NO/COPY                    STATUS

GENERAL COLL      HE9779 .H83 1986 c.1                 Available

(END) Press RETURN to continue or /ES to start a new search:
```

```
        HE9779
        .H83         Hubbard, David G., 1920-
        1986    ⟋      Winning back the sky : a tactical
                    analysis of terrorism / David G.
                    Hubbard. -- San Francisco : Saybrook ;
                    New York, NY : Distributed by W.W.
                    Norton, c1986.
                      xvi, 140 p. ; 22 cm.
                      279716   $14.95
                      ISBN 0-933071-04-3


                      1. Highjacking of aircraft--
                   Prevention.  2. Criminal psychology.
                   3. Terrorism--Prevention.  I. Title


        NcWU    23 APR 86 DP          NXWWsl      85-22169
```

Reprinted by permission of Ameritech Information Systems and
OCLC Online Computer Library Center, Inc.

to "related terms". "Aircraft theft" is not necessarily the same as hijacking, but may prove useful in a search on this topic. Finally, NT directs you to "narrower terms" such as "Trials (Hijacking of aircraft)", or to specific hijacking incidents such as "Entebbe Airport Raid, 1976" and "TWA Flight 847 Hijacking Incident, 1985".

The *Library of Congress Subject Headings* tell you how a concept will be listed in your library's catalog and will eliminate a lot of guesswork. However, using LCSH does not eliminate the necessity of using your imagination. The "BT" list under "Hijacking of aircraft" does not list "Terrorism" as a broader term. Similarly, under "Terrorism" (see Figure 2-7), we find narrower terms that are acts of terrorism such as "Bombings" but not any of the hijacking terms found in Figure 2-6, "Hijacking of aircraft", "Hijacking of ships", "Hijacking of trains", and "Hijacking of yachts". These are certainly viable topics in a study of terrorism.

Figure 2-4: Johnny Hart, "B.C." comic strip

Los Angeles: Creators Syndicate, 1971. By permission of Johnny Hart and Creators Syndicate, Inc.

Now that you know that "Hijacking of aircraft" is the most precise subject heading that you want to search, you can go to your library's catalog and see what is available under that topic. Figure 2-8 is a list of four books found in an online catalog search. The

Figure 2-5: *Library of Congress Subject Headings*, 14th ed., 1991

Skovbakken family *(Not Subd Geog)*
Skovell family
  USE Scoville family
Skovile family
  USE Scoville family
Skovsgård (Denmark)
  BT Manors—Denmark
Skræp family *(Not Subd Geog)*
Skram family
  USE Schramm family
Skrimsher family
  USE Scrimshire family
Skrimshire family
  USE Scrimshire family
Skrjabinia cesticillus
  USE Raillietina cesticillus
Skrjabinoptera *(May Subd Geog)*
  [QL391.N4]
  BT Physalopteridae
  NT Skrjabinoptera phrynosoma
Skrjabinoptera phrynosoma
  (May Subd Geog)
  [QL391.N4]
  BT Skrjabinoptera
Skrimshire family

— Artificial deformities
  [GN477.6 (Anthropology)]
  UF Head—Artificial deformities
      Head-binding
      Skull-binding
— **Diseases** *(May Subd Geog)*
  NT Craniosynostoses
      Craniotabes
      Skull—Radiography
— Fracture
  USE Skull—Fractures
— **Fractures** *(May Subd Geog)*
  [RD529]
  UF Skull—Fracture
— **Growth**
— Measurement
  USE Craniometry
— **Radiography** *(May Subd Geog)*
  BT Skull—Diseases
— **Surgery** *(May Subd Geog)*
  BT Head—Surgery
  NT Craniotomy
— — **Complications and sequelae**
      (May Subd Geog)
— **Wounds and injuries** *(May Subd Geog)*

  BT Meteorological optics
Sky disk (Art environment)
  USE Rosenthal, Howard. Sky disk
Sky divers
  USE Skydivers
Sky diving
  USE Skydiving
Sky-gods
  BT Gods
      Mythology
Sky hijacking
  USE Hijacking of aircraft
Sky Lakes Wilderness (Or.)
  (Not Subd Geog)
  BT National parks and reserves—Oregon
      Wilderness areas—Oregon
Sky radiation
  USE Atmospheric radiation
Sky sailing
  USE Hang gliding
Sky-troops
  USE Airborne troops
Skydivers *(May Subd Geog)*
  UF Parachutists
      Sky divers

Figure 2-6: *Library of Congress Subject Headings*, 14th ed., 1991

```
— Employees
     NT  Highway engineers
— Malpractice
     USE  Tort liability of highway
            departments
— Tort liability
     USE  Tort liability of highway
            departments
Highway design
  USE  Roads—Design and construction
Highway drainage
  USE  Road drainage
Highway drawings
  USE  Roads—Drawings
Highway driving
  USE  Automobile driving on highways
Highway engineering  (May Subd Geog)
     [TE]
  UF  Road engineering
  BT  Civil engineering
       Transportation engineering
  RT  Highway planning
       Roads
  NT  Highway departments
       Highway relocation
       Photography in highway engineering
       Roadside improvement
       Traffic engineering
Highway engineers  (May Subd Geog)
  BT  Civil engineers
       Engineers
       Highway departments—Employees
Highway finance
  USE  Roads—Finance
Highway geometrics
  USE  Roads—Design and construction
Highway guard fences
  USE  Roads—Guard fences
Highway law  (May Subd Geog)
     Here are entered works on the law governing the
     laying out, construction, repair, and use of highways
     and streets. Works on laws regulating traffic on high-
     ---- and streets are entered under Traffic regula-
```

```
— Citizen par----
Highway post offices
  BT  Mobile post offices
       Postal service
       Postal service—Transportation,
            Automotive
Highway relocation
  UF  Relocation of highways
  BT  Express highways
       Highway engineering
       Roads
       Traffic engineering
  RT  Highway bypasses
Highway research  (May Subd Geog)
  UF  Road research
       Roads—Research
  BT  Research
  NT  Road materials—Testing
       Roads, Experimental
— Information storage and retrieval systems
     USE  Information storage and retrieval
            systems—Highway research
Highway safety
  USE  Traffic safety
Highway skid resistance
  USE  Pavements—Skid resistance
Highway taxes
  USE  Motor fuels—Taxation
       Transportation, Automotive—Taxation
Highway traffic noise
  USE  Traffic noise
Highway transport workers
     (May Subd Geog)
  UF  Automotive transport workers
       Road transport workers
       Transportation, Automotive—
            Employees
  BT  Transport workers
  NT  Bus drivers
       Truck drivers
       Wages—Highway transport workers
— Collective bargaining
     USE  Collective bargaining—Highway
            ---------ort workers
```

```
Higrah
  USE  Muḥammad, Prophet, d. 632—Hijran
Higuchi family  (Not Subd Geog)
Higuera family  (Not Subd Geog)
  UF  De la Higuera family
       La Higuera family
Hihatl language
  USE  Chamalal language
Hiin Finiin (Horse)  (Not Subd Geog)
  UF  Xiin Finiin (Horse)
  BT  Horses
Hijacking of aircraft  (May Subd Geog)
     Subdivided by national registry of aircraft.
  UF  Air piracy
       Airlines—Hijacking
       Seizure of aircraft in transit
       Sky hijacking
       Skyjacking
  BT  Crimes aboard aircraft
  RT  Aircraft theft
  NT  Trials (Hijacking of aircraft)
— France
     NT  Entebbe Airport Raid, 1976
— United States
     NT  TWA Flight 847 Hijacking
            Incident, 1985
Hijacking of ships  (May Subd Geog)
  UF  Ships—Hijacking
  BT  Ships
— Italy
     NT  Achille Lauro Hijacking Incident,
            1985
Hijacking of the Achille Lauro, 1985
  USE  Achille Lauro Hijacking Incident, 1985
Hijacking of trains  (May Subd Geog)
  UF  Railroads—Trains—Hijacking
       Trains, Hijacking of
  BT  Railroads—Trains
Hijacking of TWA Flight 847, 1985
  USE  TWA Flight 847 Hijacking Incident,
         1985
Hijacking of yachts  (May Subd Geog)
  UF  Yachts and yachting—Hijacking
  -- Pirates
```

second book is one that we have already found, *Winning Back the Sky*. A more recent title is listed first, *Kidnap, Hijack, and Extortion* by Clutterbuck. Figure 2-9 shows the complete record for this book.

FINDING MORE TERMS: CATALOG RECORD TRACINGS

Another way to find additional relevant subject headings is to note the *tracings* on the catalog record of a relevant book. The tracings list the ways in which this item is entered in the catalog—LC subject headings, additional authors, and/or variant titles. For example, the book by Richard L. Clutterbuck entitled *Kidnap, Hijack, and Extortion: The Response* (see Figure 2-9), which we found under "Hijacking of aircraft" is also listed under the headings "Terrorism—Case studies", "Kidnapping—Case studies", and "Extortion—Case studies". All three are authorized subject headings, but none was cross-referenced under "Hijacking of aircraft" in the LCSH.

Figure 2-7: *Library of Congress Subject Headings*, 14th ed., 1991

```
        Leased territories                    Terrey family               foreign speakers
        Territorial waters                    Tery family          Tesla coils
Terror  (May Subd Geog)               Terry's syndrome                UF  Coils, Tesla
     ₍RC535 (Psychiatry)₎                 USE  Retrolental fibroplasia          Tesla transformers
        Here are entered works on intense, prolonged fear   Terschelling (Netherlands)              Transformers, Tesla
     caused by either recurring frightening imageries or    BT  Islands—Netherlands           BT  Electric transformers
     imagined or actual present or future dangers. Works        West Frisian Islands (Netherlands)      Induction coils
     on the expression of shock, fear or repulsion caused  Terskaia oblast' (Russia)       Tesla transformers
     by an atrocity or a danger directed toward oneself or   — History                      USE  Tesla coils
     others are entered under Horror.               —— Revolution of 1905          Teso (African people)  (May Subd Geog)
     BT  Fear                             ₍DK264.2.T₎                 UF  Ateso (African people)
     RT  Terrorism                    Tersteeg family                     Bakedi (African people)
Terror, Reign of                          USE  Tersteegen family              Bakidi (African people)
     USE  France—History—Revolution, 1789-  Tersteegen family  (Not Subd Geog)          Bateso (African people)
          1799                            UF  Tersteeg family                 Elgumi (African people)
Terror tales                                  Terstegen family                Etossio (African people)
     USE  Horror tales               Terstegen family                    Ikumama (African people)
Terrorism  (May Subd Geog)                USE  Tersteegen family              Iteso (African people)
     ₍JX1981.T45 (League of Nations)₎    Terthrothrips                       Itesyo (African people)
     ₍JX5420 (International offenses)₎       ₍QL598.3.P45₎                Kedi (African people)
     UF  Political violence             BT  Phlaeothripidae                 Teso tribe
     BT  Direct action                Tertiaries                          Wamia (African people)
         Insurgency                       USE  Third orders           BT  Ethnology—Uganda
         International offenses        Tertiaries, Franciscan                 Nilo-Hamitic tribes
         Political crimes and offenses     USE  Secular Franciscans     Teso language
         Subversive activities         Tertiary/Cretaceous boundary         ₍PL8726₎
     RT  Terror                           USE  Cretaceous/Tertiary boundary    UF  Ateso language
     NT  Bombings                     Tertiary Period                         Iteso language
         Embassy buildings—Takeovers      USE  Geology, Stratigraphic—Tertiary  BT  Kenya—Languages
         Genocide                              Paleobotany—Tertiary            Nilo-Hamitic languages
         Hostages                              Paleontology—Tertiary           Uganda—Languages
         Nuclear terrorism           Teruel, Lovers of (Legend)          NT  Karamojong language
         Sabotage                         USE  Lovers of Teruel (Legend)
         Terrorists
         Trials (Terrorism)

                                  4413
```

USING CALL NUMBERS TO FIND YOUR BOOKS

As you probably know, most books in libraries are arranged so that those on the same subject are shelved together. However, several other systems of organization are sometimes used. For example, oversized books are often shelved in a separate location because they simply will not fit on the standard-sized shelves with the other books. Books for special audiences, such as children's books, may be shelved separately. Fiction collections are usually arranged by author rather than subject. Whatever the method of arranging the book collection, all libraries use a call number system to identify the specific shelf location of each book.

The first part of a call number indicates the subject of the book. Since there can be many aspects of the subject, there may be several areas in the library with books relevant to your topic. Most college and university libraries now use the Library of Congress (LC) classification system for their call numbers. See Table 2-1 for a brief outline of the LC call number scheme.

Of the four books about hijacking of aircraft that we found (see Figure 2-8), one has a call numbers beginning with HV for the criminal aspects of the hijacking of aircraft, two begin with HE for the transportation aspects, and the fourth book's call number

**Table 2-1: Library of Congress Classification of Books
(Condensed to Focus on Political Science and Related Fields)**

A General Works
    AE   Encyclopedias
    AI   Indexes
    AY   Almanacs

B Philosophy/Psychology/Religion
    B-BD Philosophy
    BF   Psychology
    BL-BX Religion

C History: Related Fields
    CC   Archaeology
    CT   Biography

D History: (except America)

E History: America (General)
and United States (General)

F History: United States (Local)
and North America (except United
States), Central and South America

G Geography/Anthropology/Recreation
    G-GF Geography
    GN   Anthropology
    GV   Recreation

H Social Sciences
    HA   Statistics
    HB   Economics (General)
    HJ   Public Finance
    HM   Sociology (General)
    HN   Social History, Social
            Problems, and Social Reform
    HT   Communities, Classes, and
            Races
    HV   Social Pathology, Social
            and Public Welfare, and
            Criminology
    HX   Socialism, Communism, and
            Anarchism

J Political Science
    JA   General Works
    JB   Political Theory
    JF   Constitutional History and
            Administration
    JK   United States and Confederate
            States of America
    JL   British American and Latin
            America
    JN   Europe
    JQ   Asia, Africa, Australia,
            and Oceania
    JS   Local Government
    JV   Colonies and Colonization.
            Emigration and Immigration
    JX   International Law and
            International Relations

K Law
    KF   Law of the United States

L Education

M Music

N Fine Arts

P Languages and Literature

Q Science

R Medicine

S Agriculture

T Technology

U Military Science

V Naval Science

Z Bibliography and Library Science

begins with JX for international policy aspects. In order to locate each book quickly in the stacks, be sure to note its complete call number.

In order to use that call number to locate the book in the stacks, you need to understand the following rules used to shelve books classified by the LC system:

Figure 2-8: LS/2000 Online Catalog Subject Search

```
┌─────────────────────────────────────────────────────────────────────────────┐
│ LC SUBJECT HEADING - MAIN HEADING ONLY:     HIJACKING OF AIRCRAFT             │
│                            FOUND:    4                                         │
│ REF  DATE   TITLES                          AUTHOR          CALL NUMBER        │
│ ---  ----   ------                          ------          -----------        │
│ R1   1987   Kidnap, hijack, and extortion : Clutterbuck,    HV6431 .C549      │
│ R2   1986   Winning back the sky :          Hubbard, Davi   HE9779 .H83       │
│ R3   1985   D.B. Cooper :                   Gunther, Max,   HE9803.Z7 H5354   │
│ R4   1971   Aerial piracy and international                 JX5775.C7 A35     │
│ (END)                                                                          │
│                                                                               │
│ CHOICE: R                                                                     │
│         Enter a REF number to see details of a title; or /ES to restart.     │
└─────────────────────────────────────────────────────────────────────────────┘
```

Reprinted by permission of Ameritech Information Systems.

Figure 2-9: LS/2000 Online Catalog and Card Catalog Records for *Kidnap, Hijack, and Extortion*, by Richard Clutterbuck

```
┌───────────────────────────────────────────────────────────────────────────┐
│   HV6431  .C549 1987                                                        │
│        AUTHOR:        Clutterbuck, Richard L.                               │
│        TITLE:         Kidnap, hijack, and extortion :  the response /       │
│                       Richard Clutterbuck ; foreword by Sir Robert Mark.    │
│        PUBLISHER:     New York : St. Martin's Press, 1987.                  │
│        PHYSICAL DESC: xxii, 228 p. ; 23 cm.                                 │
│  ──►                                                                         │
│        SUBJECTS:      Terrorism - Case studies.                             │
│                       Kidnapping - Case studies.                            │
│                       Hijacking of aircraft - Case studies.                 │
│                       Extortion - Case studies.                             │
│                                                                             │
│   LOCATION        CALL#/VOL/NO/COPY                   STATUS                │
│                                                                             │
│   GENERAL COLL    HV6431 .C549 1987 c.1               Available            │
│                                                                             │
│   (END) Press RETURN to continue or /ES to start a new search:             │
│   ─────────────────────────────────────────────────────────              │
│                                                                             │
│        HV6431                                                               │
│        .C549     Clutterbuck, Richard L.                                   │
│        1987         Kidnap, hijack, and extortion : the                    │
│                  response / Richard Clutterbuck ;                          │
│                  foreword by Sir Robert Mark. -- New                       │
│                  York : St. Martin's Press, 1987.                          │
│                  xxii, 228 p. ; 23 cm.                                     │
│                  Bibliography: p. [217]-219.                               │
│                  Includes index.                                           │
│                  ISBN 0-312-00906-2                                         │
│                                                                             │
│            ──►   1. Terrorism--Case studies.                               │
│                  2. Kidnapping--Case studies.                              │
│                  3. Hijacking of aircraft--Case studies.                   │
│                  4. Extortion--Case studies.  I. Title                     │
│                                                                             │
│        NcWU    05 JUL 88 DP        NXWWsl      87-4809                      │
└───────────────────────────────────────────────────────────────────────────┘
```

Reprinted by permission of Ameritech Information Systems and OCLC Online Computer Library Center, Inc.

1. Every LC call number begins with one to three letters, followed by various combinations of whole numbers, decimal numbers, and/or letters. Sometimes at the end of the call number will be a year, a volume number, and/or a copy number.

2. Single-letter call numbers are shelved ahead of multiple-letter call numbers. Thus "J11 .A6" is shelved *ahead of* "JA1 .A3" because "J" alphabetizes ahead of "JA".

3. Numbers to the left of the decimal point in LC call numbers are whole numbers. Thus "JX238 .A7" is shelved *ahead of* "JX1226 .A6" because both start with "JX" and "238" is a smaller whole number than "1226".

4. Numbers to the right of the decimal point in LC call numbers are decimal numbers. Thus "J11 .A513" is shelved *ahead of* "J11 .A6" because ".513" is a smaller decimal number than ".6" (which is the same as ".600").

The following list of LC call numbers are in correct shelf order for the reasons given:

J11 .A513	
J11 .A6	(.6 is larger than .513)
JK609 .L5	(JK is after J)
JK609.5 .L4	(609.5 is larger than 609)
JK2312 .A44	(2312 is larger than 609.5)
JX1226 .P55	(JX is after JK)
JX1226 .P55 1982	(1982 comes after no year)

SHELF AND CATALOG SCANNING: SERENDIPITY IN THE STACKS

As you look for books in your library's catalog, you might notice that the several books on your subject are not scattered at random across all possible shelf numbers, but instead are clustered in a few or even one area of the classification scheme. This means that once you have located a particular book's location in the stacks, you should examine the titles, tables of contents, and indexes of other books adjacent to yours. In doing so, you will often find books that are useful to your research that you did not locate in the library's catalog.

With the advent of online catalogs, additional browsing opportunities are available. If you can search by call number on your library's online catalog, you can retrieve a list of books with adjacent call numbers. This is especially useful in identifying books that may have been checked out or mis-shelved when you did your stack search. Figure 2-10 shows a search of the first line of the call number of the Clutterbuck book, HV6431, that produced a list of nine other books on terrorism, some of which may contain useful information on hijacking. In addition, if you can do a keyword search on your library's online catalog, you may come across items you have missed with other search methods.

Figure 2-10: LS/2000 Online Catalog Search by Call Number

```
►CALL NUMBER: HV6431

 REF   CALL NUMBER           TITLES                     AUTHOR
 ---   -----------           ------                     ------
 R1    HV6431 .A33 1986      The financing of terror :  Adams, James,
 R2    HV6431 .B43           A time of terror :         Bell, J. Bowyer,
 R3    HV6431 .B44           Transnational terror /     Bell, J. Bowyer,
 R4    HV6431 .B87 1976      Urban terrorism;           Burton, Anthony M
 R5    HV6431 .C54 1980      Guerrillas and terrorists  Clutterbuck, Rich
 R6    HV6431 .C87 1988      Current perspectives on i
 R7    HV6431 .C549 1987     Kidnap, hijack, and extor  Clutterbuck, Rich
 R8    HV6431 .C554 1990     Terrorism and guerrilla w  Clutterbuck, Rich
 R9    HV6431 .C648 1986     Contemporary terrorism /
 R10   HV6431 .C654 1987     Contemporary trends in wo
 (MORE)

 CHOICE: R
```

Enter a REF number to see details of a title; or /ES to restart.

EVALUATING BOOKS:
BOOK REVIEW DIGEST AND *BOOK REVIEW INDEX*

You may find several books about your subject in the card catalog, perhaps more than you can read in the time allotted to you for the project. There are several efficient ways to evaluate the books you find.

You can tell much about the value of a book to your project from information in the catalog record. To illustrate this point, we refer to the catalog record of Hubbard's *Winning Back the Sky* in Figure 2-3. Note the date of publication (for Hubbard's book, 1986) and consider its importance to your topic. If you are writing about a particular terrorist incident (e.g., the TWA hijacking in 1985), but the book you find was published before the incident occurred, it will probably be of little use to you. (Hubbard's book does, in fact, include material on the 1985 TWA hijacking.) The existence of a bibliography, index, or illustrations in the book may or may not be noted in your library's catalog record for that book. You should consult a reference librarian to determine which pieces of information are included in your library's catalog records.

A bibliography can be very useful in locating other materials on your topic. An index makes it easier to get to specific facts within the book. Although some books lack an index, all books provide a table of contents. This serves as an outline of the major topics covered in the text. Some books have illustrations that may also help you understand the subject better and may be reproducible for your project. (Hubbard's book does not offer illustrations, a bibliography, or an index but the table of contents informs us that four of the seven chapter titles include the word "skyjacking" while the remaining three chapter titles appear to deal with related topics.)

There are other aspects to consider in evaluating books that may not be apparent from the catalog record. One such aspect is the author's expertise to write about the topic. Are the author's credentials given in the book? Is there a forward by another expert whose name you recognize? Also consider the appropriateness of this book's intended audience to your purposes.

Figure 2-11: *Book Review Digest*, page 780, 1986 Cumulation

BOOK REVIEW DIGEST

HUBBARD, DAVID G., 1920-. Winning back the sky; a tactical analysis of terrorism. 140p $14.95 1986 Saybrook Pubs.; for sale by Norton

   364.1 1. Hijacking of airplanes 2. Criminal psychology 3. Terrorism

   ISBN 0-933071-04-3   LC 85-22169

"This book examines terrorism, terrorists, and the U.S. response. . . . [The author suggests] that terrorists are often docile, unsuccessful, self-centered people who use the terrorist act to get their 'message out to the world.' The response of the United States has been to elevate these acts into massive threats through [media] coverage. . . . Hubbard suggests specific ways in which we can control terrorist situations." (Libr J)

"[The author] correctly directs his harshest criticisms toward U.S. attitudes and actions: we inflate the threats, overreact, paralyze our government, and demand impossible responses. This book should be widely read, first as an antidote to inaccurate assumptions and expectations and second as a most valuable insight into terrorism."

   Libr J 111:69 Ja '86. Richard B. Finnegan (150w)

"If one is unfortunate enough to end up in a terrorist's hands, one might not want Dr. Hubbard planning a rescue operation. There probably would not be any. . . . One way to attack terrorism is to bash the news media, which Dr. Hubbard does, repeatedly. . . . Unfortunately, this book bounces off recent acts of terrorism rather than studying them in any depth. 'Winning Back the Sky' lacks an index but does have a final note soliciting reader correspondence. Maybe for the next book."

   N Y Times Book Rev p17 F 16 '86. George James (290w)

Figure 2-12: *Essay Review Index 1986 Cumulation*, edited by Barbara Beach

1986 Cumulation   **HUBBARD**

c CE - v62 - Ja '86 - p222
    F '86 - p75
KR - .
   PW - v230 - S 26 8o - p.
Howes, Elizabeth B - *Jesus' Answer to God*
   TT - v42 - O '85 - p411
Howes, M J - *Gallium Arsenide*
   New Tech Bks - v71 - Ap '86 - p444
Howes, Wright - *US-iana*
 r AB - v76 - O 7 '85 - p2474
Howie, Sherry H - *A Guidebook for Teaching Writing in Content Areas*
   J Teach Ed - v36 - S '85 - p60
Howker, Janni - *Badger on the Barge and Other Stories*
 c BFYC - v21 - Summer '86 - p11
 y Bks for Keeps - My '86 - p21
 y J Read - v29 - Ap '86 - p689
 y N Dir Wom - v14 - N '85 - p19
 y Obs - Ap 6 '86 - p26
 c Par - v60 - N '85 - p64
   42 - Spring '86 - p244

c GP - v24 - N '85 - p4535
c TES - N 1 '85 - p25
Hoy, Linda - *An Alternative Assembly Book*
   Brit Bk N C - Mr '86 - p39
   Je '86 - p204
   PW - .
   TLS - O 3 '86 - p1113
The Man in the Iron Mask
   BL - v83 - O 1 '86 - p189
Hoyos, Ladislas De - *Klaus Barbie: The Untold Story*
   Spec - v255 - S 7 '85 - p23
   TLS - N 15 '85 - p1282
Hoyt, Charles A - *Witchcraft*
   CAY - v7 - Spring '86 - p7
   CAY - v7 - Spring '86 - p7
Hoyt, Edwin P - *Japan's War*
 y BL - v82 - Ja 15 '86 - p707
   BS - v46 - Ag '86 - p189
   LATBR - Ap 6 '86 - p2
   LJ - v111 - Mr 15 '86 - p66
   Nat R - v38 - Ap 11 '86 - p48
   NYTBR - v91 - Ap 6 '86 - p23
   PW - v229 - F 14 '86 - p65
 Pictorial History
   57

Hsieh, Ping-Ying - *Autobiography of a Chinese Girl*
   NY - v62 - Je 30 '86 - p89
Hsiung, James C - *Beyond China's Independent Foreign Policy*
   APSR - v80 - Je '86 - p722
   Rights in East Asia
   Pac A - v.
Hubback, David - *No Ordinary Press Baron*
   JQ - v62 - Winter '85 - p909
Hubbard, David A - *Unwrapping Your Spiritual Gifts*
   CC - v103 - Ja 29 '86 - p97
Hubbard, David G - *Winning Back the Sky*
 y BL - v82 - Ja 1 '86 - p646
   LATBR - F 23 '86 - p4
   LJ - v111 - Ja '86 - p69
   NYTBR - v91 - F 16 '86 - p17
   PW - v228 - N 29 '85 - p42
Hubbard, Edward - *Clwyd*
   TLS - Je 27 '86 - p713
Hubbard, Ethan - *First Light*
   LJ - v111 - Je 15 '86 - p74
   Nat R - v38 - Jl 4 '86 - p38
   PW - v229 - My 16 '86 - p64
   T T W - *The Race: An Inside Account*
   in the Observer

It is often helpful in evaluating books to see what criticism or praise the book has received in published reviews. Several sources will help you locate these reviews, among them, the *Book Review Digest* (BRD) and the *Book Review Index* (BRI). In Figure 2-11,

Figure 2-13: *Essay and General Literature Index*, page 1634, 1985-1989 Cumulation

Terminally ill
See also Death

K. Breaking ~~Care~~ and treatment

Terror tales *See* Horror tales

Terrorism
See also Genocide; Terrorists
Burtchaell, J. T. Moral response to terrorism. (*In* Burtchaell, J. T. The giving and taking of life p209-36)
Eco, U. A photograph. (*In* Eco, U. Travels in hyperreality p213-17)
Eco, U. Striking at the heart of the state. (*In* Eco, U. Travels in hyperreality p113-18)
Eco, U. Why are they laughing in those cages? (*In* Eco, U. Travels in hyperreality p119-23)
Krauthammer, C. The three faces of terror. (*In* Krauthammer, C. Cutting edges p167-70)
Merkl, P. H. Approaches to the study of political violence. (*In* Political violence and terror; ed. by P. H. Merkl p19-59)
Paz, O. A bird's-eye view of the Old World. (*In* Paz, O. One earth, four or five worlds p3-20)

Prevention
Government policy—United States
Friedlander, R. A. United States policy towards armed rebellion. (*In* The Year book of world affairs 1983 p39-62)

Germany (West)
Wasmund, K. The political socialization of West German terrorists. (*In* Political violence and terror; ed. by P. H. Merkl p191-228)

stage; ed. by ~~...~~ ~~Italy~~
Jones, B. The day laborer and the ~~...~~ (*In* Performance and reality; ed. by B. Sonnenberg p334-42)

Terry, Michael, 1948-
Shop stewards and management: collective bargaining as co-operation. (*In* Technological change, rationalisation and industrial relations; ed. by O. Jacobi and others p161-75)

Tertz, Abram, 1925-
About
Solotaroff, T. Tertz/Sinyavsky: a secret agent of the imagination. (*In* Solotaroff, T. A few good voices in my head p79-87)

Tesser, Abraham
(jt. auth) See Beach, Steven R. H., and Tesser, Abraham

Tessler, Mark A.
Libya in the Maghreb: the union with Morocco and related developments. (*In* The Green and the black; ed. by R. Lemarchand p73-105)

Test bias
Gould, S. J. Jensen's last stand. (*In* Gould, S. J. An urchin in the storm p124-44)

we find excerpts from two reviews of David Hubbard's *Winning Back the Sky* in the *Book Review Digest*. To find any book review, you need to know the year of publication. Hubbard's book was published in 1986, so we began our search with the 1986 volume of *Book Review Digest*. Following the **bibliographic reference** is a generally nonevaluative summary of the book's content. This is followed by excerpts from one or more critiques of the book. In our example, we find excerpts from both a positive and a negative review. Following each is its **citation**. Note that the periodical title may be abbreviated. A list of abbreviations with full titles is available at the front of each volume. By looking in this list, we find that *Libr J* stands for *Library Journal*. Another valuable piece of information in the citation is the number of words in the review. You can generally assume that a longer review will provide a more thorough evaluation of your book.

The *Book Review Index* also identifies published reviews. Although the *Book Review Index* provides only a citation, it offers the advantage of indexing book reviews found in more than 460 publications. In comparison, *Book Review Digest* indexes book reviews published in less than 100 publications. Since the two excerpts we found in the *Book*

Figure 2-14: *Essay and General Literature Index*, page 2022, 1985-1989 Cumulation

Writers, readers, and occasions. See Altick, Richard Daniel, 1915-.
Writers, readers, and occasions

Writing and madness (literature/philosophy/psychoanalysis). See ...... and madness

Yanowitch, Murray (ed) New directions ...
See New directions in Soviet social thought

Yanowitch, Murray (ed) The Social structure of the USSR. *See*
The Social structure of the USSR

Yeager, Robert F. (ed) Fifteenth-century studies. *See*
Fifteenth-century studies

➤ The Year book of world affairs; 1983; Editors: George W. Keeton
and Georg Schwarzenberger. Published under the auspices of
The London Institute of World Affairs [v37]. Westview Press
1983 312p ISBN 0-86531-519-1 LC 47-29156

The Year book of world affairs; 1984; Editors: George W. Keeton
and Georg Schwarzenberger. Published under the auspices of
The London Institute of World Affairs [v38]. Westview Press
1984 377p ISBN 0-86531-796-8 LC 47-29156

Review Digest were contradictory in their evaluations of Hubbard's *Winning Back the Sky*, we want to get additional viewpoints.

Checking the 1986 cumulation of *Book Review Index*, we find in Figure 2-12 citations to five reviews of Hubbard's book. Since the publication abbreviations used in the *Index* are different than those in the *Digest*, you should consult the list of publications indexed at the front of the volume. In addition to the two reviews we identified in the *Digest*, we now have citations to three additional reviews. Notice that one of the reviews was printed in *Publishers Weekly* in 1985 before the book was even published! More often reviews are printed and indexed in the first year or two following a book's publication. Hence, it is a good practice to search the year of publication (1986) and at least the following year (1987) when using *Book Review Digest* and *Book Review Index* or other indexes to book reviews.

LOCATING PARTS OF BOOKS:
ESSAY AND GENERAL LITERATURE INDEX

One limitation of the library catalog is that it can only lists books by general subjects and usually not parts of books that may relate to your topic. You will find that, in spite of the uniformity provided by *Library of Congress Subject Headings* (LCSH), you will still have to look under several headings from broad to narrow aspects of your topic, and that even then you may miss something valuable. Several strategies are helpful in casting your net wider to locate relevant parts of books. One is to use *Essay and General Literature Index*. This source indexes essays and chapters in selected books. It allows you to look under a specific topic and find material in books you may have missed in the library catalog.

In the example from *Essay and General Literature Index* (see Figure 2-13), there is a heading for "Terrorism—Prevention—Government policy—United States". Under this heading we find a reference to an essay entitled, "United States Policy towards Armed Rebellion", by R.A. Friedlander. The essay is published in *The Year Book of World Affairs 1983* on pages 39-62. Complete bibliographic information about the book is given in the "List of Books Indexed" (see Figure 2-14) at the back of the *Essay and General Literature Index* volume. Since this book does not deal primarily with terrorism, you probably would not have found it when you looked under "Terrorism" in your library's catalog. You may not have considered *The Year Book of World Affairs* as a likely source for information about the prevention of terrorism without the precise indexing provided by the *Essay and General Literature Index*.

SUMMARY

1. Determine which types of materials (e.g., books, audio-visual materials, government documents, periodicals) are listed in your library's catalog and which access methods (e.g., author, title, subject, keyword) are available for searching that catalog.

2. When looking for materials by subject, be sure you use subject headings that are valid. Use the *Library of Congress Subject Headings* to check for valid headings.

3. Evaluate the importance of materials to your research by considering date of publication, ease of use (e.g., arrangement of contents, index), authoritativeness, and intended audience. You might also consider the evaluations published in book reviews.

4. In addition to locating entire books on your topic, be sure to use the *Essay and General Literature Index* to identify essays or chapters in books that relate to your topic.

CHAPTER 3

USING PERIODICAL AND NEWSPAPER ARTICLES

Supplementing the information found in books with that found in periodical and newspaper articles will add another dimension to your knowledge of a subject. Most topics simply cannot be thoroughly examined without them. New information, opinion, and interpretation appear daily.

TYPES OF PERIODICALS

Newspapers and *periodicals* (general interest magazines, professional magazines, and scholarly journals) provide access to this new material in a timely manner. Periodicals differ based upon their different audiences and scholarly rigor.

General interest magazines are obviously aimed at the widest audience and present the least amount of documentation of research methods and sources. Examples are *Newsweek*, *Time*, and *U.S. News & World Report*. In contrast, both *professional magazines* and *scholarly journals* aim at a much narrower, intellectually demanding, and more sophisticated audience of practitioners and scholars in a specialized field. Examples of such periodicals are *Public Opinion* magazine and *Public Opinion Quarterly*, a scholarly journal.

Two characteristics distinguish an article in a professional magazine from one in a scholarly journal. First, the latter is *"blind" peer-reviewed* (critiqued by experts in the field who do not know the name or institutional affiliation of the author) before publication. Second, a journal article must contain extensive documentation of methods and sources in the form of footnotes, endnotes, and/or bibliography. While articles in professional magazines may deal with the same specialized concepts, they are usually not "blind" peer-reviewed before publication and generally do not include notes or bibliography. Compared to general interest magazines, professional magazines focus on more serious questions using more complex logical reasoning and more technically rigorous methods of measurement and analysis.

ADVANTAGES AND DISADVANTAGES
OF USING PERIODICAL AND NEWSPAPER ARTICLES

Several characteristics of periodical and newspaper articles make them valuable sources of information for research into politics and government. Since these articles are shorter than books, you can gather several different viewpoints about an issue faster than by reading as many books. Periodical and newspaper articles, by virtue of their length, also tend to be narrower in scope. This may help you pare your topic to a manageable size. Although one usually thinks of the advantage of currentness when thinking of periodicals and newspapers, they are also a valuable historical source. You can follow an issue as it unfolds by reading articles published during or immediately after its occurrence in order to compare different accounts of the same event or idea. Reading contemporary accounts gives you a feel for the prevailing attitudes toward the event or idea. Or, you can compare opinions appearing at the time an event occurred with the evaluations given by historians after the passage of time has revealed new information. Finally, you may wish to compare a current event with a similar historic event.

On the other hand, you should be wary of relying too heavily on information and interpretation contained in articles from magazines, journals, and newspapers. The contemporary accounts in such sources may be inadequate in time perspective (i.e., written with incomplete knowledge of secret or as yet undiscovered information). Periodical or newspaper articles may also be too brief to deal with the depth and complexity of an incident or topic. With all research you should seek balance and variety in your sources of information. Periodical and newspaper sources should be supplemented with information and interpretation from books, government documents, and other sources.

FINDING AIDS

The volume of articles published in periodicals and newspapers can seem overwhelming. However, access to articles about a specific subject is simplified with the use of *indexes* such as *Readers' Guide to Periodical Literature, New York Times Index*, or *United States Political Science Documents* (USPSD). Just as the subject scope and audience of periodicals and newspapers vary, so do the scope of indexes. *Readers' Guide* indexes popular magazines. *PAIS International in Print* (PAIS),[1] *General Periodicals Index—Academic Library Edition* (GPI-A), *Periodical Abstracts Ondisc* (PAO), and *Social Sciences Index* (SSI) all index a mixture of scholarly journals and news and professional magazines. *United States Political Science Documents* is an index to scholarly periodicals only. Think of these indexes as being on a continuum of popular to scholarly, with *Readers' Guide* and the newspaper indexes on the popular end of the scale and USPSD on the scholarly end. You must decide which index is best suited to your audience and purpose. It is very likely you will find it advantageous to have a combination of popular and scholarly sources in your information pool.

---

[1]PAIS stands for Public Affairs Information Service.

Table 3-1: Selected Periodical and Newspaper Indexes by Format and Years Covered

Index	Print	Years	CD-ROM	Years	Online	Years
Public Affairs Information Service	Y	1915-	Y	1976-	Y	1976-
General Periodicals Index—Academic Library Edition	N	--	Y	1980-[a]	N	--
Periodical Abstracts Ondisc	N	--	Y	1986-	N	--
Social Sciences Index[b]	Y	1907-	Y	1983-	Y	1983-
United States Political Science Documents	Y	1975-	N	--	Y	1975-
Social Sciences Citation Index	Y	1972-	Y	1986-	Y	1972-
Readers' Guide to Periodical Literature[c]	Y	1890-	Y	1983-	Y	1983-
New York Times Index	Y	1851-	N	--	N	--
National Newspaper Index	N	--	Y	4 yrs[d]	Y	1979-
NewsBank	Y	1981-	Y	1981-	N	--

==

Indexes are listed in the order we recommend that you search for most topics. PAIS, GPI-A, PAO, and SSI give the broadest coverage of both popular and scholarly publications. USPSD and SSCI focus more specifically on scholarly social science publications. *Readers' Guide* and the newspaper indexes give access to articles in mass-audience publications.

[a]CD-ROM format includes coverage since 1980, if your library subscribes to the backfile disk; otherwise, it covers the most recent four years.
[b]Years covered include former titles, *Social Sciences and Humanities Index* (1965-74) and *International Index* (1916-1965), and *Readers' Guide to Periodical Literature Supplement* (1907-1915).
[c]Years covered include *Nineteenth Century Readers' Guide to Periodical Literature* (1890-1899).
[d]CD-ROM format includes citations published during most recent four years only.

There are indexes on practically any subject imaginable, but fortunately there are only a few basic formats in which these indexes are produced. Once you have mastered these arrangements and know what common features to look for, you should be able to retrieve information on any subject. The most common types of periodical finding aids are 1) basic periodical indexes, 2) abstracts, 3) citation indexes, 4) mass-audience periodical indexes, and 5) newspaper indexes. We will examine each type in the pages that follow.

You will also find these indexes published in different mediums. Sometimes the same index is published in different ways. For instance, an index may be in paper copy (in bound volumes), online through a computer terminal, or on a CD-ROM (compact disk—read only memory disk). Thus, PAIS is available in paper copy, online through database vendors such as Dialog Information Service and BRS Information Technologies, and on a CD-ROM. Table 3-1 displays the major periodical and newspaper indexes, their various formats, and years covered by each.

In this chapter, we will illustrate searching the print versions of periodical and newspaper indexes when that format is published. In Chapter 7, "Computer Database Searching", we will introduce you to the principles necessary for successfully searching the newer and more powerful machine-readable computer format. There are a couple of practical reasons why we are focusing on print indexes first. Probably the most important is that the time period covered by most computer-format periodical and newspaper indexes begins in the 1970s or 1980s. To search for earlier articles, you must know how to use the print versions of periodical and newspaper indexes. Another reason to become familiar with the principles of searching print indexes is that many libraries cannot afford to purchase the computer-format of every periodical and newspaper index.

Table 3-2: Selected Periodical and Newspaper Indexes by Type and Extent of Publication Indexed

	TYPE OF PUBLICATION INDEXED					
Index	Social Science Scholarly Journals	Political Science Scholarly Journals	Social Science Professional Magazines	Social Science General Interest	Government Documents	News-papers
PAIS	S	S	S	S	S	S
GPI-A	S	S	S	B	S	S
PAO	S	S	S	S	S	-
SSI	B	S	B	S	-	-
USPSD	S	B	-	-	-	-
SSCI	B	B	B	-	-	-
RG	-	S	B	-	-	-
NYTI	-	-	-	-	-	S
NNI	-	-	-	-	-	B
NewsBank	-	-	-	-	-	B

S = selective coverage   B = broad coverage

Do not let computer-based indexes intimidate you. Their bibliographic references will most likely use the same format you may be familiar with from using the corresponding printed index. And, the effort of learning to use the computer-based versions will provide special benefits (discussed in Chapter 7) that are not available when using print indexes.

DON'T MISS THE FOREST FOR THE TREES: USE YOUR COMMON SENSE IN CHOOSING INDEXES

In the remaining pages of this chapter, we will provide you with a lot of details about searching particular periodical and newspaper indexes. However, in applying these details to a real-world library search, you should remember that a successful search always requires a large measure of common sense. We can offer two forms of assistance here—Table 3-2 and four related rules of thumb.

Indexes are listed in the order we recommend that you search for most topics. PAIS, GPI-A, PAO, and SSI give the broadest coverage of both popular and scholarly publications. USPSD and SSCI focus more specifically on scholarly social science publications. *Readers' Guide* (RG) and the newspaper indexes give access to articles in mass-audience publications.

First, in deciding how many indexes to use, consider the nature of your assignment. How short or long should your project be? Does your assignment require an exhaustive or only a selective bibliography?

Second, in choosing which indexes to use, think about which index is most likely to include references to the literature that you need. Generally, PAIS is a good index to start with because it provides access not only to periodicals but also to other types of publications, including books and government documents. While not exhaustive in coverage, it will give you an overview of what published information is available on a variety of public affairs issues. If original sources and scholarly analyses are required by your assignment, then you must go to an index which includes those types of materials. USPSD is a likely place to start because it indexes only scholarly journals; *Readers' Guide* is not as good an initial choice since it provides access to primarily general-audience periodicals.

Third, in choosing an index, consider what time period it covers. For some research, you will want to start with indexes that are quickly updated, such as *General Periodical Index: Academic Library Edition* (GPI-A). Prevention of terrorism is currently a "hot" topic, so lots of recent information is available. However, if you are working with an older topic, such as the 1976 Entebbe hostage rescue incident, much of the information was likely to have been published soon after the event. Hence, in this example, you would logically start with indexes that go back that far—GPI-A does not.

Finally, in choosing an index, consider whether most of the periodicals indexed are readily available in your library. With a very comprehensive index (such as *Social Sciences Citation Index*) or with a very specialized index (such as *Criminal Justice Abstracts*), many of the periodicals referenced may not be in your library's collection. If time permits, you can usually obtain such elusive periodical articles through interlibrary loan. See a reference librarian to discuss this service.

Stop to consider these four common-sense decisions. They will help you save time and be more systematic in your library research.

FOUR BASIC PERIODICAL INDEXES

Basic periodical indexes may provide references to both popular or scholarly articles. In this section, we will introduce you to four basic periodical indexes—*PAIS International in Print, General Periodicals Index—Academic Library Edition, Periodical Abstracts Ondisc*, and *Social Sciences Index*. In the following section on abstracts, we will discuss a fifth periodical index—*United States Political Science Documents*—which also focuses on scholarly periodicals. And, in the section on citation indexes, we will illustrate searching another finding aid—*Social Sciences Citation Index*—which also identifies scholarly sources.

The journal articles indexed by these six search aids are distinguished by several characteristics: 1) they are "blind" peer-reviewed (i.e., the journal articles are critiqued and screened before publication by other experts on the topic who do not know the name or institutional affiliation of the author); 2) consequently, the ideas and data reported in these articles are considered to be of a high degree of validity and reliability; 3) the articles cite their author(s) by name and typically contain extensive reference notes and bibliographies; and 4) the publications are read by a relatively small audience of persons knowledgeable of the specialty. In many of your assignments, large and small, you will be expected to rely primarily upon such scholarly sources of information.

The remaining two sections in this chapter illustrate searching the finding aids designed to provide access to mass-audience articles in magazines and newspapers. Such articles differ from the scholarly sources in that: 1) they are not "blind" peer-reviewed, 2) thus you cannot have as much confidence in the validity and reliability of the information presented, 3) the articles typically do not cite sources, and 4) the publications are intended for a large and less specialized audience.

You will see a lot of similarity in the structure—and hence your use—of most types of periodical indexes. One common feature used by many of these finding aids is the practice of abbreviating periodical titles. Therefore, it is important to look up the full title in the periodicals abbreviations list usually found at the front of each volume. While this may seem a waste of time, there are at least three reasons why verifying the periodical title can save you time and frustration.

First, finding the periodical in your library's catalog or *periodicals holdings list*[2] requires using a precise title. It is common for two or more scholarly periodicals to have similar titles, so it is difficult to guess the correct title from the index entry's abbreviation. For example, *Social Sciences Index* abbreviates *Public Opinion* as "Public Opin" and *Public Opinion Quarterly* as "Public Opin Q". Haste in this instance could lead you on a lengthy, wild goose chase.

A second reason for consulting the index's abbreviations list is that unfortunately the choice of abbreviations rarely matches those universally used in the individual social science disciplines or even other indexes. For example, the major political and social science journal commonly known as "the Annals" is abbreviated by *PAIS International in Print* as "Ann Am Acad" while the *Social Sciences Index* uses "Ann Am Acad Polit Soc Sci".

This particular title may present a third reason for consulting the abbreviations list. In many libraries, when an association name appears anywhere in the periodical title, that periodical will be listed in the catalog or holdings list by the association name first, for example, "American Academy of Political and Social Scientists. Annals", rather than "Annals of the American Academy of Political and Social Scientists", the periodical title as it appears on the cover or title page. Ask a librarian which practice your library uses.

As we discuss each periodical finding aid, we will point out other similarities and differences in their structure and use.

PAIS International in Print[3] (PAIS)

PAIS is a good index to begin with when starting a periodical search because it currently scans and selectively indexes over 1600 news magazines and scholarly journals of public administration and politics published in English, French, German, Italian, Portuguese, and Spanish. Approximately 80 percent of the entries are to English-language

---

[2]A periodicals holdings list is an alphabetically arranged list of periodical titles contained within the library's collection. In addition to the title, each entry indicates which volumes (and/or years) the library owns and their location in the library. Some libraries shelve their bound periodicals in the main collection, others maintain a separate area for bound periodicals. The volumes and location of periodical holdings in microform are also specified in the periodicals holdings list.

[3]Until 1991, only English-language publications were indexed in *PAIS Bulletin* and publications in other languages were indexed in *PAIS Foreign Language Index*. In 1991, these two indexes were combined as *PAIS International in Print*. PAIS is also available in CD-ROM and online versions.

publications. PAIS also includes references to selected books, pamphlets, government documents, and research reports. As Table 3-1 shows, the printed version of PAIS began in 1915 and the CD-ROM and online versions began in 1976. The printed and online versions of PAIS are updated monthly and the CD-ROM version is updated quarterly. A cumulated subject index is available for the years 1915-1974. Public Affairs Information Service, Inc., a nonprofit educational corporation, publishes PAIS. You can search the printed version of this index by either subject heading or author's name; the computer-searchable versions offer many other access points. In a separate volume, titled *PAIS Subject Headings,* is the list of controlled vocabulary terms used to create the subject index.[4] If you do not find *PAIS Subject Headings* shelved with PAIS, ask a reference librarian if your library has this available.

Most of the time, you will begin your search in the subject section of the index. Figure 3-1 shows that if you look under "Hijacking of airplanes" in the 1987 PAIS, you will find references to three periodical articles and a U.S. government document. The first reference is to an article by Graham Norton, entitled "Tourism and International Terrorism", which appeared in *World Today*, from London. The remainder of the entry tells you that it was printed in volume 43 on pages 30 to 33 in the February 1987 issue.[5] At the end of the entry is a brief note describing the content of the article. Since it suggests remedies for hijacking of airplanes, this article would be useful for our research on the prevention of terrorist hijackings.

Notice that the second entry under "Hijacking of airplanes" is much different in format from the first and subsequent entries. This reference is to a U.S. government document issued by the Government Activities and Transportation Subcommittee of the U.S. House Committee on Government Operations. The title of this document is "FAA Review of Security at Foreign International Airports: Hearing, September 18, 1986". The entry tells you that this subcommittee hearing was published in 1987, and contains 3 preface pages and 102 text pages. The hearing was held during the 99th Congress, second session. The Superintendent of Documents classification number is Y4.G74/7:F31/70. This document is available in paper copy from the Superintendent of Documents. Both the document's title and entry note indicate that the hearing dealt with the FAA's role in preventing airline hijacking, so it too is relevant to our topic.

Just as you used more than one subject heading in locating books in the library catalog, so should you use several subject headings in searching periodical indexes. Although the subject headings used by PAIS are very similar to Library of Congress subject headings, you will find that there are differences. Instead of using LCSH's "Hijacking of aircraft", PAIS uses "Hijacking of airplanes", a seemingly minor difference in this case; however, when searching computer-format indexes, this difference in

---

[4]Such a subject heading list is generally referred to as a thesaurus.

[5]The "User's Guide" in the front of each volume of PAIS will introduce you to both the subject and author indexes as well as individual elements of the index entries. Because the PAIS includes references to periodical articles, government documents, books, and other types of publications, you may need to consult the "User's Guide" to determine what type of reference you have found.

Figure 3-1: *Public Affairs Information Service Bulletin*, 1987 Cumulation

Environmental aspects

† United Nations. Econ. Comm. for Europe. Application of environmental impact assessment: highways and dams. '87 xix+210p tables charts maps (Sales no. E.87.II.E.14) (ECE/ENV/50) (Environmental ser. 1) (ISBN 92-1-116387-) pa $25—*U N Agent*
Canada, Finland, West Germany, Netherlands, Norway, Portugal, and the U.S.; report of a task force with the Netherlands as lead country.

Finance

� Charles D. State-local responsibilities for financing
⸱⸱⸱ '87 8p table map
(ISBN 0-···
Conference sponsored by the U.S. ····
Administration.

Finance

Cervero, Robert and John Greitzer. Money for mobility: lessons from California on off-site road financing. tables *Urban Land* 46:2-6 Ag '87
Developer financing of off-site road improvements.

McCarthy, Robert J. Rebuilding New York: expressway to a new system or a momentary detour? il *Empire State Rept* 12:13-16+ Ja '87
The "Rebuild New York" bond issue of 1983; political considerations in future infrastructure finance.

Research

See Highway research.

Right of way

United States. House. Com. on Public Works and Transportation. Feasibility of allowing fiber optic cable along the interstate system: joint hearing, April 15, 1986, before the Subcommittee on Economic Development and the Subcommittee on Surface Transportation. '87 iv+227p il table diags charts maps (99th Cong., 2d sess.) ([Pubn. no.] 99-63) (SD cat. no. Y 4.P 96/11:99-63) pa—*Supt Docs*

Tolls

See Toll roads.

Great Britain

··· ·Britain. Sec. of State for Transport. Policy for roads ··· ···charts maps (Cm.
Docs
Selected statistics relating to highway use, ······ , and plant.

HIJACKING OF AIRPLANES

Norton, Graham. Tourism and international terrorism. *World Today (London)* 43:30-3 F '87
Recent incidents in air travel; suggested remedies.

United States. House. Com. on Govt. Operations. Govt. Activities and Transportation Subcom. FAA review of security at foreign international airports: hearing, September 18, 1986. '87 iii+102p (99th Cong., 2d sess.) (SD cat. no. Y 4.G 74/7:F 31/70) pa—*Supt Docs*
Adequacy of FAA inspections in light of the Sept. 6, 1986 hijacking of a Pan American flight in Karachi, Pakistan.

Wilensky, Roberta L. Flying the unfriendly skies: the liability of airlines under the Warsaw Convention for injuries due to terrorism. *Northwestern J Internat Law and Bus* 8:249-72 Spring '87

Press coverage

Atwater, Tony. Terrorism on the evening news: an analysis of coverage of the TWA hostage crisis on "NBC Nightly News." tables *Pol Communication and Persuasion* 4:17-24 no 1 '87
Hijacking of TWA Flight 847 by Islamic militants, June 14, 1985.

HIKING
See also

HOLDING COMPANIES
See also
Banking - Holding companies.
Directories - Banking - Holding companies.

HOLIDAY INNS, INC.

Helyar, June. Altered landscape: the Holiday Inns trip: a breeze for decades; bumpy ride in the '80s. charts *Wall St J* 209:1+ F 11 '87
Effect of changing public tastes on the former U.S. motel chain leader.

HOLIDAYS
See also
Vacations, Employees'.

Bur. of Nat. Affairs, Inc. Paid holiday and vacation
··· · N '86 62p il tables (Personnel Policies Forum.
···· ···) pa $30—*Bur*

Figure 3-2: *PAIS International in Print*, May-August 1991 Cumulation

Peru

Pilar Tello, María del. Perú: el precio de la paz. '91 367p tables charts maps pa —*Departamento de Relaciones Públicas, Petroperú S.A., Paseo de la République 3361, San Isidro, Lima, Peru*
Examines the extent of violence perpetrated by leftist groups in Peru, especially the Movimiento Revolucionario ˙᠆᠆᠆ (MRTA) and Sendero
᠆᠆ ᴀᴛ ᴘ᠆᠆
$4 payment with order—*Rana Corp*
Analyzes the relationship between explosive population growth in and around cities and terrorism.

United States

\# Beliaev, Igor and John Marks, ed. Common ground on terrorism: Soviet-American cooperation against the politics of terror. '91 183p (LC 90-21173) (ISBN 0-393-02986-7) U.S. $22.50; Can. $31.95—*Norton*
Examines the links to religious extremism, narco-terrorism, techno-terrorism, and concrete steps in a US-Soviet cooperative response, including cooperation between the CIA and the KGB.
Based on findings from the US-Soviet Task Force to Prevent Terrorism.

Boynton, Homer. Air carrier security programs: statement before the U.S. House of Representatives' Government Activities and Transportation Subcommittee. *Terrorism (New York) 13:353-7 Jl/O '90*
Testimony of the American Airlines' representative, given Sept. 25, 1989, critiquing present baggage screening methods and security personnel training, and suggesting possible remedies.

Terrorism: no one law enforcement agency, no one intelligence organization, no one country, regardless of its resources, can combat terrorism alone; this is a war that the international community must fight, and win, together. il *Police Chief 58:36-8+ Je '91*
US, chiefly; 6 articles.

Yeffet, Isaac. American carrier security: an oral statement. *Terrorism (New York) 13:373-80 Jl/O '90*
Testimony of Sept. 25, 1989, critiquing the training of US airline security personnel and overall airport security.

TESSIN (CANTON), SWITZERLAND. See Ticino (canton), Switzerland.

TEST TUBE BABIES. See Fertilization (in vitro)

TESTS, EDUCATIONAL
United States

Fuhrman, Susan H. and Betty Malen, ed. The politics of curriculum and testing: the 1990 yearbook of the Politics of Education Association. '91 278p bibls tables index (Educ. policy perspectives ser.) (ISBN 1-85000-974-0) $55; (ISBN 1-85000-975-9) pa $25—*Falmer Pr*
State-level changes in curriculum policy; changes in testing policy and accountability ᠆᠆᠆᠆ ᠆ of instructional

Cross, Frank B. The Texas economy: compulsory unitization of Texas oil reservoirs. table charts *Tex Bus R p [1-4] Ap '91*
Advocates cooperative unitary development of an entire reservoir for its oil rather than limiting ownership to the extractor.

Jurisprudence

Keith, Darrell L. Medical expert testimony in Texas medical malpractice cases. *Baylor Law R 43:1-138 Winter '91*
Discusses roles of rule of evidence in the admissibility of medical expert testimony under traditional Texas case law.

Phillips, B. Lee. Open adoption: a new look at adoption practice and policy in Texas. *Baylor Law R 43:407-29 Spring '91*
Policy as established through statutes and court cases, focusing on the termination of the parent-child relationship.

Law enforcement

Cromwell, Paul F. and others. Breaking and entering: an ethnographic analysis of burglary. '91 130p bibl tables chart index (Studies in crime, law, and justice v. 8) (LC 90-21366) (ISBN 0-8039-4026-2) $29.95; (ISBN 0-8039-4027-0) pa—*Sage Pubns*
Extent to which rational processes influence the decision to burglarize a residence, impact of drug use, environmental cues, the market for stolen property; based in part on a study of 30 active burglars in Texas.

United States. House. Select Com. on Narcotics Abuse and Control. The federal strategy on the Southwest border: hearing, December 10, 1990. '91 iii+149p tables (101st Cong., 2d sess.) (SCNAC-101-2-16) (SD cat. no. Y 4.N 16:101-2-16) pa—*Supt Docs*
Issues in law enforcement and border controls in preventing drug trafficking across the Texas section of the US-Mexican border.

Legislature
Rules and practice

Texas legislative manual. rev ed '91 110p tables chart map (ISBN 0-934367-15-9) pa $7.50 —*Texas Directory Press, Inc., P.O. Box 12186, Austin, TX 78711*
Covers rules and procedures of the Legislature and the function of the officers and officials.

Transportation sector

Taylor, Gary. Deep in the ports of Texas. table *Internat Bus 9:45-6+ My '91*
᠆᠆᠆᠆ ᠆᠆᠆ ᴛᵉˣᵃˢ port cities for
economic development. ᴅ᠆᠆᠆ ᠆᠆
role. bibl tables *World Competition 14:97-11/ Mr '91*
Analyzes the change in comparative advantage in manufactured exports in the region, and the implications for industrial competitiveness.

Shen, Jing and Duo Qin. Aspects and prospects of joint ventures and foreign trade in China's textile industry. bibl table *In* Advances in Chinese industrial studies, 1990: pt. B *p 213-22 '90*
Recent foreign investments, the import of machinery and raw materials, and the export of textiles.
Chapter of the book, "Advances in Chinese industrial studies, 1990: pt. B." '90 xi+317p (v. 1, pt. B) $63.50--JAI Pr.

Asia

Anderson, Kym. Textiles and clothing in global economic development: East Asia's dynamic role. bibl tables *World Competition 14:97-117 Mr '91*
Analyzes the change in comparative advantage in manufactured exports in the region, and the implications for industrial competitiveness.

China (People's Republic)

Shen, Jing and Duo Qin. Aspects and prospects of joint ventures and foreign trade in China's textile industry. bibl table *In* Advances in Chinese industrial studies, 1990: pt. B *p 213-22 '90*
Recent foreign investments, the import of machinery and raw materials, and the export of textiles.
Chapter of the book, "Advances in Chinese industrial studies, 1990: pt. B." '90 xi+317p (v. 1, pt. B) $63.50--JAI Pr.

United States
Southern states

† Leiter, Jeffrey and others, ed. Hanging by a thread: social change in southern textiles. '91
᠆᠆᠆ ᠆᠆᠆ charts index (LC   ᠆᠆᠆

wording is very significant. Cross-references to other subject headings are included in PAIS.

Make use of the cross-references to other subject headings in the index and the subject headings list, but do not stop there. If you will remember your search for books in the library catalog, you will recall that "Terrorism" was a very useful subject heading even though it was not cross-referenced under "Hijacking of aircraft". In PAIS, you will find that "Terrorism" is also a productive subject heading even though it is not cross-referenced under "Hijacking of airplanes".

Using the more current *PAIS International in Print*, we found no entries under "Hijacking of airplanes". However, looking under "Terrorism—United States" (see Figure 3-2), we find a number of entries dealing with prevention of terrorist acts against air carriers. You might note that the titles of these publications indicate that the focus of published research has shifted somewhat from earlier concerns with the prevention of aircraft hijacking to more recent attention to security measures necessary to screen baggage for explosive devices.

In this chapter so far, we have looked at just two volumes of one index. You will need to continue looking at other volumes of that index. Why? Because each volume of the printed index covers a different year of publication. In addition, you will also need to search for references in other periodical indexes. Why should you bother to search other periodical indexes? Because they index articles in different sets of periodicals. For example, *General Periodicals Index* is broader in subject scope than PAIS.

General Periodicals Index—Academic Library Edition (GPI-A)

GPI-A is an example of a periodical index that is available only in machine-readable (computer) format. GPI-A indexes approximately 1100 general and scholarly periodical titles published since 1980.[6] As its title implies, GPI-A is a general index covering many disciplines and is not specialized to only social science publications. This index is updated monthly by a new cumulative compact disk.

The company that produces GPI-A, Information Access Company, also publishes in machine-readable format a number of other periodical and newspaper indexes. In CD-ROM format, all of these databases are made to run on their "Infotrac" workstation. If your library has an "Infotrac" workstation, check the information displayed there or ask a reference librarian to determine which databases are available. An advantage of GPI-A and other databases produced by Information Access Company is that they all use LCSH subject headings. You can also search by keyword and, with the PowerTrac search mode, author, journal name, and date searching are available. Another useful feature of the Infotrac system is the capability to include information about which periodicals are available at your library. If your library has entered this information into the database, each reference will indicate if your library subscribes to that periodical or newspaper. By pressing function key 5 (F5), the details about its availability will display, for instance, which volumes are owned and their location and format (e.g., bound or microfilm).

Since we already know from Chapter 2 that LCSH uses "Hijacking of Aircraft" as a main heading, we can begin with a subject search on that phrase. For this search, shown in Figure 3-3, we used the backfile time period, 1980-1988, because hijackings were more prevalent then than in the 1989-1992 time period. After selecting this database and time period, then typing the subject heading on the "Start a Search" screen, we see the first screen displayed in Figure 3-3. This screen shows there are 180 articles indexed under "Hijacking of Aircraft", but also allows us to choose a display of 45 subdivisions that have been used with "Hijacking of Aircraft" to narrow the search. There are also two related headings, and we are shown that "Hijacking of Aircraft" also appears in the

---

[6]Currently, GPI-A also indexes the most recent sixty days of the *New York Times* and *Wall Street Journal*.

subject heading "Trials (hijacking of aircraft)". By moving the highlight bar with the arrow keys we can select any of these choices.

Choosing to see the subdivisions display, we then used the "Page Down" key to scroll through the subdivisions to select "prevention" (the second screen shown in Figure 3-3). This selection produced the last screen in Figure 3-3, which displays the first three of 33 references indexed under "Hijacking of Aircraft—Prevention". The first reference is to a speech transcript published in a U.S. government periodical. This periodical should be available in this library, since the "Journal Available" message is displayed in the upper right corner of the screen. The second reference is to a scholarly journal, and the third is to a news magazine. Notice that the references are listed in **reverse-chronological order** (i.e., the most recent publications are listed first).[7] As the highlight bar is placed on each of these references, the journal availability message will appear if the library subscribes to the periodical.

GPI-A also allows keyword searching. Returning to the "Start a Search" screen, we selected "Key Word" searching instead of "Subject" searching. This screen is shown in Figure 3-4. This search produces 54 references and takes us directly to the brief citations list (see the second screen in Figure 3-4). Notice that the first and third references were not included in the list produced for Figure 3-3 while the second and fourth references were. By pressing the Enter key while each of these references is highlighted on the search screen, it is possible to see a full display for each citation which includes a list of subject headings used to index each reference (not shown in this figure). The first reference was retrieved because it was indexed under "Achille Lauro **Hijacking** Incident, 1985 - Analysis" and under "Terrorism - **prevention**". The third reference had "**Hijacking** of aircraft - Japan" and "Terrorism - **prevention**" as subject headings. While the first reference does not directly relate to our topic, the third may prove useful. The ability to do a keyword search may turn up additional useful references, but because it is less precise, this type of search requires you to carefully examine each reference (or the article itself) to judge its relevance to your topic.

Periodical Abstracts Ondisc (PAO)

Periodical Abstracts Ondisc (PAO) is a comparable periodical index that is published by University Microfilms International (UMI). PAO is available as either a CD-ROM or main-frame computer database. As Table 3-1 indicates, PAO is not issued in print format. Over 450 English-language periodicals that UMI classifies as "high-demand" magazines and journals are indexed from 1986 forward. Brief abstracts are included. Like GPI-A, PAO is a general periodical index that is interdisciplinary in coverage and thus not limited to only social science publications. Cumulative compact disks are issued each month to update PAO. Because searching PAO requires the use of Boolean logic, use of this index will be illustrated in Chapter 7, "Computer Database Searching".

---

[7]Reverse-chronological ordering of entries is common to most computer-format indexes. It is unusual in print indexes because they typically cumulate only one year's entries.

Figure 3-3: *General Periodicals Index—Academic Libraries Edition*™

```
Infotrac EF    General Periodicals Index-A              Subject Guide
  ┌────────────────────────────────────────────────────────────────┐
  │ Subjects containing the words: Hijacking of Aircraft             │
  │                                                      ┌─Rec.´s─┐  │
  Hijacking of Aircraft                                       180  ◄──
    (45) subdivisions
    (2) related subjects
  Trials (hijacking of aircraft)                                1

  ══════════════════════════════════════════════════════════════════
      Press Enter <-- to view    │ Esc Return to start
      the citation(s) for the    │ F1 Help   F2 Start over   F3 Print
      highlighted subject        │ F4 Mark   F10 PowerTrac
```

```
Infotrac EF    General Periodicals Index-A              Subject Guide
  ┌────────────────────────────────────────────────────────────────┐
  │ Subdivisions of: Hijacking of Aircraft                           │
  │                                                      ┌─Rec.´s─┐  │
            -prevention                                       33  ◄──
            -public opinion                                    2
            -research                                          1
            -safety and security measures                      2
            -safety measures                                   1
            -security measures                                 4
            -seychelles                                        4
            -social aspects                                    2
            -soviet union                                      5
            -statistics                                        2
            -syria                                             1
            -television use                                    2
            -turkey                                            1
            -united states                                     2
                See also twa flight 847 hijacking incident, 1985

  ══════════════════════════════════════════════════════════════════
      Press Enter <-- to view    │ Esc Return to prior subject list
      the citation(s) for the    │ F1 Help   F2 Start over   F3 Print
      highlighted subject        │ F4 Mark   F10 PowerTrac
```

```
Infotrac  EF        General Periodicals Index-A      Brief Citations
  ┌──────────────────────────────────────────────────────────────┐  ◄──
  │ Subject: Hijacking of Aircraft          Journal Available      │
  │ Subdivision: prevention                 Press F5 for details   │
  └──────────────────────────────────────────────────────────────┘
  1        Countering terrorism: successes and failures.  (L. Paul Bremer,
     III (address) (transcript) Department of State Bulletin Sept ´88 v88
     n2138 p59(4).
  2        Intervention policy analysis of skyjacking and other terrorist
     incidents. Jon Cauley and Eric Iksoon Im. American Economic Review,
     May 1988 v78 n2 p27 (5).
  3        Carry-on bags: sky no longer the limit. (airlines security) U.S.
     News & World Report, Dec 28, 1987 v103 n26 p14(1).

  ══════════════════════════════════════════════════════════════════
  Display  Narrow  Explore   │ Esc Return to prior subject list  F3 Print
                             │ F1 Help   F2 Start over   F4 Mark
  Display full record        │          F10 PowerTrac
```

Figure 3-4: Expanded Search of *General Periodicals Index—Academic Libraries Edition*™

```
 Infotrac EF     General Periodicals Index-A              Start a Search

   EasyTrac provides two ways to search.  Try the Subject Guide first.


            Enter KEY word(s) and press Enter <--

            HIJACKING PREVENTION

 Subject Guide      Browse subject listings for subjects such as energy
                    conservation or taxation.  Use one or two words for
                    best results.

 Key Word Search    Search using words important to your topic.  This works
                    best when searching for names of persons, products, or
                    companies.

                          Esc  Exit to database list
                          F1  Help   F10  PowerTrac

                          V Search using key words


 Infotrac EF      General Periodicals Index-A              Brief Citations

   Key Words:  hijacking prevention              Journal Available
                                                 Press F5 for details

 ─────────────────────────1 of 54──────────────────────────
 1          Arafat and the Bush transition. (Yasir Arafat, George Bush)
    (Washington Notebook) (includes related articles) Daniel Schorr. The
    New Leader, Dec 12, 1988 v71 n21 p3(2).
 2          Countering terrorism: successes and failures.  (L. Paul Bremer,
    III address) (transcript)  Department of State Bulletin Sept '88 v88
    n2138 p59(4).
 3          Face terrorism with strength. (column) Hidejiro Kotani. Business
    Japan, July 1988 v33 n9 p7(1).
 4          Intervention policy analysis of skyjacking and other terrorist
    incidents. Jon Cauley and Eric Iksoon Im. American Economic Review,
    May 1988 v78 n2 p27 (5).
 5          Carry-on bags: sky no longer the limit. (airlines security) U.S.
    News & World Report, Dec 28, 1987 v103 n26 p14(1).


 Display  Narrow  Explore      Esc Return start      F3 Print
                               F1 Help  F2 Start over  F4 Mark
 Display full record                    F10 PowerTrac
```

Copyright © 1992 by Information Access Company. Reprinted by permission.

Social Sciences Index[8] (SSI)

SSI is one of several well-known indexes published by the H.W. Wilson Company. The 300-plus English language periodicals indexed in SSI are from the fields of

---

[8]*Social Sciences Index* was previously titled *Social Sciences and Humanities Index* (1965-74), *International Index* (1916-65), and *Reader's Guide to Periodical Literature Supplement* (1907-15).

Figure 3-5: *Social Sciences Index*, page 23, Volume 2, 1975-1976

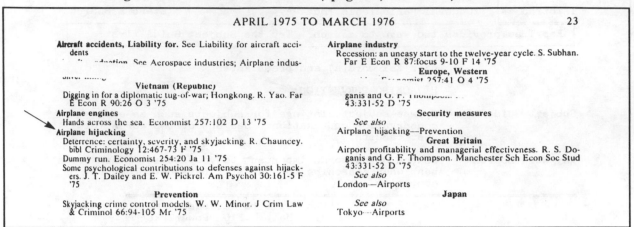

APRIL 1975 TO MARCH 1976   23

Aircraft accidents, Liability for. See Liability for aircraft acci-
    dents
    ·   ·   ·   ·   ·   ·   ·   See Aerospace industries; Airplane indus-

                    Vietnam (Republic)
    Digging in for a diplomatic tug-of-war; Hongkong. R. Yao. Far
        E Econ R 90:26 O 3 '75
Airplane engines
    Hands across the sea. Economist 257:102 D 13 '75
Airplane hijacking
    Deterrence: certainty, severity, and skyjacking. R. Chauncey.
        bibl Criminology 12:467-73 F '75
    Dummy run. Economist 254:20 Ja 11 '75
    Some psychological contributions to defenses against hijack-
        ers. J. T. Dailey and E. W. Pickrel. Am Psychol 30:161-5 F
        '75
                    Prevention
    Skyjacking crime control models. W. W. Minor. J Crim Law
        & Criminol 66:94-105 Mr '75

Airplane industry
    Recession: an uneasy start to the twelve-year cycle. S. Subhan.
        Far E Econ R 87:focus 9-10 F 14 '75
                    Europe, Western
    ·   ·   Economist 257:41 O 4 '75

    ganis and G. F. Thompson. · ·
    43:331-52 D '75
                    Security measures
    See also
    Airplane hijacking—Prevention
                    Great Britain
    Airport profitability and managerial effectiveness. R. S. Do-
        ganis and G. F. Thompson. Manchester Sch Econ Soc Stud
        43:331-52 D '75
        See also
    London—Airports
                    Japan
        See also
    Tokyo—Airports

Copyright © 1976 by The H.W. Wilson Company. Material reproduced with permission of the publisher.

anthropology, economics, geography, law and criminology, political science, psychology, sociology, and related subjects. The printed format, which began publication in 1907, is updated quarterly with annual cumulations. The print version provides author and subject access. Many additional access points are available with the computer version of SSI. The CD-ROM and online versions include coverage from 1983 forward. The compact disks are issued with quarterly, cumulative updates. The online version is updated twice a week.

Now that you are familiar with the format of PAIS, you can easily use several other periodical indexes that use basically the same arrangement, including SSI. Compare Figure 3-2 (PAIS) with Figure 3-5 (SSI). Where the entries in PAIS list author's name first, SSI entries begin with the title of the article. However, the name of the periodical, volume, page(s), and issue date are in the same configuration in both indexes.

An advantage of using SSI compared to any of the general periodical indexes discussed above is that SSI indexes many more social science publications. For example, in Figure 3-5 you will find excerpts from a page from the 1975-76 volume of SSI with four entries under "Airplane hijacking". Three of these entries are in periodicals that are not also indexed by PAIS. The reference from the *Economist* is the only article that you might have found in your search of PAIS.

ABSTRACTING SERVICES

Abstracting services not only index but also summarize the content of publications. The advantage of such abstracting services is that you can often eliminate from your search some publications whose abstracts indicate that they are not relevant to your topic. This is especially important if your library does not have these publications, so that you can determine whether or not you wish to order them through interlibrary loan. An apparent disadvantage of some abstracting services is that they do not index as many publications as comparable indexes without abstracts. However, some abstracting services

Figure 3-6: *United States Political Science Documents*, Volume 12 (1986), Part 1: Indexes

86002980• Gottmann, Jean• *The Role of the University in Modern Urban Development• POLICY STUDIES JOURNAL*, Vol. No. 14, Iss. No. 3, (March, 1986), 429-436.

86002981• Greenfield, Franz• *The Changing Role of Universities in a ____ ____ The Case of the Netherlands• POLICY ____ ____ 1986) 437-444.

86002987• Throburn, ~~n. G.~~ ____ dian Experience• *POLICY STUDIES JOURNAL*, Vol. No. ____ No. 3, (March, 1986), 478-486.

HIGHJACKING

86000224• Holden, Robert T.• *The Contagiousness of Aircraft Hijacking• AMERICAN JOURNAL OF SOCIOLOGY*, Vol. No. 91, Iss. No. 4, (January, 1986), 874-904.

86001689• Miller, Reuben• *Acts of International Terrorism: Governments' Responses and Policies• COMPARATIVE POLITICAL STUDIES*, Vol. No. 19, Iss. No. 3, (October, 1986), 385-414.

86003206• Quester, George H.• *Cruise-Ship Terrorism and the Media• POLITICAL COMMUNICATION AND PERSUASION*, Vol. No. 3, Iss. No. 4, (1986), 335-370.

HIGHWAY POLICY

86001721• Pagano, Michael A.• *Old Wine in New Bottles? An Analysis and Preliminary Appraisal of the Surface Transportation Assistance Act of 1982• PUBLIUS*, Vol. No 16, Iss. No. 1, (Winter, 1986), 181-197.

86002521• Cervero, Robert• *Unlocking the Suburban Gridlock• JOURNAL OF THE AMERICAN PLANNING ASSOCIATION*, Vol. No. 52, Iss. No. 4, (Autumn, 1986), 389-406.

86002031• Tienda, Marta; Ortiz, Vilma• *"Hispancity" and the 1980 Census• SOCIAL SCIENCE QUARTERLY*, Vol. No. 67, Iss. No. 1, (March, 1986), 3-20.

86002039• Lowell, B. Lindsay; Bean, Frank D.; De La Garza, Rodolfo O.• *The Dilemmas of Undocumented Immigration: An Analysis of the 1984 Simpson-Mazzoli Vote• SOCIAL SCIENCE QUARTERLY*, Vol. ____ No. 1 (March, 1986) 118-127.

grant *Characteristics* ____ ____ *Bilingualism and TERNATIONAL MIGRATION REVIEW*, Vol. No. 20, ____ (Fall, 1986), 657-671.

86002834• Garcia, John A.• *The Voting Rights Act and Hispanic Political Representation in the Southwest• PUBLIUS*, Vol. No. 16, Iss. No. 4, (Fall, 1986), 49-66.

86002835• Cotrell, Charles L.; Polinard, Jerry• *Effects of the Voting Rights Act in Texas: Perceptions of County Election Administrators• PUBLIUS*, Vol. No. 16, Iss. No. 4, (Fall, 1986), 67-80.

86003112• Fraga, Luis Ricardo; Meier, Kenneth J.; England, Robert E.• *Hispanic Americans and Educational Policy: Limits to Equal Access• JOURNAL OF POLITICS*, Vol. No. 48, Iss. No. 4, (November, 1986), 850-876.

86003204• Tienda, Marta; Jensen, Leif• *Immigration and Public Assistance Participation: Dispelling the Myth of Dependency• SOCIAL SCIENCE RESEARCH*, Vol. No. 15, Iss. No. 4, (December, 1986), 372-400.

HISTORIAN

86000102• Kolodziej, Edward A.• *Raymond Aron: A Critical Retrospective and Prospective• INTERNATIONAL STUDIES QUARTERLY*, Vol No. 29, Iss. No. 1, (March, 1985), 5-11.

____ and the Theory of Inter-

are very thorough in their coverage of periodicals in a particular discipline. An example is the following.

United States Political Science Documents (USPSD)

USPSD abstracts articles in nearly 150 political science scholarly journals published since 1975. It is produced by the NASA Industrial Applications Center at the University of Pittsburgh. USPSD is issued only once a year in the print version. However, its online version is updated quarterly. Both versions provide author, subject, geographic-area, proper-name, and journal-name searching. The online version also provides keyword searching. The controlled vocabulary for USPSD subjects and geographic areas was published separately under the title, *Political Science Thesaurus*. A rotated subject descriptor display is also printed in each index volume.

Using an abstracting service usually involves a two-step process. First, look in the index section for your subject; and then look up the ***accession number***(s) in the abstract section for the article summary. Using USPSD as an example, Figure 3-6 shows a page from the index volume with the subject heading "Highjacking".[9]

Note that USPSD does provide a bibliographic reference to the periodical article in the index section. Some abstracting services give only an entry or accession number,

---

[9]Incidentally, notice that USPSD uses a different spelling for hijacking than do the other indexes that we have searched. This spelling difference is important if you are doing a computer search of USPSD. More information about computer searching is given in Chapter 7.

Figure 3-7: *United States Political Science Documents*, Volume 12 (1986), Part 2: Document Descriptions

32 / 86000221

Attributes of Establishments and Jobs in Mixed Occupations; Table 3 - Sex Segregation Among Occupations and Job Titles by Major Occupational Groups; Table 4 - Distributions of Establishments by Levels of Segregation Computed Across Major Occupational Groups, Detailed Occupations, and Job Titles; Table 5 - Determinants of Sex Composition (% Female) of Work in Mixed Occupations, Metric Coefficients for Regression (N ' 2,997); Table 6 - Determinants of Likelihood That Women Are Excluded from Jobs in Mixed Occupations, Logistic Regression Coefficients (N ' 2,997); Table 7 - Staffing Patterns for Packaging Jobs in Same Nine-Digit DOT Classification: 1968, Pharmaceutical Manufacturing; Table 8 - Gender Composition of Jobs in California Personnel System, Full-Time Workers, Jobs with Two or More Incumbents: December 31, 1984; **KEY SUBJECTS:** Job Discrimination; Womens Studies; Economic Decision Maker; Segregation Policy; Sex Discrimination; Division of Labor; Classification Process; Bias; Organization Cleavage Characteristics; Statistical Data; Occupation Characteristics; **KEY GEOGRAPHIC AREAS:** United States of America;

86000222 AUTHOR(S): Hirsch, Paul M.; **TITLE:** *From Ambushes to Golden Parachutes: Corporate Takeovers as an Instance of Cultural Framing and Institutional Integration.* **SOURCE:** *AMERICAN JOURNAL OF SOCIOLOGY,* Vol. No. 91, Iss. No. 4, (January, 1986), 800-837. **ABSTRACT:** Hostile takeovers -- in which over 50 percent of the shares of a large, publicly held corporation are bought over the protests of stockholders, managers, and/or board of directors -- are examined organizationally and culturally. Both the structural transformations and their symbolic framing are considered. The history and diffusion of hostile takeovers are traced, beginning with the first wave (1960-70). During 1973-80, this initially deviant innovation became common and accepted practice. The linguistic framing of these contests for ownership has changed along with the growing legitimacy of such takeovers. From negative images, the newer terms are more balanced, as well as complex, specialized, and routinized. Institutionalization of hostile takeovers was eased by ideological and linguistic shifts. The cognitive, social-psychological, and institutional functions represented linguistically and their roles in the diffusion process are further explored. **SPECIAL FEATURES:** Table 1 - Tender Offers, 1974-84; Table 2 - Genres and Image Clusters; Table 3 - Language and Ideology Characterizing the Hostile ... Institutional Core from Periph-

AREAS: United States of America (19th Century); United States of America; California, San Francisco Area (19th Century); California, San Francisco Area;

86000224 AUTHOR(S): Holden, Robert T.; **TITLE:** *The Contagiousness of Aircraft Hijacking.* **SOURCE:** *AMERICAN JOURNAL OF SOCIOLOGY,* Vol. No. 91, Iss. No. 4, (January, 1986), 874-904. **ABSTRACT:** The view of aircraft hijacking as a contagion spread by media coverage was examined, focusing upon 1968-72, the peak period for US hijacking attempts. The contagion hypothesis attributes these acts to mental derangement and to the desire for attention or to rational goal seeking. Beginning with a distinction between transportation and extortion hijackings, the study traces their historical development since the late 1950s. Five hypotheses are tested, using a model of hijacking as a stationary stochastic process. Data from the records of the Federal Aviation Administration (FAA) were mathematically analyzed to predict the rates of US hijacking attempts. It was demonstrated that successful US-based episodes produced contagion effects, as did US media coverage of foreign incidents. Each type of hijacking inspired only its own type, suggesting rationality in the hijackers. The influence of exogenous factors -- such as the Vietnam war and the civil rights movement during 1968-72 -- must also be accounted for. **SPECIAL FEATURES:** Figure 1 - Annual Aircraft Hijacking Attempts, 1953-82; Table 1 - Destinations Desired by US Hijackers, 1968-72; Figure 2 - Monthly Hijacking Attempts -- US-Boarded Aircraft; Figure 3 - Monthly Hijacking Attempts -- Foreign-Boarded Aircraft; Table 2 - Summary of Hijacking Attempts, 1968-72; Table 3 - Estimates of Contagion Effects on US Hijacking Attempts; Table 4 - Estimates of Contagion Effects on US Transportation Hijacking Attempts; Table 5 - Estimates of Contagion Effects on US Transportation Hijacking Attempts; **KEY SUBJECTS:** Highjacking; Air Piracy; Epidemic; Contextual Analysis; Motivational Analysis; News Coverage; Hypothesis Testing; Influence Process; Stochastic Model; **KEY GEOGRAPHIC AREAS:** United States of America;

86000225 AUTHOR(S): Apostle, Richard; Clairmont, Don; Osberg, Lars; **TITLE:** *Economic Segmentation and Politics.* **SOURCE:** *AMERICAN JOURNAL OF SOCIOLOGY,* Vol. No. 91, Iss. No. 4, (January, 1986), 905-931. **ABSTRACT:** Segmentation theory -- previously confined to dual labor market analysis and other economic areas -- is applied to ... relationships and activities among establishments and workers in ... level the anal-

requiring that you look up the abstract to get the bibliographic reference. Since USPSD gives the full bibliographic reference in the index section, you may be able to deduce from the title and date of publication whether the article is relevant to your topic; and if so, you have sufficient information to locate the article. Such is the case with the second entry, an article by Rueben Miller, which focuses on government anti-terrorist policies. It is less certain that the Robert T. Holden article will be relevant to prevention of aircraft hijacking. In order to determine this from the information in USPSD, you can use the accession number (86000224) to find the summary of its contents (see Figure 3-7). The abstract tells us that this article focuses on a cause (or consequence) of hijacking (i.e., media coverage), but does not seem to deal with government policies in response to this cause.

Other Political Science Abstracting Services

In the field of political science, there are two other major abstracting services. *International Political Science Abstracts* summarizes articles published in 600 English-language and foreign-language periodicals. *Political Science Abstracts* summarizes articles in about 250 journals. There are also some very specialized abstracting services within the political science or related fields, such as *Peace Research Abstracts Journal* or *Criminal Justice Abstracts*. Related social science disciplines also have their own periodical abstracting services, such as *Sociological Abstracts,*

Figure 3-8: *Social Sciences Citation Index*™, 1987, Volume 1

Reprinted with the permission of the Institute for Scientific Information™ (ISI™). Copyright © 1992.

Psychological Abstracts, Communication Abstracts, and *America: History and Life*. These abstracting services concentrate on scholarly works. However, there are a few sources, such as *Readers" Guide Abstracts*, which provide summaries or abstracts of popular magazine articles.

CITATION INDEXING:
SOCIAL SCIENCES CITATION INDEX

There is one more type of specialized index you will find useful in undergraduate political science research. You already know to save for later use those bibliographic references relevant to your topic that you found while searching indexes and abstracts or reading books and periodical articles. However, this search strategy will (with a very few exceptions) take you to works older than the source in which they are mentioned. On the other hand, a citation index takes you forward in time to more recently published works. For political science research, you can use the *Social Sciences Citation Index* (SSCI). With this index you can search key, older articles and see who has cited them since they were published.

Figure 3-9: *Social Sciences Citation Index*™, 1987, Volume 4

VANDERTA.HG—THE DEBT PROBLEM ...
WORLD DEV 14(9):1107-1124 86 NO R F4311
WORLD BANK, WASHINGTON, DC 20433, USA

SELSER JN
see RICHARDS.JL HEALTH PSYC 6 183 87

SELTH A
INTERNATIONAL TERRORISM AND THE CHALLENGE TO DIPLOMACY
TERRORISM 10(2):103-112 87 29R J7434
AUSTRALIAN DEPT FOREIGN AFFAIRS,COUNTER TERRORISM POLICY SECT, CANBERRA, AUSTRALIA

(ANON)	84 PATTERNS GLOBAL TERR		5
ARON R	70 PEACE WAR THEORY INT		25
ASTON CC	84 CONFLICT STUDIES	157	1
BAUMANN CE	73 DIPLOMATIC KIDNAPPIN		110
BELL JB	78 TIME TERROR REVOLUTI		64
"	81 TRANSNATIONAL RELATI		167
BULL H	71 ADELPHI PAPER	83	31
CLUTTERBUCK R	75 LIVING TERRORISM		33
DAM KW	84 CURRENT POLICY	618	2
JENKINS BM	75 INT TERRORISM WORLD		25
"	77 P5905 RAND CORP RAND		2
"	81 NEWSWEEK 0209		19
"	81 R2651RC RAND CORP RE		146
"	83 R3009DNA RAND CORP R		14
"	84 N2114RC RAND CORP RA		4
MACK A	81 AUSTR NZ J CRIMI DEC		199
MCDERMOTT G	73 NEW DIPLOMACY ITS AP		67
MILLER JDB	81 WORLD STATES		35
MOWAT RB	35 DIPLOMACY PEACE		199
PALLISER M	84 EXPANSION INT SOC		372
PEREZ FH	82 CURRENT POLICY 0610		402
SAYRE RM	84 CURRENT POLICY	608	2
SCHLESINGER P	83 TELEVISING TERRORISM		12
SHULTZ GP	84 COMMUNICATION 1025		
WARDLAW G	84 AGE 0418		13
WATSON A	82 DIPLOMACY DIALOGUE S		140
WIGHT M	78 POWER POLITICS		113
WILKINSON	86 TERRORISM LIBERAL ST		194
WILKINSON P	81 CONFLICT Q SPR		5

SELTZER MM
—FAMILY MEMBERS AS CASE MANAGERS
... AND INFORMAL

SSCI contains references to articles published since 1972 in 1500 social science journals as well as selected articles relating to the social sciences from about 3000 journals in the natural and physical sciences. SSCI is one of several citation indexes published by the Institute for Scientific Information. The print version of SSCI is issued three times a year with annual and multi-year cumulations. The online version is updated weekly. The CD-ROM version is updated quarterly with annual cumulations containing one year per disk.

The most powerful and unique use of SSCI is to locate more current articles by searching from citations of previously published books and articles. One author writing on the topic of aircraft hijacking that we have encountered in our research so far is Richard Clutterbuck. To see who has recently cited his work, we look in the "Citation Index" under Clutterbuck (see Figure 3-8). Here we see that ten authors have cited Clutterbuck during 1987, the year of the *Social Sciences Citation Index* we are using.

Figure 3-10: *Social Sciences Citation Index*™, 1986, Volume 6

19TH - - - - - POSCETTI M	¨- - - -	PUBLIC - - - - BOWER	HILL,REUBEN
1984-AND-1. - GREENEWA.CH	HIGHS	RECENT - - - - "	SOUVENIRS - ADAMS BN
37TH - - - - - ROTHSCHI.VM	CANNABINOID CONE EJ	REQUIREMEN. EDNER SM+	
56TH - - - - - RENDERO T	CONTACT - - - "	RESOURCE - - - "+	HILL,REUBEN,L
57TH - - - - - LEVINE HZ@	EXCRETION - - "	ROADS - - - - "+	OLSON DH
	EXPOSURE - - "	STATE - - - - "+	
HIGHLY	JUMPED - - -STINSON JF	STREETS - - - "+	HILL,RICHARD
ADAPTATION ROUTMAN EM	MARIJUANA - CONE EJ	TRANSPORTA. - BOWER RW	ESSAYS - - - PERKINS KJ+
ADAPTATIONS MAHONEY SA	MOONLIGHTL - STINSON JF		HONOR - - - - "+
AFRICAN - - INT MIGR	PASSIVE - - CONE EJ	HIJACKED	
AGGRESSIVE NIKULINA EM	RECORD - - - STINSON JF	HIJACKERS - BREITHAU.GL	HILLFORT
POTEGAL M	SMOKE - - - CONE EJ	- NEIER A	ANATOMY - - CLARK G+
ALKALINE - - MAHONEY SA	URINARY - - - "		BRITAIN - - - AVERY M
ARCHAEOLOGY KAPLAN MF	WOMEN - - - - STINSON JF	HIJACKERS	ENTRANCES - -
ASCVD - - - DRINKWAT.D		HIJACKED - - BREITHAU.GL	EXCAVATIONS CLARK G+
ATHEROSCLE. - "	HIGHTECH	- NEIER A	FIRE - - - - AVERY M
ATHLETES - - "	COMPANIES - NAKAMURA GI	HINDER - - - TRACY EJ	HAMPSHIRE - - CLARK G+
BEHAVIOR - - - NIKULINA EM	JAPANESE - - "	NEW - - - - "	WAINWRIG.GJ+
BEHAVIORS - - POTEGAL M	MAJOR - - - - "	X-RAY-SCAN. - "	IRON-AGE - - - CLARK G+
BUILDING - - GILBERT GR	MANAGEMENT "		WAINWRIG.GJ+
CARDIOVASC. - DRINKWAT.D	STRATEGIC - - "	HIJACKING	SOUTHERN - - AVERY M
CBA - - - - - NIKULINA EM		AIRCRAFT - - HOLDEN RT	STONING - - - "
CHANGING-R. GRUNFELD F	HIGHWAY	CONTAGIOUS. - "	VOL - - - - - - CLARK G+
CHROMOSOMES PEACOCK WJ	ACT - - - - - LYNCH J	RIPOSTE - - NATURE	
CLASSIFICA. PAWLAK Z	AGE - - - - - WAGENAAR AC		HILLIER
CONTRAST - COX WM	ALASKA - - - DUCKER JH+	HIJAZ	FACILITIES - KAKU BK
COUNTRIES - - INT MIGR	ALLOCATION FWA TF	CONTROL - - - SAAB AP+	IMPROVE - - - "
CREATION - - LAURENCE JR	AMERICAN - BOUCHER M	OTTOMAN - - - "+	LAYOUT - - - - "
DD - - - - - NIKULINA EM	ANIMALS - - CLARKE PH		PERTURBATL. - "
DEVELOPED - - GRUNFELD F	APPROACH - - FWA TF	HIJAZ-RAILWAY	PROBLEM - - - "
DIFFERENTL - POTEGAL M	ARCHAEOLOG. SUTTON DG+	CHANGING - OCHSENWA.W+	SCHEME - - - "
DISORDER - - GRINOLIN.HM	AREA - - - - FEARNSID.PM	SIGNIFICAN. - - "+	SOLUTION - - - "
SVRAKIC DM	ASSIGNMENT JANSON BN		
DISPOSAL - - - KAPLAN MF	BEAUTIFICA - LYNCH J	HIJRAS	HILLIERS
DISSOCIATL. - LAURENCE JR	BID - - - - JOYNER AD	INDIA - - - - NANDA S	FACILITIES - PICONE CJ
DNA-SEQUEN. - PEACOCK WJ	BRAZILS - - - FEARNSID.PM		IMPROVE - - - "
DROSOPHILA. -			

Reprinted with the permission of the Institute for Scientific Information™ (ISI™). Copyright © 1992.

Look at the third entry, a book by Clutterbuck published in 1975, listed as *Living Terrorism*.[10]

The *Living with Terrorism* entry tells us that another author, A. Selth, writing in the journal *Terrorism*, Volume 10, page 103, in 1987, cited Clutterbuck's book. We can then go back to the "Source Index", to find the complete bibliographic reference to Selth's source article (see Figure 3-9). The "Source Index" lists all the articles from which citations are taken for indexing in a given time period, in this case the year 1987. The articles are listed alphabetically by author. In addition to providing the full bibliographic reference, each entry includes the author's address and the article's bibliography in abbreviated format. Therefore, even if we cannot obtain a copy of Selth's article, we have its bibliography.

Because the title of Selth's article—"International Terrorism and the Challenge to Diplomacy"—is clearly relevant to our research, and because his institutional affiliation—Australian Department of Foreign Affairs, Counter Terrorism Policy Section—indicates Selth's active involvement in the prevention of terrorism, we can therefore conclude that

---

[10]Unfortunately, in order to save space, this index deletes "insignificant" words from titles of works indexed. The full title of Clutterbuck's book is *Living with Terrorism*.

this article should be searched in later issues of the *Social Sciences Citation Index* as a cited work. This "recycling" allows you to update and expand your bibliography.

Another expansion of your terrorism-prevention bibliography results from pursuing the seven other Clutterbuck publications listed in Figure 3-8 besides his book, *Living with Terrorism*. Your next search step in tracking down these additional Clutterbuck works is to read their abbreviated titles to determine whether any of them might be relevant to your topic. At least six of the seven titles seem to focus upon political violence and terrorism.

Only one of these citations is to a journal title; others are to book titles. The 1981 entry, "Terrorism", includes a volume number (5) and a page number (125), indicating that this is a periodical citation to a Clutterbuck article in the journal, *Terrorism*. None of the other Clutterbuck citations include both volume and page numbers, indicating that these citations are to books written by Clutterbuck. Since books are not included in the "Source Index", finding more information about Clutterbuck's seven books requires using the techniques of Chapter 2 to locate either the work or a more complete reference to it. However, since journal articles are included in the "Source Index", you can obtain the full title and complete bibliography of the 1981 *Terrorism* article in the 1981 issue of the "Source Index". Or, you can use the periodicals holding list to see if your library has the 1981 volume of the journal, *Terrorism*, so that you can go directly to the article itself.

The *Social Sciences Citation Index* also provides a second access method in its "Permuterm Index". This is a keyword index that combines every two significant words from the title of the work. Starting our search with the keyword "hijacking", we find that "aircraft" and "contagious" are both linked to an article by R.T. Holden (see Figure 3-10). When we go to the "Source Index" and look under Holden's name (see Figure 3-11), we find a citation to his 1986 article in the *American Journal of Sociology*. To the right of that citation we find the notation "52R" indicating that Holden's article contains fifty-two references. An abbreviated citation to each of the fifty-two references is listed below. Notice that the 1975 Clutterbuck book, that we searched in the "Citation Index" for 1987 (see Figure 3-8), is one of the works that Holden cites in 1986.

An Index to Mass-Audience Periodicals: *Readers' Guide to Periodical Literature*

There are occasions, especially at the undergraduate level, when you will find useful information that bears upon your research questions in less scholarly and more mass-audience periodicals. You should not rely upon such sources for most of your information, because they are not peer-reviewed, often do not cite the author(s) by name, and are intended for a less knowledgeable audience. However, news magazine and newspaper articles can provide useful contemporary accounts of events, as well as analyses and interpretations of political phenomena, and even raw data. Articles in these mass-audience sources are selectively indexed in two search aids that we already have covered—PAIS and *Social Sciences Index*. Two other periodical indexes provide broad coverage of mass-audience magazines. We have already discussed GPI-A. Now, we turn to probably the most well-known index to popular literature—*Readers' Guide to Periodical Literature*.

Figure 3-11: *Social Sciences Citation Index*™, 1986, Volume 4, Source Index

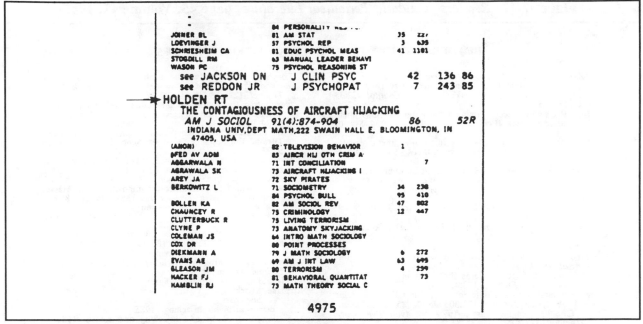

Readers' Guide indexes articles in about 200 popular magazines by subject[11] and author. Entries are listed under each heading in alphabetical order by title. In Figure 3-12 note the use of subdivisions to make it easier to get to the most relevant articles quickly. Under the main subject heading of "Airplane hijacking" you find the subdivision "Prevention". The eight entries listed here are from the general-audience periodicals *World Press Review, U.S. News & World Report, Time*, and *Jet*.[12] Notice that all of the *Readers' Guide* entries are in exactly the same format as the SSI entries. Another finding aid offered is the see-also reference; under "Prevention" you are referred to "Airports—Security measures".

So far, we have covered several print and computerized indexes to journal and magazine articles. In the following section, you will learn to apply the same search techniques to indexes of newspaper articles. For many types of undergraduate political science research, whether brief or lengthy, you will find newspaper articles a valuable source of information and interpretation.

---

[11]Note that *Readers' Guide*, like many periodical indexes, does not strictly adhere to the LCSH authority list. However, if you begin with a LC subject heading, you are likely to find a cross-reference if they use a different term.

[12]While primarily indexing mass-audience periodicals, *Readers' Guide* also indexes some special-interest periodicals, for example, *Aviation Week and Space Technology*.

Figure 3-12: *Readers' Guide to Periodical Literature*, page 45, Volume 45, 1985

Airplane engines, Jet—Standards—cont.
FAA making final evaluation of overwater rules [twin-engine transports] *Aviat Week Space Technol* 122:33 F 18 '85

IFALPA seeks voice in twin-engine extended-range flight standards. *Aviat Week Space Technol* 122:34 My 13 '85

Pilots cite economic pressures in twin-engine overwater safety. W. H. Gregory. *Aviat Week Space Technol* 123:37+ D 9 '85

Singapore A310-200 uses 90-min. limit on overwater route. *Aviat Week Space Technol* 123:30-1 Ag 5 '85

. . . . N. Moll. *Flying* 112:35 My '85

Airbus . . . . . . testbed. il *Aviat Week Space Technol* . . . . . . '85

Allison-powered TurBonanza [1979 Bonanza A36 converted to turboprop] B. Brechner. il *Flying* 112:52-6 Ja '85

B-1B engines damaged during flight, ground run at Offutt. *Aviat Week Space Technol* 123:25-6 Jl 8 '85

CF6-powered A310-300 joins flight test program. il *Aviat Week Space Technol* 123:42-3 O 7 '85

French facility to evaluate fanwheel for CFM56-5. *Aviat Week Space Technol* 122:305 Je 3 '85

GE CF6-80C2 engine nears certification. *Aviat Week Space Technol* 122:304-5 Je 3 '85

GE expands facility for unducted fan engine. K. F. Mordoff. il *Aviat Week Space Technol* 123:153+ Jl 22 '85

General Electric flight tests CF6-80C2 engine on Airbus A300B2. il *Aviat Week Space Technol* 122:31 F 4 '85

General Electric, McDonnell Douglas to flight test unducted fan on MD-80. il *Aviat Week Space Technol* 122:67-8 Je 3 '85

General Electric test series confirming unducted fan concept. S. W. Kandebo. il *Aviat Week Space Technol* 122:53+ My 13 '85

Large-scale propfan built by Hamilton Standard set for high-speed tests. il *Aviat Week Space Technol* 123:28 S 2 '85

Lockheed gears for propfan assessment flights in 1987 [Gulfstream tests] S. W. Kandebo. il *Aviat Week Space Technol* 123:81-2 Jl 15 '85

Lockheed to fly propfan on Gulfstream in 1987. il *Aviat Week Space Technol* 122:66-7 Je 10 '85

McDonnell Douglas nears commitment to fly propfan on MD-80 testbed. B. A. Smith. il *Aviat Week Space Technol* 122:32-3 My 20 '85

Navy tests begin on GE F110 engine for F-14s. *Aviat Week Space Technol* 122:110 Je 10 '85

. . . . . F-4 Phantom. il *Aviat Week*

Lockheed installs advanced facilities as part of factory modernization. J. C. Lowndes. il *Aviat Week Space Technol* 122:113-18 My 27 '85

Negotiating the factory of the future [GE's aircraft parts factory work rules changes] J. Schlefer. il *Technol Rev* 88:24-7 Ja '85

New materials, computers spur engine design [Garrett Turbine Engine] il *Aviat Week Space Technol* 123:119 S 23 '85

Production management concept cuts delays, budget over-runs [Optimized Production Technology] J. C. Lowndes. *Aviat Week Space Technol* 122:85+ My 13 '85

Teams vie for USAF contract in composites. A. K. Marsh. *Aviat Week Space Technol* 122:135+ My 20 '85

Location

. . . . . . with state of New . . . . .

Beech plans to close plant at Liberal, Kan. *Aviat Week Space Technol* 122:27 F 18 '85

Wales

Norman establishing facility in Wales. *Aviat Week Space Technol* 123:26 Jl 8 '85

Airplane fares *See* Airlines—Fares

Airplane hijacking
See also
Beirut airplane hijacking, 1985
EgyptAir Flight 648 hijacking and rescue, 1985

Destination Teheran: anatomy of a hijacking [Kuwaiti airliner] N. M. Adams. il *Read Dig* 127:71-80 O '85

Outwitting the terrorists [Kuwaiti airline hijacking] W. F. Buckley. *Natl Rev* 37:62-3 F 8 '85

Undeclared war [Iranian terrorism] D. Pipes. *New Repub* 192:12-14 Ja 7-14 '85

Prevention
See also
Airports—Security measures

Combating terrorism. O. Ward. *World Press Rev* 32:43 Ag '85

European pilots' groups differ on safety issues after hijacking [EgyptAir hijacking] il *Aviat Week Space Technol* 123:31-3 D 2 '85

IFALPA urges cessation of Beirut operations. *Aviat Week Space Technol* 122:31 Jl 1 '85

In the skies: matching wits with the pirates. C. Skrzycki. il *U S News World Rep* 99:35 Jl 1 '85

Making the sky secure. il *Time* 125:21 Jl 1 '85

Rep. Collins vows to aid FAA in security upgrade. *Jet* 69:6 N 11 '85

Terrorist hijack spurs U.S. review of international security [Beirut hostage crisis] *Aviat Week Space Technol* 122:30-2 Je 24 '85

U.S. seeks international aid in campaign against air piracy. *Aviat Week Space Technol* 123:31-2 Jl 8 '85

Airplane industry
See also

NEWSPAPER INDEXES

Most newspaper indexes list references to only one newspaper. For example, the *New York Times Index* is a meticulous index to just the Late City Edition of the *New York Times*. Other major newspapers that are separately indexed include *Boston Globe, Christian Science Monitor, Los Angeles Times, New Orleans Times-Picayune, St. Louis Post-Dispatch, Wall Street Journal* and *Washington Post*. Your campus library is likely

Figure 3-13: ***New York Times Index*, 1986**

ncea composites, ...
l in airplane bodies; Hexcel had net income
' million, an increase of 31 per cent; revenues
ıt to $235 million and in 1986 analysts
; of $2.30 to $2.40 a share and revenues of
raphs; drawing (M), O 15,IV,1:3
ts third quarter earnings of $2 million, up 11.1
ear-earlier $1.8 million (S), O 16,IV,21:3
also
–Quantum Universe, The (Book), O 5
e L. See also
ils, Je 21
. See also
–Vic Holyfield and the Class of 1957

ee also
ıttempted Murders, Ag 29
r. See also
–Maldive Mystery, The (Book), S 21
on 3d. See also
y & Co Inc, My 28
See also
8
el J. See also
Corp, Ja 4,9
en D. See also
r Inc, My 9
r. See also
s, O 5
p (Prof). See also

on. See also
Mr 27
rdo. See also
Mr 27
ert L. See also
5

poration appoints H L Williamson president
4
ries Inc
ustries, Long Island, NY, maker of space and
nent, names S Gerard Benford vice president
cial officer (S, Ap 8,IV,2:3
See also

Hicks & Haus. See also
A&W Brands Inc, Ap 24
Dr Pepper Co, Ag 21,25
Seven-Up Co, O 1,4
Squirt & Co, N 14
Hicksville (NY). See also
Postal Service, N 16
Roads and Traffic, O 6
Article, If you're thinking of living in Hicksville (NY); photos; map (M), N 9,VIII,1:1
Hiebert, Nancy. See also
Douglas County (Kan), N 8
Hier, Marvin (Rabbi). See also
Austria, My 15
United Nations Commission on Human Rights, My 25
Hieroglyphics. See also
Archeology and Anthropology, My 13
Higbee Beach (NJ). See also
Beaches, Ag 3
Higgins, George V. See also
Baseball, Ag 10
Book Reviews–Impostors (Book), My 12, Je 29
Football, Ja 26
Massachusetts, Ag 3
Higgins, Jay F. See also
Salomon Brothers Inc, Mr 7
Higgins, Joel. See also
Television–Search for Tomorrow (TV Program), Ag 19
Higgins, Margaret. See also
East New York Savings Bank, F 6
Higgins, Michael (Actor). See also
Theater–In This Fallen City (Play), O 24
Higgins, Stephen E. See also
Wines, Ag 6
Higgins, Thomas A (Judge). See also
Banks and Banking, S 1
Higgins Armory Museum (Worcester, Mass)
Higgins Armory Museum in Worcester, Mass, is undergoing $2 million renovation project aimed at preparing building and its artifacts for 21st century; museum's trustees have fended off merger requests by Worcester Art Museum and by Boston Museum of Fine Arts; trustee Mary Louise Wilding-White comments; photo (M), O 19,I,52:3
Higgs, David. See also
Music, Jl 31
... See also

Highway Safety, Insurance Institute for. See also
Roads and Traffic, Ag 23
Highway Safety, Office of (NJ). See also
Roads and Traffic, Mr 9
Highway Safety Representatives, National Assn of Governors'. See also
Roads and Traffic, Ag 23
Highway Traffic Safety Administration, National. See also
Automobiles, F 23, Jl 29, Ag 3,8,17, D 24
Liquor, Ap 21
Motorcycles, Motor Bikes and Motorscooters, Ag 16
Roads and Traffic, Ja 9, S 30
Highways. Use Roads and Traffic
Highways, Bureau of (NYC). See also
Roads and Traffic, My 7
Higson, Allison. See also
Commonwealth Games (1986), Jl 27
Hijacking. See also
Airlines and Airplanes, Ja 7, F 6,9,23,28, Mr 14, Ap 5,9,26, My 4,14,15,23,24, Je 12,13, Jl 27, Ag 5,31, S 5,6,7,8,9,10, 12,13,14,16,18,23,28, O 2,19,29, D 6,26,27,28,29
Armored Car Services, D 28
Crime and Criminals, S 11
India, D 1,2,7
Ireland, Northern, Je 9
Israel, State of, My 27, Je 26
Middle East, My 28,30, Je 1,2,3,27,30, Jl 1,2,4,7,11,14,15, Ag 7,12,25, D 29,31
Ships and Shipping, F 1,10,13, Mr 23, Ap 7,18, My 7,9,11, 18,21,25, Je 8,11,17,18,19,20,21,22,28, Jl 6,11,12,24, Ag 1, 2, O 30, D 6
Hijazi, Ihsan A. See also
Middle East, Ag 11
Hiking. Use Walking
Hildegard, Saint (1098-1179). See also
Music, Mr 27
Hildegarde (Entertainer). See also
Music, Ja 30
Hilditch & Key. See also
Apparel, My 23
Hildreth, Horace A. See also
Caribous, S 14
Hildt, Robert. See also
Sturtevant & Hildt Advertising, Je 23
... Patrick (Repr). See also

to have at least one of these newspaper indexes; and, the library may have indexes to other newspapers in your region.[13]

There are also indexes that provide access to articles in more than one newspaper. In this chapter, we will illustrate searching two of these—*National Newspaper Index* and *NewsBank*. While *National Newspaper Index* provides more-or-less exhaustive indexing to five major U.S. newspapers, *NewsBank* provides very selective access to hundreds of newspapers in all 50 states and the District of Columbia.

New York Times Index (NYTI)

Perhaps the most commonly found newspaper index is the *New York Times Index*. Looking in the 1986 volume of NYTI, under the subject heading "Hijacking" in Figure 3-13, we find no index entries but a series of cross-references to different subject headings. The first of these is "Airlines and airplanes" followed by the abbreviated dates for articles listed in the index under "Airlines and airplanes" which deal with hijacking. When we turn to the subject heading "Airlines and airplanes", we find hundreds of

[13]Your library may also provide access to full-text, computer-searchable versions of one or more newspapers. Among other advantages, this capability allows searching for keywords in headlines, datelines, and the newspaper articles as well. The text of these articles can be printed out even when the library does not subscribe to that newspaper.

Figure 3-14: *New York Times Index*, 1986

Airlines and Airplanes — Cont

Atlantic Southeast Airlines Inc orders 22 Brasilia aircraft from Empresa Brasileira de Aeronautica of Brazil at cost of about $115 million (S), S 4,IV,4:4

British Aerospace PLC wins orders worth about $65 million for six Jetstream 31 airlines and seven 125-800 business jets (S), S 4,IV,4:5

Alaska Air Group Inc buys an additional 520,000 shares of Jet America Airlines Inc, bringing its total holdings to 18 percent (S), S 4,IV,5:6

→ Pakistani officials say that four men dressed as security guards and firing machine guns seized Pan American World Airways jumbo jet filled with nearly 400 people at Karachi airport and at least four people were wounded; say gunmen appear to be Arabs and are demanding to be flown to Cyprus; say three-man cockpit crew escaped through emergency hatch; say plane had just arrived from Bombay, India, en route to New York; say about 41 Americans are

→ among passengers (M), S 5,I,3:1

New book by Seymour M Hersh, The Target is Destroyed, says Soviet Union shot down South Korean airliner at time when US intelligence had vast array of listening devices directed at that area of East Asia, including installations in Japan unknown to Japanese Government (M), S 5,I,6:3

Los Angeles County Coroner Dr Ronald N Kornblum has offered to perform second autopsy of William C Kramer, pilot of small plane that collided with Aeromexico jetliner; Kornblum originally concluded that Kramer had suffered heart attack 'minutes before' collision, but John Lauber, who is leading Federal inquiry into accident, says he doubts that was case (M), S 5,I,16:3

Aircraft Owners and Pilots Association says it will lobby against renewed calls for restrictions on noncommercial aviation in wake of midair collision between private aircraft and Mexican airliner that killed all 67 passengers and crew and many people on ground in Los Angeles suburb (M), S 5,I,16:4

Continental Airlines, in effort to increase ridership, sharply reduces ticket prices on many routes, including $99 one-way transcontinental fare on flights booked 30 days in advance (S), S 5,IV,3:6

At least 15 people are killed and scores wounded when Arabic-speaking hijackers of New York-bound Pan American jumbo jet suddenly begin shooting and detonating grenades inside darkened passenger cabin; hundreds of passengers escape as Pakistani commandos outside plane apparently fire shots, killing two of gunmen; at least two other hijackers are reportedly taken into custody, one claiming to be Palestinian; one American passenger, Rajesh Kumar, is shot early in 16-hour hijacking; map; photos (M), S 6,I,1:6

Pres Reagan condemns seizure of Pan American jet as 'cruel and sinister terrorist act,' and accuses hijackers of 'dispicable and cowardly crime'; praises Pakistani Government for acting 'boldly and decisively to bring this nightmare to an end'; spokesman indicates that there is no immediate evidence indicating whether Libya, Iran or any other nation was involved in attack (M), S 6,I,1:5

Pan American World Airways says Federal Aviation Administration issued 'general alert' for possible terrorist acts to all US airlines 10 days ago; says that even though security system at Karachi airport passed three inspection by FAA in 12 months, 'airport perimeter was penetrated by terrorists'; photo (M), S 6,I,1:6

Passengers aboard Pan American airliner hijacked in Karachi, Pakistan, describe 16-hour ordeal and its bloody ending; photo (M), S 6,I,4:1

Investigation begins into identities and political affiliation of gunmen who seized Pan American plan at Karachi International Airport in Pakistan; fact that they spoke Arabic and wanted to be flown to Cyprus to secure release of colleagues in Cypriot prison suggests that hijackers were Palestinian guerrillas (M), S 6,I,4:1

Excerpts from briefing by Larry Speakes, Pres Reagan's spokesman, and State Department spokesman Charles E Redman on hijacking of Pan American World Airways ～～ ～～ Pakistan; photo (L), S 6,I,5:1

- 39 -

S 7,I,1:2

Chronology of events in hijacking at Karachi airport; photo (page 15A), S 7,I,15:1

Responsibility for two terrorist acts in Middle East within 24 hours--the attack on Istanbul synagogue and hijacking of jet in Karachi, Pakistan--remains unclear; speculation centers on two possibilities: either or both acts could have been carried out by Islamic fundamentalists who had forged links with Palestinian guerrillas infiltrating back into southern Lebanon in recent months, or either or both acts were work of renegade Palestinian terrorist Abu Nidal; what is known is that both attacks were carried out by Arab extremists; photo (M) (page 15B), S 7,I,15:1

Reagan Administration sends team of American investigators to Pakistan to help in learning identities and affiliation of hijackers of Pan American jet in Karachi airport; White House continues to express confidence in way incident was handled by Pakistani authorities; photo (page 15B) (M), S 7,I,15:1

Partial list of casualties on Pan American flight hijacked at airport in Karachi, Pakistan (page 15B) (M), S 7,I,15:4

Seizure of Pan American World Airways jet at Karachi airport was not first attempted hijacking in Pakistan; there were two thwarted hijacking attempts made in 1978 (page 15A) (M), S 7,I,15:5

Among victims of hijacking at Karachi airport was Syed Nesar Ahmad, Pakistani citizen and permanent United States resident who taught at Friends World College on Long Island (page 15A) (M), S 7,I,15:5

Prime Min Rajiv Gandhi of India criticizes Pakistan's handling of hijacking of jet, saying Pakistani security forces 'bungled' rescue mission 'very badly'; also accuses Pakistani authorities of encouraging hijackers by not promptly convicting them and by allowing hijackers to acquire weapons; photo (M) (page 15B), S 7,I,15:5

Article by Professor Peter Cappelli says public has already enjoyed major benefits of airline deregulation and that its drawbacks will become increasingly apparent; says industry has become increasingly concentrated, with some carriers having virtual monoply in certain regions; sketch (M), S 7,III,2:3

Article by economist Gary J Dorman says that despite some calls for renewed Government regulation of airline fares and routes, numerous studies show that deregulation has produced more efficient airlines, lower fares and improved services for most cities (M), S 7,III,2:3

Profile of Lockheed Corporation chairman and chief executive, Lawrence O Kitchen, including his recent handling of scandal regarding company's inability to account for documents relating to Stealth airplane project; his photo; financial chart (L), S 7,III,6:1

Review of seizure of Pan American jumbo jet, Karachi, Pakistan, by Arabic-speaking gunmen, who killed 16 persons and wounded more than 100 others; photos (M), S 7,IV,1:1

Recent crash between small private plane and Aeromexico jet revives question of whether small planes should be kept away from big airports; photo; chart on major midair collisions over US (M), S 7,IV,5:1

Passengers from Pan American Flight 73 recall hijacking terror in Karachi, as soothing words of terrorists were followed by machine-gun massacre when lights went out on plane (S), S 8,I,1:3

Reagan Administration says US Army counterterrorism team was sent to scene of Pan American hijacking in Karachi but failed to arrive before violence erupted; Pakistan Pres Mohammad Zia ul-Haq apparently dismisses idea that such help was needed; says hijackers were four 'volatile' Palestinians, with no known link to any government, who will be prosecuted and possibly executed; incident raises question of stationing special forces close to where such incidents occur (M), S 8,I,1:4

Pakistan Pres Mohammad Zia ul-Haq says four Palestinians who hijacked Pan American airliner have no apparent link to any government and may receive death penalty; says hijacking will not lessen Pakistani support for Palestinian cause; death toll now 18, with 43 other people in hospitals; Zia and other officials say commandos arrived 2- ～～ ～ fire but passengers say

Airlines and Airplanes — Cont

winds causes flight to arrive e～
Christopher Lehmann-Haupt
Destroyed. What Really Happ
America Knew About It by S～
of shooting down of Korean A～
interceptor in 1983; photo, S ～

Delta Air Lines and Western million deal that will open ma～ Atlanta-based Delta; terms ca～ to get $12.50 for each share tł～ balance in Delta stock; Wester～ Delta subsidiary, although ope～ within a year of merger, appar～ and statistical table on airlines～ corporate data (M), S 10,I,1:1

Defense Sec Caspar Weinber～ indications--but no proof--that～ by Abu Nidal was involved in～ S 10,I,11:1

Tennessee Air National Gua～ plane crashes and burns durin～ Campbell, Ky, killing three cr～ (S), S 10,I,12:4

Authorities say 'communicat～ order to two Air National Gu～ unidentified aircraft off coast ～

Trans World Airlines is orde～ senior flight attendants who st～

Delta Air Lines' proposed m～ being seen as belated admissio～ on its conservative internal gr～ competitive (S), S 11,IV,4:3

Airbus Industrie says it has f～ McDonnell Douglas Corp to t～ liner (S), S 11,IV,4:6

Association of European Air～ forecast for 1986 growth in in～ to 3 percent from 5.2 percent～

Market Place column notes ～ airline mergers in near future ～

Senior Pakistani Governmen～ arrested Libyan man as suspec～ Pan American jetliner last wee～ breakthrough in probe into po～ helped four gunmen who seize～ Pres Qaddafi has denied any l～ S 12,I,3:1

Pakistan has not yet provide～ interrogation of terrorists who～ World Airways aircraft in Kar～

Pan American World Airway～ agreement with Texas Air Cor～ landing and takeoff slots at th～ enable Pan Am to start more ～ from La Guardia Airport next～ development, sources say Peo～ buyer or partner to strengthen～ talked to Texas Air (M), S 12,～

Government says proposed s～ ahead early next year; sale is e～ billion (US) (S), S 12,IV,4:6

Delta Air Lines Inc ends its～ result of inability to reach agr～ creditors (S), S 12,IV,4:6

Photo of Raymond Johnson～ US from Cuba, to which he all～ Nov 1968; Johnson, charged w～ returned to see his ailing moth～ Government of Fidel Castro, S～

Texas Air Corp says it has s～ Pan American World Airways～ make it possible for Pan Am t～ service that would be competit～ with Eastern Air Lines shuttle～

Transportation Department a～ proposed merger of Ozark Air～ lines, creating nation's sixth la～ (S), S 13,I,35:1

Two Palestinians are arrested～ ～～ with hijacking in Pakis～

entries relating to many aspects of that topic, including labor disputes and corporate mergers. However, since we are interested in only those entries dealing with hijacking of aircraft, we can use the specific dates given to us under "Hijacking" to limit our search to only those entries. Since the index entries are arranged in chronological order under the subject headings, the cross-reference under the original heading ("Hijacking") gives you both an alternate heading ("Airlines and airplanes") and the dates of the specific index entries referred to. You need the dates to easily locate the articles which relate to both "Airlines and airplanes" and "Hijacking".

Note in Figure 3-13 that the *New York Times* published many articles about aircraft hijacking during 1986 appearing in issues dated 7 January through 29 December. Beginning on 5 September, there is a series of articles in the paper almost daily. In order to find the index entries for these articles, we turn now to Figure 3-14. Here we find that this series of articles recounts the takeover of a Pan American World Airways jet at the Karachi, Pakistan airport.

Under each subject heading in the *New York Times Index* you will find entries describing, but not usually giving the title of, the articles. After a brief content statement, the month, day, section (if there is one), page, and column are given. Notice that the year is not part of the entry. This is determined by the year of the index you are using, 1986 in our example. It is important that you write down the year of the volume you use, especially if you search the index over several years. As mentioned earlier, the entries are listed under each heading in chronological order. This makes it easy to follow news coverage of an event as it unfolded. The first entry for 5 September is the first report about the plane's takeover. The article is of medium length, indicated by (M), printed in section I (or A), on page 3, column 1. The information you need to find the article is given in logical order: first you must know the date, then the section (if sections are used they are indicated by letters or roman numerals), then the page number, then the column number.

National Newspaper Index (NNI)

A finding aid that covers several newspapers is *National Newspaper Index (NNT)*. NNI indexes five newspapers of national prominence: *New York Times, Christian Science Monitor, Los Angeles Times, Wall Street Journal*, and *Washington Post*. NNI is another Information Access Company index that is available in CD-ROM format on Infotrac workstations (like GPI-A) and as an online index. As Table 3-1 shows, the CD-ROM format includes citations published during the most recent four years only while the online version goes back to 1979.

Figure 3-15 shows a screen from the CD-ROM format of NNI that is produced by searching the heading "Hijacking of aircraft" with the subheading "Prevention". Notice that, as with GPI-A, the newspaper article citations are arranged in reverse-chronological order. Another thing to watch out for when using this index is the different editions of two of the newspapers indexed. The Late City Edition and the National Edition of the *New York Times*, as well as the Western Edition and the Eastern Edition of the *Wall Street Journal*, are indexed here. For example, in the first citations in Figure 3-15, the article entitled "Machines Won't End Air Terrorism" appeared in the *Wall Street Journal*, on 20 June 1989. This article appeared on page A16 of the Western Edition (W) and on page A18 of the Eastern Edition (E). You will need to find out which edition your library owns.

Figure 3-15: *National Newspaper Index*™

```
Infotrac EF        National Newspaper Index            Brief Citations

  Subject: Hijacking of Aircraft              Journal Available
  Subdivision: prevention                     Press F5 for details
                          1 of 4
1          Machines won't end air terrorism. (column) by S. Fred Singer.
    The Wall Street Journal, June 20, 1989 pA16(W) pA18(E)   33 col. in.◄───
2          Peak season in the skies. (air safety measures) (editorial) The
    Washington Post, June 3, 1989 pA14 9 col in.
3          FAA warns of possible hijacking; alert on Palestinians given to
    U.S. airlines operating in Europe. Laura Parker.  The Washington Post,
    March 24, 1989 v112 pA1 27 col in.
4          F.A.A. tells airlines of threat, paper says. (Federal Aviation
    Administration, hijacking threat in Europe)  The New York Times, March
    23, 1989 v138 pA9(1) 5 col in.


Display  Narrow  Explore      Esc Return to prior subject list  F3 Print
                              F1 Help   F2 Start over  F4 Mark
Display full record                      F10 PowerTrac
```

NewsBank

NewsBank is both an index and a microfiche service. Articles are selected from newspapers in over 450 U.S. cities. The articles are reproduced on microfiche and a monthly index to this collection is issued in print and CD-ROM formats.

Figure 3-16 illustrates using the CD-ROM version of the *NewsBank Index*. We began this search by typing in "aircraft hijacking". In the first screen, a list of subject headings is displayed showing 51 index entries within the time period January 1986 to May 1991 that relate to our topic. In the second screen, the first seven of these 51 index entries are displayed. Each entry contains very brief information—the airline affected along with the microfiche locator code that allows you to locate the full text of that article. This code includes the year, an abbreviation for the microfiche category, the microfiche card number, and grid coordinates. The microfiche categories are broad subject categories that are used to group together similar articles in the microfiche collection. Occasionally, you will find several related articles grouped together on the same microfiche.

Figure 3-16: *NewsBank Index*

```
Enter: AIRCRAFT HIJACKINGS ◄——
Topic:                                                              NewsBank Index
                                                               January 1986 - May 1991

Headings                              No. of Articles

AIRCRAFT                                    1              Type in a subject to move to that
AIRCRAFT AND AEROSPACE IN                1021              term in the list of subject headings
AIRCRAFT CARRIERS                           *
AIRCRAFT HIJACKINGS                        51 ◄——          Press the SEARCH key to search the
AIRD JOHN S                                 1             index for the highlighted topic
AIRDOCKS                                    3                             or
AIRFONE INC                                 1             Press the HEADINGS key to narrow
AIRLINES                                 2158             your search.
AIRLITE ALUMINUM CORP                       1
AIRPLANE HIJACKINGS                         *             Press LINE FRWD, LINE BACK to
AIRPLANES                                                 Scroll thru the index.
AIRPORTS                                 2288
AKAKA DANIEL                                5             Press the Backspace ( <- ) key to type
AKANA BERNARD                               2             in a new subject.
AKEBONO BRAKE INDUSTRY CO LTD               1
AKERS FRED                                  1             Press HELP for more help assistance.
AKERS JOHN                                  1
AKIHITO CROWN PRINCE OF JAPAN               1             Press F6 to BACKTRACK.

Highlight a topic and press HEADINGS to narrow search, PRINT REF to print.
```

```
Current    AIRCRAFT HIJACKINGS               Last
Search                                       Search
            January 1986 - May 1991
              NewsBank Index                              Microfiche Locator Code ◄——

AIRCRAFT HIJACKINGS
   Aeroflot                                          1988    INT 24:E6
   Air Afrique
     French passenger killed                         1987    INT 100:C9
   Air China
     landing in Japan                                1989    INT 130:A14
   Alaska Airlines
     Alaska:  Anchorage                              1987    TRA 20:G7
   America West Airlines
     hijacker's trial
        1990-Jan-18:  Hijacker admits guilt in America West incident
                                                     1990    TRA 1:F6
   American Airlines
     termination                                     1989    TRA 32:E3
   Delta Airlines
     Texas:  Dallas-Fort Worth International Airport
                                                     1986    TRA 5:G10

Press LINE FORWARD or BACK, HEADINGS for headings list, PRINT REF to print.
```

SUMMARY

1. Searching the periodical and newspaper literature for information on your topic is valuable for at least four reasons. First, current topics, such as aircraft hijacking, simply cannot be thoroughly researched without the new information that continuously appears. Second, periodical and newspaper articles often examine in detail aspects of larger topics that may not be covered in monographs. Third, because they are shorter than books, such articles make it easier to survey diverse interpretations of your topic in a briefer period of time. Fourth, the evolution of a real-world phenomenon and its scholarly interpretation can be traced by reading articles published over a period of time.

2. There are a couple of limitations to the use of periodical and newspaper articles that you should keep in mind. Articles written during or immediately following an event can be flawed by incomplete information. Since articles are brief, they may not adequately deal with the depth and complexity of your topic. Similarly, magazine and newspaper articles usually lack the methodological rigor found in articles in scholarly periodicals, which are peer-reviewed.

3. As with books, you should evaluate the appropriateness of various periodical and newspaper articles by considering the nature of your assignment, and the subject scope, authoritativeness, timeliness, and reading level of the articles that you retrieve. This evaluation will determine which indexes you should use in your research.

4. Periodical and newspaper indexes generally are arranged by one of four methods: basic periodical indexes, newspaper indexes, abstracts, and citation indexes. For any particular index, the medium may vary from print, to CD-ROM, to online database; however, the index's arrangement and your search tactics will remain basically the same.

5. Take the time, as you begin your periodical search, to choose indexes most appropriate to your needs. Do you need general or scholarly sources? Historical or current sources? An exhaustive or selective bibliography? Must your sources be immediately available or can you wait for interlibrary loan to obtain them?

6. Once you have developed a bibliography of periodical and newspaper articles, check your library's holdings list to determine which are immediately available. For those articles that your library does not own, you may consider using interlibrary loan to obtain photocopies of them.

CHAPTER 4

LOCATING U.S. GOVERNMENT DOCUMENTS

When trying to find information about practically any topic, *government documents* are often a prime source of information. Your library may have United Nations documents, United States documents, other nations' documents, and even state and local government documents which offer statistics, analysis, law, policy, and opinion on a wide array of concerns. This chapter will cover U.S. government documents. Chapter 5, "Legal Research", also includes a discussion of those U.S. government publications that deal with that subject. Since U.S. government documents are the most commonly available government documents, you are more likely to use them in your undergraduate political science research.

In any study of public policy, government documents are at least as important as—and in many cases more important than—other published sources. If you are trying to find information about a problem and its effects on the public, or the public's reaction to the problem, government documents are essential to your research. In the case of our sample topic, prevention of aircraft hijacking, U.S. government documents are clearly a relevant source of primary information.

WORLD'S LARGEST PUBLISHER

The U.S. government is the largest publisher in the world. Practically every imaginable topic can be found in a U.S. documents collection, from assassinations to zealots. The Government Printing Office (*GPO*) has established a vehicle to distribute items it publishes through a system of *depository libraries*. These libraries receive documents free of charge from GPO, but they are obligated to maintain the collection and make the documents available to the public. Some libraries are *partial depositories* and select only those categories of documents most likely to be of interest to the people they serve. Even non-depository libraries will probably have some U.S. government documents. Check printed guides to your library or ask a reference librarian if your library is a depository and how U.S. government documents are selected and arranged.

Many libraries do not include information about U.S. government documents in their main library catalogs. Most periodical indexes and abstracts do not cover U.S.

government documents. Of the indexes and abstracts that we discussed in Chapter 3, only *PAIS International in Print* includes any appreciable number of government documents.

Because of this lack of general cataloging, indexing, and abstracting, you will probably need to use one of the specialized indexes to U.S. government documents to identify those particular documents relevant to your research. There are several guides to U.S. government documents, some published by the government itself and some by commercial publishers. Even if your library catalogs U.S. government documents, these indexes will help you identify documents to look for in your library or those not in your library's collection which you may decide to order through interlibrary loan. Since many documents are surprisingly inexpensive, if time allows, you have the option to purchase documents directly from the Government Printing Office.

Libraries that maintain a separate U.S. government document collection usually arrange the materials by the ***Superintendent of Documents Classification System (SUDOC)***. The SUDOC system uses an alpha-numeric scheme which arranges documents by the department or agency that created them, or for which they were created. For instance, Transportation Department publications have SUDOC numbers beginning with "TD". The documents of one of its subordinate agencies, the Federal Aviation Administration, are classified as "TD 4.". Table 4-1 presents an outline of the SUDOC classification system.

THE FEDERAL GOVERNMENT'S DOCUMENT INDEX: *MONTHLY CATALOG OF UNITED STATES GOVERNMENT PUBLICATIONS*

The *Monthly Catalog of United States Government Publications* (*MoCat*) is issued by the Government Printing Office.[1] Locating documents by subject, title, title keyword, author, or series or report numbers in MoCat is a two-step process. First, use one of the appropriate indexes to get the MoCat entry (accession) number; second, use the entry number to find the document description and SUDOC number.[2] Library of Congress subject headings are used to standardize the subject index. Note that there are no cross-references provided in the index section of MoCat; therefore, if you have not already done so, you should now consult *Library of Congress Subject Headings* (discussed in Chapter 2) to locate the appropriate subject headings for your topic.

In the 1987 MoCat Subject Index (Figure 4-1), we look under "Hijacking of aircraft—Prevention" and find one entry, a U.S. House subcommittee hearing on the FAA's review of security at foreign international airports. Each subject index entry provides the document's title, author (beginning in 1987), SUDOC number, and MoCat entry number.

---

[1]The format of MoCat was completely revamped in 1976. This discussion explains the format used since then.

[2]Beginning in 1987, you are given the SUDOC number in the subject and title indexes. Prior to 1987, you are required to look up the document description in order to find the SUDOC number.

Table 4-1: A Selective Outline of the SUDOC Classification System

A	Agriculture Department	L	Labor Department
AE	National Archives and Record Administration		L 2. Labor Statistics Bureau
			L 35. Occupational Safety and Health Administration
C	Commerce Department	LC	Library of Congress
	C 3.Census Bureau	LR	National Labor Relations Board
CC	Federal Communications Commission	NAS	National Aeronautics and Space Administration
D	Defense Department		
		Pr	President
E	Energy Department	PrEx	Executive Office of the President
ED	Education Department		
EP	Environmental Protection Agency		PrEx 2.Management and Budget Office
			PrEx 3.National Security Council
FR	Federal Reserve System		PrEx 3.10Central Intelligence Agency
FT	Federal Trade Commission		
		S	State Department
GA	General Accounting Office	SBA	Small Business Administration
		SE	Securities and Exchange Commission
HE	Health and Human Services Department	SI	Smithsonian Institution
	HE 20.Food and Drug Administration		
HH	Housing and Urban Development Department	T	Treasury Department
			T 17. Customs Service
			T 22. Internal Revenue Service
			T 70. Alcohol, Tobacco, and Firearms Bureau
I	Interior Department		
IC	Interstate Commerce Commission	TD	Transportation Department
			TD 4. Federal Aviation Administration
			TD 5. Coast Guard
J	Justice Department		
	J 1.14Federal Bureau of Investigation	VA	Veterans Affairs Department
	J 29.Justice Statistics Bureau	X	Congress (joint documents)
Ju	Judiciary		
	Ju 6.Supreme Court	Y	Congress (chamber documents)
			Y 4. Committees

In order to find a more complete description of this document, we use the MoCat entry number (87-12220) to locate the information displayed in Figure 4-2. The main body of each issue contains these document descriptions which look like typical catalog entries, arranged by issuing agency and numbered consecutively. From reading the document's title, we surmise that it should be a highly relevant source about prevention of aircraft hijacking. In fact, if you looked at this subcommittee hearing you would find that it contains testimony from concerned representatives from the Air Line Pilots Association, the U.S. Department of Transportation, the U.S. Department of State, and a private company dealing in civil aviation security.

Figure 4-1: *Monthly Catalog of United States Government Publications,* Cumulative Subject Index, 1987

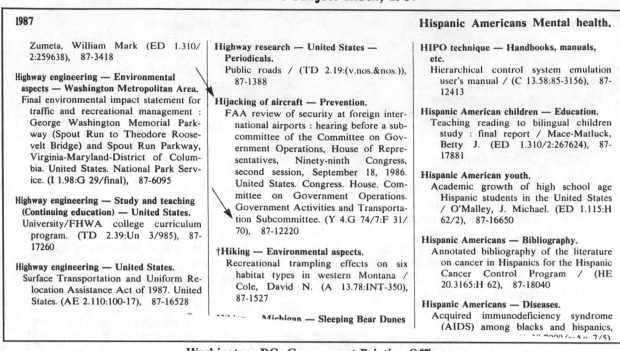

1987

Zumeta, William Mark (ED 1.310/2:259638), 87-3418

Highway engineering — Environmental aspects — Washington Metropolitan Area.
Final environmental impact statement for traffic and recreational management : George Washington Memorial Parkway (Spout Run to Theodore Roosevelt Bridge) and Spout Run Parkway, Virginia-Maryland-District of Columbia. United States. National Park Service. (I 1.98:G 29/final), 87-6095

Highway engineering — Study and teaching (Continuing education) — United States.
University/FHWA college curriculum program. (TD 2.39:Un 3/985), 87-17260

Highway engineering — United States.
Surface Transportation and Uniform Relocation Assistance Act of 1987. United States. (AE 2.110:100-17), 87-16528

Highway research — United States — Periodicals.
Public roads / (TD 2.19:(v.nos.&nos.)), 87-1388

Hijacking of aircraft — Prevention.
FAA review of security at foreign international airports : hearing before a subcommittee of the Committee on Government Operations, House of Representatives, Ninety-ninth Congress, second session, September 18, 1986. United States. Congress. House. Committee on Government Operations. Government Activities and Transportation Subcommittee. (Y 4.G 74/7:F 31/70), 87-12220

†Hiking — Environmental aspects.
Recreational trampling effects on six habitat types in western Montana / Cole, David N. (A 13.78:INT-350), 87-1527

Michigan — Sleeping Bear Dunes

Hispanic Americans Mental health.

HIPO technique — Handbooks, manuals, etc.
Hierarchical control system emulation user's manual / (C 13.58:85-3156), 87-12413

Hispanic American children — Education.
Teaching reading to bilingual children study : final report / Mace-Matluck, Betty J. (ED 1.310/2:267624), 87-17881

Hispanic American youth.
Academic growth of high school age Hispanic students in the United States / O'Malley, J. Michael. (ED 1.115:H 62/2), 87-16650

Hispanic Americans — Bibliography.
Annotated bibliography of the literature on cancer in Hispanics for the Hispanic Cancer Control Program / (HE 20.3165:H 62), 87-18040

Hispanic Americans — Diseases.
Acquired immunodeficiency syndrome (AIDS) among blacks and hispanics,

Washington, DC: Government Printing Office.

Do not confuse the entry number in MoCat with the SUDOC number. The MoCat entry number is used to find the document description in MoCat. The SUDOC number (Y4.G74/7:F31/70) is used to find the document in the library's collection. A third number useful in your search for a U.S. government document is the "Item number" (Item 1016-A, 1016-B [microfiche] in Figure 4-2). The presence of such an item number indicates that the document was issued as one of a set of depository items with that same number. This number is easy to locate because it is always preceded by a large black dot.

If your library is a full depository, it should receive all depository items. If your library is a partial depository library, its staff selects the most appropriate item numbers (categories) for the library's users. Some of the documents indexed in MoCat are not issued as depository items. You will need to ask a documents or reference librarian how you can find out what documents are received by your library.

There are a variety of ways in which libraries indicate what government documents are received. First, documents may be cataloged, either in the main catalog or separately. Second, there may be a public *shelf list* in which document descriptions are arranged alpha-numerically by call number. If your library has such a government documents shelf list, you will need to find out what call number system is used. Most commonly you will find either SUDOC or LC classification call numbers used. Third, some depository libraries make available to users an *Item List* indicating those depository item numbers received by that library. If your library has such an Item List, to find the document described in Figure 4-2, you would now look to see if Item 1016 was received; and, if so, whether in paper (1016-A) or microfiche (1016-B). If your library does not use a

Figure 4-2: *Monthly Catalog of United States Government Publications*, Main Entry Section, 1987

Government Operations, Committee on — House

1. United States. Congress. House. Committee on Foreign Affairs Bibliography Periodicals. I. United States. Congress. House. Committee on Foreign Affairs. sn-87042696 OCLC 08321912

GOVERNMENT OPERATIONS, Committee on, House
Washington, DC 20515

87-12219

Y 4.G 74/7:Et 3

United States. Congress. House. Committee on Government Operations. Environment, Energy, and Natural Resources Subcommittee.

EDB pesticide disposal problems : hearing before a subcommittee of the Committee on Government Operations, House of Representatives, Ninety-ninth Congress, second session, November 10, 1986. — Washington : U.S. G.P.O. : For sale by the Supt. of Docs., Congressional Sales Office, U.S. G.P.O., 1987.

iv, 140 p. : ill., 1 form ; 24. Distributed to some depository libraries in microfiche. Shipping list no.: 87-203-P. ●Item 1016-A, 1016-B (microfiche)

1. United States. Environmental Protection Agency. 2. Ethylene dibromide. 3. Pesticides — Toxicology — United States. 4. Pesticides policy — United States. 5. Hazardous substances — United States — Physiological effect. I. Title. OCLC 15526975

87-12220

Y 4.G 74/7:F 31/70

United States. Congress. House. Committee on Government Operations. Government Activities and Transportation Subcommittee.

FAA review of security at foreign international airports : hearing before a subcommittee of the Committee on Government Operations, House of Representatives, Ninety-ninth Congress, second session, September 18, 1986. — Washington : U.S. G.P.O. : For sale by the Supt. of Docs., Congressional Sales Office, U.S. G.P.O., 1987.

iii, 120 p. ; 23 cm. Distributed to some depository libraries in microfiche. Shipping list no.: 87-179-P. ●Item 1016-A, 1016-B (microfiche)

1. International airports — Security measures. 2. Hijacking of aircraft — Prevention. I. Title. OCLC 15506993

87-12221

Y 4.G 74/7:G 76/9

United States. Congress. House. Committee on Government Operations. Intergovernmental Relations and Human Resources Subcommittee.

Office of Human Development Services grants programs : hearing before a subcommittee of the Committee on Government Operations, House of Representatives, Ninety-ninth Con-

a subcommittee of the Committee on Government Operations, House of Representatives, Ninety-ninth Congress, second session on H.R. 4784 ... May 15, 1986. — Washington : U.S. G.P.O. : For sale by the Supt. of Docs., Congressional Sales Office, U.S. G.P.O., 1987.

iii, 64 p. ; 24 cm. Distributed to some depository libraries in microfiche. Shipping list no.: 87-211-P. ●Item 1016-A, 1016-B (microfiche)

1. Land titles — Registration and transfer — Washington (D.C.) 2. Housing — Law and legislation — Washington (D.C.) 3. Homelessness — Law and legislation — Washington (D.C.) I. Title. OCLC 15564110

GOVERNMENTAL AFFAIRS, Committee on, Senate
Washington, DC 20510

87-12223

Y 4.G 74/9:S.prt.100-17

United States. Congress. Senate. Committee on Governmental Affairs. Permanent Subcommittee on Investigations.

Rules of procedure / Senate Permanent Subcommittee on Investigations of the Committee on Governmental Affairs, United States Senate. Washington, DC : U.S. G.P.O. : For sale by the Supt. of Docs., Congressional Sales Office, U.S. G.P.O., Supt. of Docs., Congressional Sales Office, U.S. Govt. Print. Off., Washington, DC 20402

v. ; 15 cm. (S. prt. ; 100-17)

Biennial Shipping list no.: 87-184-P. Feb. 26, 1987. Description based on: Feb. 26, 1987. Vols. for ⟨1987-⟩ distributed to some depository libraries in microfiche. ●Item 1037-B, 1037-C (microfiche)

1. United States. Congress. Senate. Committee on Governmental Affairs. Permanent Subcommittee on Investigations Rules and practice Periodicals. I. Title. II. Series. sn-87042314 OCLC 15507159

HOUSE ADMINISTRATION, Committee on, House
Washington, DC 20515

87-12224

Y 4.H 81/3-11:987

United States. Congress. House. Committee on House Administration.

Calendar of business / United States House of Representatives, Committee on House Administration. [Washington, D.C.] : U.S. G.P.O. : For sale by the Supt. of Docs., Congressional Sales Office, U.S. G.P.O., Supt. of Docs., Congressional Sales ... Off., Washington, D.C. 20402

Washington, DC: Government Printing Office.

---

catalog, shelf list, or Item List to indicate what government documents are in its collection, ask a documents or reference librarian if other finding aids are available.

As its title implies, the *Monthly Catalog of United States Government Publications* is published monthly. Semiannual and annual cumulations of the MoCat indexes save time in locating appropriate documents. MoCat is also issued in CD-ROM versions by several commercial publishers. Check with a reference librarian to find out if MoCat is available on CD-ROM in your library. In Chapter 7, "Computer Database Searching", you will find hints on constructing search statements for online retrieval of computer-stored information.

While MoCat is the official record of publications issued by the U.S. Government Printing Office, it is not the only search tool available for identifying U.S. government documents. Several commercial publishers issue indexes that can be very useful in research involving government policies and programs. Each commercial index has special features that make them attractive for different types of research.

A major drawback of MoCat is that it describes and indexes documents as a whole, but does not analyze or index parts of documents. In this respect, MoCat is like the library catalog, which describes the overall subject matter of a book, but not individual chapters within the book. Three of the commercially produced indexes that provide this more detailed indexing of parts of documents are *CIS/Index, Index to U.S. Government Periodicals*, and *American Statistics Index*. In order to accomplish such detailed indexing, *CIS/Index* limits its scope to Congressional documents, *Index to U.S. Government Periodicals* provides access to individual articles in periodicals published by many government agencies, and *American Statistics Index* pinpoints statistical tables included within U.S. government documents. While *CIS/Index* is limited by agency (U.S. Congress), *Index to U.S. Government Periodicals* is limited by type of document (periodical). *American Statistics Index* is not limited by agency or document type, but rather by type of information (statistics). This latter index is discussed in detail in Chapter 6, "Locating General Information".

Coverage of Congressional Documents:
CIS/Index

In fulfilling its investigative and legislative duties, the U.S. Congress gathers a tremendous amount of information on a wide variety of topics. This information is supplied to committees and subcommittees by reports and testimony offered by: 1) congressional staff; 2) congressional research agencies, such as Congressional Research Service, Congressional Budget Office, General Accounting Office, and Library of Congress; 3) individuals and agencies within the other two branches of the federal government; 4) American state and local governments; 5) foreign governments; and 6) private individuals and organizations from the U.S. and abroad.

Providing detailed access to all of these reports and testimony is the *CIS/Index*, published by Congressional Information Service, Inc. It is issued monthly in two parts: "Index of Subjects and Names" and "Abstracts of Congressional Publications". The index cumulates quarterly. Both the index and abstracts cumulate annually. In addition, a third part is issued annually, "Legislative Histories of U.S Public Laws". Collectively, these publications are intended to provide prompt access to all working papers of Congress, except the *Congressional Record*.

CIS/Index is another two-step index. Starting in the "Index of Subjects and Names" section of the *1987 CIS/Index* cumulation, we looked under "Hijacking of aircraft" and were told to see "Air piracy" (see Figure 4-3). Here we find three entries. Each index entry contains a brief phrase describing the content of the document. This guides your selection of documents that are relevant to your topic. While all three entries do appear related to our sample topic of preventing aircraft hijacking, the description of the third

Figure 4-3: *CIS/Index*. 1987 Annual, Index of Subjects and Names

Index of Subjects and Names

Authorization, FY88-FY89, for personnel
programs, S201-15
Authorization, FY88-FY89, for tactical
warfare R&D programs, H201-31.6
B-1B bomber program status and problems,
H201-32, H202-5
Budget proposal, FY88, review, S251-5.5
"Development of Productivity Indexes from
the RAND Air Force Study", J932-22
DOD and armed services governing laws,
US Code Title 10 text, H202-12

Air Force contracts and procurement
  see Defense contracts and procurement
Air Force personnel
  see Military personnel
Air Force Sergeants Association
  Veterans and military personnel educ
  assistance programs permanent authority
  estab, H761-10.6, S761-5.1
Air freight service
  see Air cargo
Air Line Pilots Association, International
  Air traffic control system safety review,

Air pollution

Air piracy
  Airport security in foreign countries, FAA
  assessment program, H401-24
  Guns not detectable by airport security
  systems, trade restrictions estab, H521-45
  Terrorism control efforts, laws, treaties, and
  docs compilation, H382-20
Air pollution
  Acid rain and ozone control programs,
  S321-17
  Acid rain control and clean coal technology
  R&D, S311-20
  Agric Research Service programs, FY88

looks especially useful since it compiles information about various types of control efforts. The brief description is followed by an accession number that must be used in the second step of locating a complete bibliographic reference and abstract of the document located in the abstracts volume of the *1987 CIS/Index*. Notice that all three "Air piracy" index accession numbers in Figure 4-3 begin with an "H" indicating that they are U.S. House documents. Elsewhere, you will find entries beginning with "J" for joint committee publications and "S" for U.S. Senate materials.

Figure 4-4 shows the abstract for index accession number H382-20 titled, *International Terrorism: A Compilation of Major Laws, Treaties, Agreements, and Executive Documents*. Notice part "1. International Civil Aviation Organization Document (p. 939-962)". This section appears to be the part of the document most relevant to our research on prevention of terrorist hijacking of aircraft. The document also has a subject index to aid in finding other sections bearing on our topic.

It is important to realize that because the title of this document indicates a very broad treatment of terrorism policy, it is not indexed under "Hijacking of aircraft" in the MoCat. Therefore, without the detailed indexing provided by *CIS/Index*, you would have no efficient means of determining this document's relevance to our research topic.

As mentioned earlier, *CIS/Index* includes a third part, "Legislative Histories of U.S. Public Laws". A *legislative history* is a bibliographic record that traces the documents recording the development of acts of Congress that become public laws. Such a history in the *CIS/Index* typically includes bibliographic references to committee reports, hearings, and prints; predecessor or companion bills; *Congressional Record* of floor debate; House or Senate documents including messages to Congress from the President; the enacted bill or joint resolution; and the presidential statement on signing the bill from the *Weekly Compilation of Presidential Documents*.

Using the "Index of Subjects and Names" in the *1984 CIS Annual Legislative Histories*, we were referred from "Air piracy" to "Convention for the Suppression of Unlawful Acts Against the Safety of Civil Aviation" (see Figure 4-5). This reference is to Public Law 98-473 (Title II). It is the second major section of the 473d bill enacted into public law by the 98th Congress. The public law number serves as the accession number to find the legislative history in the main part of this volume of *CIS/Index*. In

Figure 4-4: *CIS/Index*, 1987 Annual, Abstracts of Congressional Publications

Foreign Affairs H382–23

Appendix (p. 213-231) includes texts and excerpts from selected arms control agreements and treaties, including SALT II.

Classified material has been deleted.

Report of a ...

East Oct. 15-30, 1986 staff study mission, led by Staff Director Michael H. Van Dusen, to Portugal, Spain, Greece, and Turkey, to review political-military issues, including NATO relationships, U.S. economic and military assistance programs, and forthcoming negotiations regarding U.S. access to military facilities in the region.

H382–17 TWENTY-EIGHTH MEETING OF THE CANADA-U.S. INTERPARLIAMENTARY GROUP, June 4-8, 1987.
July 1987. 100-1. v+59 p.
GPO $2.00 CIS/MF/3
•Item 1017-A; 1017-B.
°Y4.F76/1-11:987.

Report by Rep. Sam Gejdenson (D-Conn), Chairman of the House Delegation, on the 28th meeting of the Canada-U.S. Interparliamentary Group, held in Vancouver, British Columbia, Canada, June 4-8, 1987. Includes committee reports on trade, economic, energy, defense, fisheries, environment, and transboundary issues.

H382–18 TWENTY-SIXTH MEXICO-U.S. INTERPARLIAMENTARY CONFERENCE, Colorado Springs, Colorado, May 30-June 1, 1986.
June 1987. 99-2. v+60 p.
GPO $2.00 CIS/MF/3
•Item 1017-A; 1017-B.
°Y4.F76/1:M57/7/986/report.
MC 87-17502.

Report, also prepared for the Senate Foreign Relations Committee, by House delegation Chairman E de la Garza (Rep, D-Tex) and Senate delegation Chairman Phil Gramm (Sen, R-Tex), on the 26th meeting of the Mexico-U.S. Interparliamentary Group, held May 30-June 1, 1986 in Colorado Springs, Colo. Reviews conference deliberations on political, social, and economic issues.

H382–20 INTERNATIONAL TERRORISM: A COMPILATION OF MAJOR LAWS, TREATIES, AGREEMENTS, AND EXECUTIVE DOCUMENTS.
Aug. 1987. 100-1.
xv+970 p. GPO $27.00
CIS/MF/12
•Item 1017-A; 1017-B.
°Y4.F76/1:T27/2.
MC 87-18867.

CRS compilation, prepared by Jennifer D. Kibbe and Marjorie A. Browne, of texts of major laws, treaties and agreements, and executive documents and reports regarding U.S. and international efforts to combat and control terrorism. Organized as follows:

a. Foreign Assistance and Related Legislation (p. 1-21).
b. Department of State Legislation (p. 23-90).
c. Trade and Financial Legislation (p. 91-122).
d. Treaty-Implementing Legislation (p. 123-150).
e. Other Legislation (p. 151-165).
f. Executive Branch Documents (p. 167-196).
g. Economic Summit Conference Statements (p. 197-207).
h. Bilateral Agreements, regarding aviation security and extradition (p. 209-326).
i. Multilateral Treaties (p. 327-410).
j. Reports to Congress and to the President, from Federal departments and agencies (p. 411-893).
k. Regulations (p. 895-938).
l. International Civil Aviation Organization Document (p. 939-962).

Also includes a subject index (p. 963-970).

H382–21 U.S. ARMS CONTROL AND DISARMAMENT AGENCY 1986 ANNUAL REPORT,

28th interparliamentary ... pean Parliament, held in Madrid, Spain, Apr. 11-13, 1987. Summarizes sessions and includes texts of papers presented on common concerns, including overall U.S.-European Community (EC) relations, East-West relations and arms control issues, and U.S.-EC trade relations.

Appendices (p. 45-90) include summaries of bilateral meetings and:

– H. Res. 121, to commend the EC and the governments of the EC member nations for the EC role in development of U.S.-European relations, text as introduced and as passed by the House (p. 58-63).

H382–23 INTERPARLIAMENTARY UNION CONFERENCE.
1987. 100-1. v+41 p.
GPO $1.50 CIS/MF/3
•Item 1017-A; 1017-B.
°Y4.F76/1:In8/52/987.
LC 88-600768.

Report of the U.S. Delegation to the Interparliamentary Union meeting held at Managua, Nicaragua, Apr. 27-May 2, 1987. Summarizes conference deliberations on political and economic issues.

Includes U.S. delegation statements (p. 20-25) and texts of adopted resolutions (p. 31-40).

Volume 18, Number 1-12 CIS/INDEX 261

Figure 4-6 we find that Title II of PL 98-473 is the Comprehensive Crime Control Act of 1984. Its twenty-three chapters are outlined in the first section of the legislative history. Scanning these chapter titles and descriptions, we find that Chapter XX, Part A and Part B enact penalties for hostage-taking and crimes aboard aircraft, information pertinent to a study of the prevention of terrorist hijacking of aircraft.

Other Commercial Indexes to U.S. Government Documents

You may already be aware that the U.S. government publishes periodicals, such as the *Department of State Bulletin* or *Monthly Labor Review*. Some of these are indexed in the periodical indexes discussed in Chapter 3. However, the *Index to U.S. Government*

Figure 4-5: *CIS/Index*, 1984 Annual, Abstracts of Congressional Publications

Coronado National Forest

Fla wilderness study areas land use classification, judicial review ban, PL98–430

Ga wilderness study areas land use classification, judicial review ban, PL98–514

PL98–580

Wash State wilderness study areas land use classification, judicial review ban, PL98–339

Wis wilderness study areas land use classification, judicial review ban, PL98–321

Wyo wilderness study areas land use classification, judicial review ban, PL98–550

Congressional powers
see also Congressional-executive relations
see also Congressional-judicial relations
see also Impoundment of appropriated funds
see also Presidential powers

Congressmen
see Congress
see Senate

Connecticut

see also Civil-military relations
see also Civil rights
see also Congressional-executive relations
see also Congressional-judicial relations
see also Federal-State relations
see also Impoundment of appropriated funds
see also Interstate relations

Consumer Information Center
Approp, FY85, PL98–371

Consumer Price Index
Social security cost of living adjustment, limitation requirement waiver and SSA study requirement, PL98–604

Consumer Product Safety Commission
Approp, FY85, PL98–371
Cigarette and little cigar fire safety study, Fed advisory program estab, PL98–567
Hazardous products for children, Consumer Product Safety Commission regulatory procedures revision, PL98–491

Consumer protection
CAB termination and functions transfer, PL98–443
Cable TV regulatory revisions, PL98–549
Generic drug approval procedures revision, PL98–417

Contracts
see Defense contracts and procurement
see Government contracts and procurement
see Research and development grants and contracts

Contributions
see Campaign funds

Criminal justice procedures revision, PL98–473 (Title II)

Convention for Suppression of Unlawful Acts Against the Safety of Civil Aviation
Aircraft sabotage, intl convention implementation, PL98–473 (Title II)

Convention on the Conservation of Antarctic Marine Living Resources
Implementation, PL98–623

Conventions
see Conferences
see Political conventions
see Treaties and conventions

Coolidge Dam, Ariz.
Bur of Reclamation dam safety programs revision, PL98–404

Cooperatives
see also Rural cooperatives

Tower Umpqua and Siuslaw

Figure 4-6: *CIS/Index*, 1984 Annual, Legislative Histories of U.S. Public Laws

Public Law 98-473 (Title II)   98 Stat. 1976

Comprehensive Crime Control Act of 1984

October 12, 1984

Public Law

1.1   Public Law 98-473, Title II, approved Oct. 12, 1984 (H.J. Res. 648)

Title II, the Comprehensive Crime Control Act of 1984, is organized as follows.

CHAPTER I, the Bail Reform Act of 1984.

Amends the Bail Reform Act of 1966 to permit pretrial detention of certain dangerous defendants, and to establish penalties for violation of pretrial release conditions.

CHAPTER II, the Sentencing Reform Act of 1984.

Provides for comprehensive and consistent sentencing and a review process, and establishes the U.S. Sentencing Commission to promulgate sentencing guidelines and policy.

CHAPTER III, the Comprehensive Forfeiture Act of 1984.

Amends the Comprehensive Drug Abuse Prevention and Control Act of

Establishes as a Federal crime the receipt, transport, or possession of a firearm by persons with three prior convictions for robbery or burglary.

Establishes a mandatory minimum sentence of 15 years without parole for armed career criminal conviction.

CHAPTER XIX, the Criminal Justice Act Revision of 1984.

Increases maximum amounts of payments authorized for representation of defendants financially unable to obtain adequate representation.

CHAPTER XX, PART A, the Act for the Prevention and Punishment of the Crime of Hostage-Taking.

Establishes a penalty for hostage taking, effective on the date the International Convention Against the Taking of Hostages comes into force and the U.S. has become a party to it.

CHAPTER XX, PART B, the Aircraft Sabotage Act, amends the Federal Aviation Act, and implements the Convention for the Suppression of Unlawful Acts Against the Safety of Civil Aviation.

Establishes penalties for aircraft sabotage, attempted aircraft sabotage, acts of violence on board civil aircraft, and hoaxes endangering aircraft safety.

CHAPTER XXI, the Counterfeit Access Device and Computer Fraud and Abuse Act of 1984.

Establishes criminal penalties for unauthorized use of computers involving institutions or restricted Government data, including

Periodicals provides more comprehensive indexing to articles in government periodicals. Articles in almost 200 U.S. government periodicals are indexed by author and subject in this source.

When you find a useful entry, it will tell you where the article was published. As with many indexes, to save space, the periodical title is often abbreviated. When you look in the front of the index, you will find the full name of the periodical and its SUDOC number. Now you will need to find out if your library subscribes to this periodical. If so, is the periodical located in the documents collection, the periodicals collection, the main collection, or elsewhere? These practices vary among libraries. To be certain that you can find the article, ask a documents or reference librarian which procedure your library follows.

There are other commercially produced indexes to U.S. government publications that may be available in your library. For example, the *Government Publications Index* (*GPI*) is a convenient source for locating U.S. government documents from the entire range of federal agencies. Issued monthly by Information Access Corporation, it is like *General Periodicals Index—Academic Library Edition* in that it is not issued in paper copy. GPI is available as a CD-ROM index or in computer-output microform. A nice feature of GPI is that it cumulates several years of entries (starting with 1976). Like MoCat, GPI uses Library of Congress subject headings.

NewsBank, Inc. publishes the *Index to the Foreign Broadcast Information Service Daily Reports*. The daily reports consist of material from broadcasts, news agency transmissions, newspapers, periodicals, and government statements originating in other nations around the world. These reports are collected and published by the Foreign Broadcast Information Service (FBIS), a U.S. government agency. The FBIS reports and corresponding NewsBank indexes are divided into eight geographic regions: Asia and Pacific, China, Eastern Europe, Latin America, Middle East and Africa, South Asia, Soviet Union, and Western Europe. The *FBIS Daily Reports* offer selected but unedited perspectives on contemporary affairs from outside the United States. As such, they are a valuable primary source of information for the student of politics.

Transdex (also known as *Bell & Howell Transdex*) is another commercially published index. Issued by University Microfilms International, it is a guide to the translations and transcriptions issued by the Joint Publications Research Service (JPRS), which is now a part of FBIS. Although the emphasis of JPRS is on providing scientific and technical information from communist countries, political and sociological affairs worldwide are also covered.

These and other indexes to government documents may be available in your library. Ask your reference librarian about using them.

SUMMARY

1. Government documents provide information on a wide array of topics. In doing research on political issues, problems, or events, it is likely that your best sources for statistics, analysis, law, policy, and opinion will be found in government publications.

2. You should become familiar with the specialized indexes and abstracts to government documents because the latter are not covered comprehensively (and sometimes not at all) in the library catalog or in general periodical indexes.

3. Use MoCat to locate documents from all parts of the U.S. national government. Use narrower indexes (e.g., *CIS/Index*) to locate documents published by specific branches, departments, or agencies of the federal government. Also useful are those narrower indexes (e.g., *Index to U.S. Government Periodicals* and *CIS/Index*) that provide access to parts of government documents.

4. If your research requires locating government documents issued by American state or local governments, foreign governments, or international organizations, be sure to consult with a reference librarian to determine what finding aids and sources are available.

CHAPTER 5

LEGAL RESEARCH: STATUTES, REGULATIONS, CASES, AND TREATIES

Laws are those rules governing relations between people that are prescribed, enforced, and adjudicated by government. Given the complex distribution of governmental power in the American federal system, legal research can lead in many directions. Because of the constitutional division of power across levels of American government, you may need to research laws at the local, state, or federal level. In this chapter, we will limit our focus to legal research at the federal level including international law involving the United States. However, the search skills and strategies appropriate to legal research at the federal level apply equally well to researching state and local laws. For example, researching federal government policies intended to prevent aircraft hijacking will illustrate techniques that also can be used to find state or local government attempts to make illegal and punish this form of terrorism.

FOUR TYPES OF LAW

Because of the constitutional separation of power within each level of American government, you may need to research law making, law enforcing, or law adjudicating. You may also need to locate relevant treaties or international agreements. Hence, this chapter is divided into four sections: statute law, case law, administrative law, and international law. *Statute law* encompasses those bills and resolutions debated and enacted by legislatures. Since locating statute law entails using the same techniques (and often the same primary and secondary sources) as researching constitutional law, this chapter will not offer a separate section on the latter. Once you know the appropriate sources and search techniques for finding statutes, you can utilize them to find constitutional provisions.

Case law entails those principles and rules of law developed by courts in deciding lawsuits or cases. *Administrative law* includes those rules or regulations and orders or directives issued by administrative agencies under their quasi-legislative and quasi-judicial authority. *International law*, regulating the conduct of nations, is based largely upon treaties and international agreements. Throughout this chapter, when we use the phrase "the law", we are referring broadly to all four types of law, not just legislative-made statute law. We will illustrate legal research in all four types of law by investigating the legal dimensions of our sample topic—prevention of aircraft hijacking.

TWO TYPES OF LEGAL SOURCES: PRIMARY AND SECONDARY SOURCES

As with other forms of library research, legal research requires locating and using primary and secondary sources. In legal research, *primary sources* are publications that present the law itself, that is, the actual text of constitutions, statutes, regulations, court decisions, or treaties. Table 5-1 lists the major primary sources for legal research that are discussed in this chapter. *Secondary sources* are those publications that describe, summarize, and analyze the conflicts that created, the nature of, and consequences resulting from the application of those laws. Table 5-2 lists the major secondary sources for legal research that are discussed below. It also includes finding aids for legal research in the form of indexes to court decisions and treaties.

Two Types of Primary Legal Sources: Chronological Series and Codes

Within all four areas of legal research, we will find that primary legal sources fall into two basic types of publications: 1) chronological series that compile the full text of statutes, regulations, court decisions, or treaties in the order in which they were adopted; and 2) codes that collect or arrange the law according to topics or subjects. Table 5-1 lists the major chronological series and codes useful for research into federal and international law. Commonly used abbreviations are included in the table for the primary legal sources we will discuss and illustrate in this chapter.

A legal *chronological series* is a compilation of the full text of the law in the order that it was adopted. For example, if you knew the approximate date or legal citation (e.g., public law or PL number), you could locate the full text of enacted federal anti-hijacking legislation in slip laws or *United States Statutes at Large* (Stat). Similarly, the Federal Aviation Agency's anti-hijacking regulations are published in the *Federal Register* (FR); presidential anti-terrorism proclamations or executive orders are in the *Weekly Compilation of Presidential Documents*; announced U.S. Supreme Court decisions and opinions are given in Slip Opinions, *United States Reports* (US), *United States Supreme Court Reports, Lawyers' Edition* (LEd), or *Supreme Court Reporter* (SCt); and U.S. treaties and international agreements appear as slip treaties in *Treaties and Other International Acts Series* (TIAS) and are later collected in *United States Treaties and Other International Agreements* (UST).

Since statute, case, administrative, and international law are all continuously being adopted or modified, their respective legal chronological series are frequently updated. Hence, our most up-to-date published sources of federal and international law will usually be issued as chronological series.

A legal *code* is a subject-organized, topical, or encyclopedic arrangement of the actual text of the laws in force. In effect, it is a very detailed subject index to the law. A code is usually published as a large, multi-volume compilation or set that is updated with *pocket parts* (paperbound supplements that update some legal codes and digests—found in pockets attached inside the cover of hardbound volumes), annual

Table 5-1: Selected Primary Sources of Federal and International Law

Federal Law			International Law[a]
Statute	**Administrative**	**Case[b]**	
Chronological Series			
• Slip Laws • *U.S. Statutes at Large* (Stat) • *U.S. Code Congressional and Administrative News*[c]	• *Federal Register* (FR) • *Weekly Compilation of Presidential Documents*	• Slip Opinions • *U.S. Reports* (US) • *U.S. Supreme Court Reports, Lawyers' Edition* (Led) • *Supreme Court Reporter* (SCt)	• *Treaties and Other International Acts Series* (TIAS) • *U.S. Treaties and Other International Agreements* (UST)
Codes			
• *U.S. Code (USC)* • *U.S. Code Annotated* • *U.S. Code Service*	• *Code of Federal Regulations (CFR)* • *Code of Federal Regulations Annotated* • *Codification of Presidential Proclamations and Executive Orders*		

[a]For reasons of brevity, the primary sources listed here for international law are limited to those providing access to treaties and other international agreements to which the U.S. is a party. See the discussion in the text under international law for information about primary sources for other treaties and other international agreements.

[b]Similarly, the primary sources listed here for case law are limited to sources of U.S. Supreme Court decisions. See the discussion in the text under case law for information about analogous court reporters for lower federal courts and state courts.

[c]Even though this work includes the word "Code" in its title, it is nevertheless a chronological series much like *U.S. Statutes at Large*.

supplements, and/or new editions issued every few years. Because of the time it takes to codify and publish a code, it is not as up-to-date as a chronological series.

The basic advantage of using a code of the law is that you can do a subject search and locate all currently in-force law on your topic, regardless of when adopted. Thus,

Table 5-2: Selected Finding Aids and Secondary Sources of Federal and International Law

Federal Law			International Law[a]
Statute	**Administrative**	**Case[b]**	
• CQ Weekly Reports • CQ Almanac • CQ Congress & the Nation • CQ's Guide to Congress • Congress A to Z • Politics in America • Almanac of American Politics	• National Journal • Federal Regulatory Directory • U.S. Government Manual • Government Agencies • The Capital Source • Washington Information Directory	(LEGAL ENCYCLOPEDIAS) • American Jurisprudence 2d • Corpus Juris Secundum (COURT DIGESTS) • U.S. Supreme Court Digest • U.S. Supreme Court Reports Digest (INDEX TO DECISIONS) • U.S. Supreme Court Decisions, 2d ed. (Guenther, 1983) (CASE BRIEFS) • Preview of U.S. Supreme Court Cases • Landmark Briefs and Arguments of the Supreme Court of the U.S.	• Treaties in Force • American Foreign Policy Current Documents • Digest of U.S. Practice in International Law

[a]For reasons of brevity, the secondary sources listed here for international law are limited to those providing access to treaties and other international agreements to which the U.S. is a party.

[b]Similarly, the secondary sources listed here for case law are limited to indexes to and analyses of U.S. Supreme Court decisions.

Table 5-1 shows that you can subject search federal statute law and federal administrative law directly using the *United States Code* (USC) and *Code of Federal Regulations* (CFR), respectively.

Figure 5-1: Examples of Legal Citations

Chronological Series Citations

(statute)   Act for the Prevention and Punishment of the Crime of Hostage-Taking, 98 Stat 2186 (1984).

(regulation) FAA, Airport Security, Access to Secured Areas, 54 FR 588 (1989).

(case)   US v. Healy, 376 US 75 (1964).

(treaty)   Convention on Offenses and Certain Other Acts Committed on Board Aircraft, 20 UST 2941 (1969).

Code Citations

(statute)   18 USC §1203 (1982).

(regulation) 14 CFR §108.10 (1988).

Citation Format for Primary Legal Sources

As each primary legal source is introduced in this chapter, we will illustrate the proper citation format for that source. There is a section in the *Style Manual for Political Science* that describes and gives examples of legal citations and references (see Appendix II, pp. 197-98). The standard reference work on legal citations is *A Uniform System of Citation* (often called "the Blue Book"). Check your library's catalog to see if it is available to you.

However, since citations to all primary legal sources (chronological series or codes) follow a common pattern within each type, now is a good time to describe the two patterns.

At a minimum, a citation to an entry in a legal chronological series should contain three elements in the following order of presentation:

1) the short title or popular name of the statute, regulation, case, or treaty;

2) three pieces of information about the publication in which the statute, regulation, case, or treaty is found:

     a) volume number,
     b) the abbreviation of the main title of the chronological series,
     c) the starting page number,

3) the year in which the statute was enacted, the regulation was issued, the case was decided, or the treaty was ratified (not necessarily the year of publication).

Examples of citations to entries in legal chronological series are shown in Figure 5-1. There seems to be no universal agreement on the use of periods in acronyms and abbreviations in legal citations. In this text we will join those who drop the periods.

At a minimum, citations to entries in legal codes contain just two elements: the facts of publication which tell you where the entry is located in the code, and the year of the edition or supplement. These facts of publication are: the title number, followed by an abbreviation of the code's title, followed by the section number (§). Examples of citations to entries in legal codes are shown in Figure 5-1.

Secondary Sources for Legal Research

A cardinal rule of good library research is to use primary sources. This allows you to draw your own conclusions about the causes, nature, and consequences of the phenomenon that you are researching. However, in all library research, including legal research, there are times when it is not only appropriate but also desirable and perhaps even necessary to use secondary sources. That is, you will often want or need to locate and read what conclusions other researchers have published about your topic. Table 5-2 lists the major secondary sources for research into U.S. statutes, regulations, court decisions, and treaties.

DECISION RULES TO GOVERN YOUR SEARCH STRATEGY

The preceding two sections on primary and secondary sources have identified more than two dozen basic sources. What is obviously needed here is a set of guidelines to help you decide where to start. That, in turn depends upon the breadth and depth of the information you wish to locate and the nature of the information you already know. Table 5-3 summarizes these guidelines.

STATUTE LAW

Article I, Section 1 of the U.S. Constitution vests in Congress all legislative powers granted to the national government. In legislating, Congress debates bills and resolutions. Bills and joint resolutions become law if passed in identical form by the House and Senate and signed by the president. Most legislation becomes law in this manner.

However, there are two exceptions. Bills and joint resolutions that are vetoed by the president can still become law if two-thirds of the members present in each chamber vote to override the veto. Bills or joint resolutions not signed by the president become law if Congress remains in session for ten working days from the time that the president received the bill or joint resolution. Statute law, which involves enforcing the laws Congress has enacted, is then the responsibility of the administrative branch.

An Overview of the Legislative Process

Acts of Congress: Statutes and Joint Resolutions. Federal statutes are bills that have passed both houses of Congress. Federal statutes carry the force of law and are either

Table 5-3: Legal Search Decision Rules

Search Situation (What you already know and what you are searching for)	Search Strategy (Where to begin your search)
1) If you know the full citation and want to find the full text,	Then, go to the chronological primary source, e.g., slip laws, Stat, FR, slip opinions, court reporter (US, LEd, SCt), slip treaties (TIAS), or UST.
2) If you know the popular name but not the full citation and want to find the full text,	Then, a) for statutes, go to the "Acts Cited by Popular Name" index of the USC to get the full citation and then go the cited Stat or USC location. b) for Supreme Court cases, start with either a legal encyclopedia (Am Jur 2d or CJS) or an index to decisions to get the full citation and then go to a court reporter (US, LEd, SCt) for the full text of the opinions.
3) If you want to find law on a particular subject but do not yet know a specific citation or popular name,	Then, a) for an overview of statutory and case law, begin with the subject index of a legal encyclopedia (Am Jur 2d or CJS) or annotated code, and then go to the cited statutes or cases in a chronological series or code. b) for statutes, go to the subject index of the USC for the code citations, and then go into the code to the cited titles and sections. c) for regulations, go the subject index of the CFR for the code citations, and then go into the code to the cited titles and parts. d) for executive orders, begin with the indexes to either CFR or *Weekly Compilation of Presidential Documents*, and then go to cited EO number or page number. e) for Supreme Court cases, start with a court digest to get the full citations and summaries, then go to a court reporter (US, LEd, or SCt) for the full text of the opinions. f) for treaties, use the subject index of *Treaties in Force*. g) for recent statutes, regulations, cases, or treaties too new to be indexed, thumb through slip laws, the *Federal Register* (FR), slip opinions, and slip treaties (TIAS).

public or private laws. *Public laws* deal with government benefits or restrictions that are applicable to a broad class of individuals, such as, for example, a 1984 federal statute that set fines of up to $100,000 and prison terms of up to 20 years for any persons acting violently toward anyone on an aircraft. *Private laws* deal with more specific matters of concern to particular individuals. For example, Congress might pass a private law to settle a negligence claim against the Federal Aviation Agency made by a victim of a particular hijacking incident not adequately prevented by FAA anti-terrorist regulations.

Resolutions are either concurrent, joint, or simple resolutions; however, only joint resolutions (like statutes) carry the force of law. Like bills, joint resolutions (designated "H J Res" and "S J Res") are passed by both houses of Congress and must be signed by the president to become law. Joint resolutions are used by Congress primarily to endorse or oppose presidential initiatives in foreign affairs. Perhaps the most famous such joint resolution was the Tonkin Gulf Resolution passed in 1964 and repealed in 1970, which authorized wide latitude in presidential authority to conduct military operations in southeast Asia.

The other two forms of resolutions—simple and concurrent—are used by Congress primarily to make or amend the internal procedural rules of one or both chambers or to express the sentiment of one or both houses on some issue or event. Unlike statutes or joint resolutions, neither simple nor concurrent resolutions carry the force of law.

As you will recall from Chapter 4, you can trace the development of acts of Congress that become public laws by examining their legislative histories. Such a search typically includes locating committee reports, hearings, and prints; predecessor or companion bills; *Congressional Record* text of floor debate; House or Senate documents, including messages to Congress from the President; the enacted bill or joint resolution; and the Presidential statement on signing the bill from the *Weekly Compilation of Presidential Documents*.

An example of a legislative history, which we looked at in Chapter 4, led us to PL 98-473, an example of *omnibus legislation* that encompasses many separate acts of Congress bundled together into, in this case, one joint resolution (see Figure 4-6). We found that Title II of this joint resolution was entitled "Comprehensive Crime Control Act of 1984". We also found that Title II, Chapter XX, Part A, "Act for the Prevention and Punishment of the Crime of Hostage-Taking" pertained to our topic. In order to read the full text of this legislation, the first decision rule in Table 5-3 tells us to go to a chronological source.

Session Laws, a Chronological Source for Federal Statute Law: Slip Laws and *United States Statutes at Large*

During each session of Congress, as bills and joint resolutions are enacted into law, they are issued first as individual slip laws; at the end of the session, they are published in bound volumes entitled, *United States Statutes at Large* (Stat). A new volume number of *U.S. Statutes at Large* is assigned to each session of Congress. Typically, the first session of Congress is largely devoted to committee review of pending legislation. Therefore, so few bills and resolutions are enacted that they usually all fit into one bound volume. However, the typical second session of Congress passes a significantly larger number of bills and resolutions requiring that the second session volume be divided into two or more separately numbered parts sharing the same volume number. The subject index in any one bound part includes entries for its entire volume. The spine of each bound part gives the Congress, session, year, volume, part, and inclusive page numbers.

Returning to our example of PL 98-473, the PL number tells us that this was the four hundred seventy-third act passed by the 98th Congress. We do not know which session of the 98th Congress passed this legislation. However in searching *U.S. Statutes at Large* it is a good rule of thumb to start with the second session volume unless the PL number is very low. The 98th Congress, 2nd session *U.S. Statutes at Large* is in three separately bound parts, each sharing the volume number, 98. It is important to note that this correspondence between volume number and Congress number is purely coincidental—for any other Congress, the *U.S. Statutes at Large* volume number will probably not be the same as the Congress number.

Searching the subject index of Part 1 of *U.S. Statutes at Large* volume 98, we find an entry for the "Act for the Prevention and Punishment of the Crime of Hostage-Taking" referring us to page 2186 (see Figure 5-2). Using the cited (starting) page number, we consult the spine of the three separately bound parts and discover that Part 2 contains page 2186 (see Figure 5-3). Turning to that page in Part 2, we find the full text of this act (see Figure 5-4).

In the top and side margins of this (and every other) act five pieces of useful information are given: the Stat citation, PL number, passage date, short title or popular name, and USC citations. Each act of Congress has one Stat citation, referring to the volume and starting page number of its location in the *U.S. Statutes at Large*. However, even the simplest act typically has more than one USC citation. This is, of course, because the Code is a subject-organized work and even the shortest legislation usually deals with more than one subject covered by separate sections of the Code.

What we have done in the above search example is apply decision rule one in Table 5-3. Our next example, using slip laws, illustrates decision rule 3(g). Because a *U.S. Statutes at Large* volume is published only after that session of Congress ends and because it takes time to prepare, publish, and distribute the bound volume, there is a two- to three-year delay between passage of an act of Congress and its appearance in a bound volume of *U.S. Statutes at Large*. To cover this time period, rule 3(g) suggests thumbing through the slip laws that are available (they are typically issued within a month or two of enactment). Since the slip laws have no subject index, your options are to systematically scan each short title (popular name) printed at the beginning of each slip law or to use clues you may have found in secondary sources, such as recent periodical articles.

Figure 5-5 shows portions of a fairly recent act of Congress, available as a slip law, which is relevant to the prevention of aircraft hijacking. In response to the use of airport metal-detector screening devices, authorities fear that terrorists will switch to newly developed plastic firearms. Congress responded to this problem by prohibiting the manufacture, importation, or possession of such firearms. Besides the five marginal notations discussed in Figure 5-4, this slip law illustrates two other important marginal notations usually found in the full text of a statute: the bill or resolution number and the legislative history of the act.

Figure 5-2:
United States Statutes at Large: 98th Congress, 2d Session, 1984, Volume 98, Part 2, Subject Index

Washington, DC: Government Printing Office.

NOTE: Page references are to beginning pages of each law, with the exception of acts being amended or repealed, which cite to pages where they actually appear.

Codified Sources for Federal Statute Law:
United States Code, United States Code Annotated, and *United States Code Service*

Our discussion of federal statute codes will focus on the use of the *United States Code*, the official codification of the general and permanent federal statutes issued by the U.S. Government Printing Office. The other two commonly cited codifications are issued by commercial publishers. These commercially produced codes offer the advantage of annotations added to each title and section referring to relevant federal and state court decisions.

You will remember from Figure 5-4 that one of the marginal notations highlighted showed two *U.S. Code* citations. This tells you where this particular law has been integrated into the subject-arranged code of all federal statute laws currently in force. Figure 5-6 illustrates the page in the *U.S. Code* that contains both sections cited in the margin of a 1984 statute, PL 98-473 (18 USC §1201 and §1203). The number 18 refers to Title 18 of the *U.S. Code*, which contains all federal statutes on "Crimes and Criminal Procedure". Sections 1201 and 1203 fall within Chapter 55, "Kidnapping".

At the time this book was written, the most recently issued complete edition of the *U.S. Code* was published in 1988 as the 11th edition. The USC editions have been on a six-year publication cycle since 1934. Figure 5-6 illustrates a portion of Title 18, from the 1988 edition. USC supplements are issued annually after the main edition is complete; therefore, to determine if sections §1201 and/or §1203 were further amended you would need to look for those sections in each available supplement.

Figure 5-3:
United States Statutes
at Large: 98th Congress,
2d Session, 1984,
Volume 98, Part 2

Washington, DC:
Government Printing Office.

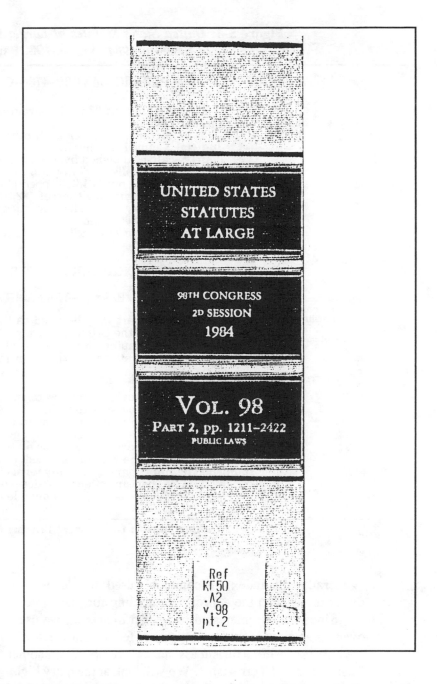

The purpose in using any code is to find other laws relevant to your search topic. In 18 USC §1201(a)(3), we find a reference to the Federal Aviation Act of 1958, 49 USC §1301(36). From the title of the act and its presence in the kidnapping section, it is obvious that this act is relevant to our topic of aircraft hijacking.

To comprehensively search a legal code, you must make use of its indexes. The *U.S. Code* offers two such finding aids, the General Index and the Acts Cited by Popular Name index. Searching the *U.S. Code* (1988 edition) General Index under "Hijacking", we find in Figure 5-7 cross-references to "Aircraft Piracy" and "Piracy." The phrase,

Figure 5-4: *United States Statutes at Large: 98th Congress, 2d Session, 1984*, Volume 98, Part 2

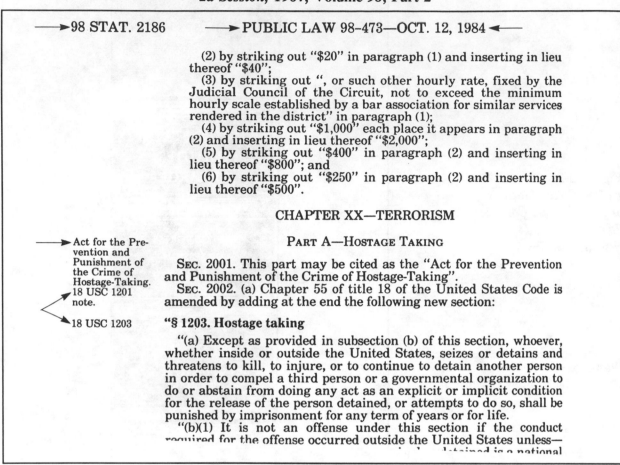

➤98 STAT. 2186 ➤PUBLIC LAW 98-473—OCT. 12, 1984 ◄

(2) by striking out "$20" in paragraph (1) and inserting in lieu thereof "$40";

(3) by striking out ", or such other hourly rate, fixed by the Judicial Council of the Circuit, not to exceed the minimum hourly scale established by a bar association for similar services rendered in the district" in paragraph (1);

(4) by striking out "$1,000" each place it appears in paragraph (2) and inserting in lieu thereof "$2,000";

(5) by striking out "$400" in paragraph (2) and inserting in lieu thereof "$800"; and

(6) by striking out "$250" in paragraph (2) and inserting in lieu thereof "$500".

CHAPTER XX—TERRORISM

PART A—HOSTAGE TAKING

➤Act for the Prevention and Punishment of the Crime of Hostage-Taking.
18 USC 1201 note.

18 USC 1203

SEC. 2001. This part may be cited as the "Act for the Prevention and Punishment of the Crime of Hostage-Taking".

SEC. 2002. (a) Chapter 55 of title 18 of the United States Code is amended by adding at the end the following new section:

"§ 1203. Hostage taking

"(a) Except as provided in subsection (b) of this section, whoever, whether inside or outside the United States, seizes or detains and threatens to kill, to injure, or to continue to detain another person in order to compel a third person or a governmental organization to do or abstain from doing any act as an explicit or implicit condition for the release of the person detained, or attempts to do so, shall be punished by imprisonment for any term of years or for life.

"(b)(1) It is not an offense under this section if the conduct required for the offense occurred outside the United States unless—

Washington, DC: Government Printing Office.

"generally, this index", is commonly used in indexes to legal sources instead of "see" to direct the user to the appropriate heading for that subject.

Since we are interested in aircraft hijacking, we use "Aircraft Piracy" and discover over 30 entries for various aspects of federal statute law covering aircraft piracy. One of the entries, "Antiterrorism assistance", refers us to another section of the General Index, "Terrorists and Terrorism". We will look at the entry highlighted, "Screening procedures to assure security against [aircraft piracy]", 49 App. USC §1356. Some of the USC titles are followed by an appendix that contains chapters and sections that are subject-related to that title but have not yet been incorporated into the "positive law" version of the USC. Hence, the chapters and sections in a USC title's appendix can be considered an interim version that may be subject to change before later incorporation into that title.

Figure 5-8 shows a portion of section 1356 in *U.S. Code* title 49 Appendix. Notice that there is a fuller section title that summarizes all major topics covered in the section. Subsection 1356(a) authorizes the Federal Aviation Administration to "...prescribe or continue in effect reasonable regulations..." concerning airline passenger and baggage

Figure 5-5: Slip law for Public Law 100-649, Undetectable Firearms Act of 1988

102 STAT. 3816   PUBLIC LAW 100–649—NOV. 10, 1988

Public Law 100–649
100th Congress

An Act

Nov. 10, 1988
[H.R. 4445]

To amend title 18, United States Code, to prohibit certain firearms especially useful to terrorists.

Be it enacted by the Senate and House of Representatives of the United States of America in Congress assembled,

Undetectable
Firearms Act of
1988.
Business and
industry.
Imports.
Commerce and
trade.
Exports.
18 USC 921 note.

SECTION 1. SHORT TITLE.

This Act may be cited as the "Undetectable Firearms Act of 1988".

SEC. 2. UNDETECTABLE FIREARMS.

(a) PROHIBITIONS.—Section 922 of title 18, United States Code, is amended by adding at the end the following:

"(p)(1) It shall be unlawful for any person to manufacture, import, sell, ship, deliver, possess, transfer, or receive any firearm—

"(A) that, after removal of grips, stocks, and magazines, is not as detectable as the Security Exemplar, by walk-through metal detectors calibrated and operated to detect the Security Exemplar; or

"(B) any major component of which, when subjected to inspection by the types of x-ray machines commonly used at airports, does not generate an image that accurately depicts the shape of the component. Barium sulfate or other compounds may be used in the fabrication of the component.

"(2) For purposes of this subsection—

"(A) the term 'firearm' does not include the frame or receiver of any such weapon;

"(B) subsection (t) of section ... 'major component' means, with respect to a ... the frame or repealed;

"(C) subsection (f) of section 925 of such title is hereby repealed;

"(D) section 924(a)(1) of such title is amended by striking ", (c), or (f)" and inserting in lieu thereof "or (c)"; and

"(E) section 925(a) of such title is amended by striking ", except for provisions relating to firearms subject to the prohibitions of section 922(p),".

Approved November 10, 1988.

LEGISLATIVE HISTORY—H.R. 4445 (S. 2180):

HOUSE REPORTS: No. 100–612 (Comm. on the Judiciary).
CONGRESSIONAL RECORD, Vol. 134 (1988):
    May 10, considered and passed House.
    May 25, considered and passed Senate, amended, in lieu of S. 2180.
    Oct. 20, House concurred in Senate amendment with an amendment.
    Oct. 21, Senate concurred in House amendment with an amendment. House
      concurred in Senate amendment.

Washington, DC: Government Printing Office.

Figure 5-6: *United States Code* (1988 edition), Title 18—Crimes and Criminal Procedures

TITLE 18 APPENDIX §§ 1201-1203

Sections 1201-1203 of Pub. L. 90-351, 82 Stat. 236, as amended, relating to Unlawful Possession or Receipt of Firearms, are set out in the Appendix to this title.

CROSS REFERENCES

Wire or oral communications, authorization for interception, to provide evidence of kidnaping, see section 2516 of this title.

§ 1201. Kidnaping

(a) Whoever unlawfully seizes, confines, inveigles, decoys, kidnaps, abducts, or carries away and holds for ransom or reward or otherwise any person, except in the case of a minor by the parent thereof, when—

(1) the person is willfully transported in interstate or foreign commerce;

(2) any such act against the person is done within the special maritime and territorial jurisdiction of the United States;

→ (3) any such act against the person is done within the special aircraft jurisdiction of the United States as defined in section 101(36) of the Federal Aviation Act of 1958, as amended (49 U.S.C. 1301(36)); [1]

(4) the person is a foreign official, an internationally protected person, or an official guest as those terms are defined in section 1116(b) of this title; or

(5) the person is among those officers and employees designated in section 1114 of this title and any such act against the person is ~~~~~~~~~~~~ in or on ac-

the Attorney General may request assistance from any Federal, State, or local agency, including the Army, Navy, and Air Force, any statute, rule, or regulation to the contrary notwithstanding.

(June 25, 1948, ch. 645, 62 Stat. 760; Aug. 6, 1956, ch. 971, 70 Stat. 1043; Oct. 24, 1972, Pub. L. 92-539, title II, § 201, 86 Stat. 1072; Oct. 8, 1976, Pub. L. 94-467, § 4, 90 Stat. 1998; Nov. 9, 1977, Pub. L. 95-163, § 17(b)(1), 91 Stat. 1286; Oct. 24, 1978, Pub. L. 95-504, § 2(b), 92 Stat. 1705; Oct. 12, 1984, Pub. L. 98-473, title II, § 1007, 98 Stat. 2139; Nov. 10, 1986, Pub. L. 99-646, §§ 36, 37(b), 100 Stat. 3599.)

HISTORICAL AND REVISION NOTES

Based on title 18, U.S.C., 1940 ed., §§ 408a, 408c (June 22, 1932, ch. 271, §§ 1, 3, 47 Stat. 326; May 18, 1934, ch. 301, 48 Stat. 781, 782).

Section consolidates sections 408a and 408c of title 18 U.S.C., 1940 ed.

Reference to persons aiding, abetting or causing was omitted as unnecessary because such persons are made principals by section 22 of this title.

Words "upon conviction" were omitted as surplusage, because punishment cannot be imposed until a conviction is secured.

Direction as to confinement "in the penitentiary" was omitted because of section 4082 of this title which commits all prisoners to the custody of the Attorney General. (See reviser's note under section 1 of this title.)

The phrase "for any term of years or for life" was substituted for the words "for such term of years as the court in its discretion shall determine" which ap~~~~~~~ in said section 408a of Title 18, U.S.C., 1940 ed. ~~~ all doubt as

Washington, DC: Government Printing Office.

screening. When we turn to search administrative law, we will locate these regulations. Notice that at the end of the subsection there are listed two relevant public laws. Hence, *U.S. Code* sections cite relevant PL numbers and Stat citations just as the public laws in *U.S. Statutes at Large* cite *U.S. Code* citations. This example illustrates decision rule 3(b) from Table 5-3.

Sometimes in legal research you will know the name of an act of Congress but not its citation. In such cases, our decision rule 2(a) suggests going to the *U.S. Code*'s "Acts Cited by Popular Name" index, which is found in the tables volume. This index lists acts of Congress cited by their short titles or popular names. You will remember that we found a reference to the Federal Aviation Act of 1958 while searching the *U.S. Code* (see Figure 5-6). In order to find its Stat and all USC citations, we can look it up in the "Acts Cited by Popular Name index. Figure 5-9 shows a portion of the page in this index of acts cited by popular names (or short titles). What you see is the PL number, date of enactment, Stat citation, and USC citations for the original statute and every amendment to it. In the case of the Federal Aviation Act of 1958, there have been numerous later amendments dealing with many different aspects of aviation. Hence many different *U.S. Code* titles are listed.

Another way to use the *U.S. Code*'s "Acts Cited by Popular Name" index is to search your subject as if it is the first word of a popular name. This is no substitute for

Figure 5-7: *United States Code* (1988 edition), General Index

HIGHWAYS—Continued

United States,
  Agreements of foreign government with U.S. relative to Inter-American Highway, 23 § 212
  Appropriation of lands, etc., owned by U.S.,
    Construction, etc., appropriations, 23 § 101 note
  Limitations,
    Items included in estimates for construction engineering on projects financed with urban funds, 23 § 106
    Payment for construction engineering on projects financed with Federal-aid highway funds, 23 § 121
    Payment to States for retirement of bonds issued for Federal-aid system projects, 23 § 122
    States of Maine and New Hampshire excluded

Utility, defined, Federal-aid, 23 § 123
Utility facilities, relocation in connection with Federal-aid system projects, 23 § 123
Vacation of highway between sections in Oklahoma, 43 § 1095
Vanpool,
  Off-street parking with preferential parking provision, etc.

Zoned industrial or commercial areas, outdoor advertising signs, etc., 23 § 131

HIJACKING

Aircraft Piracy, generally, this index
Piracy, generally, this index

HIKING

Alaska national interest lands conservation. Alaska, generally, this index
Cotton,
  Set-aside and diverted acreage, use for, addi-

AIR TRANSPORTATION—Continued

Secretary of Transportation, emergency preparedness functions concerning, 50 App. § 2251 note, Ex. Ord. No. 11490
Transportation Tax, this index

AIR TRANSPORTATION SECURITY ACT OF 1974

AIRCRAFT

See AIRPLANES OR AIRCRAFT, generally, this index

AIRCRAFT CARRIERS

Command, eligibility of officer, 10 § 5942
Navy shipbuilding policy, 10 § 7291 note
Sale, transfer or disposal, restrictions, 10 § 7307
Underage, 10 § 7295
Uniformed services, hazardous duty, incentive pay, flight deck performance, 37 § 301

AIRCRAFT ENGINE

AIRCRAFT PIRACY

Accomplice, commission of offense by, 49 App. § 1472
Aircraft leased without crew to lessee with principal place of business or permanent residence in U.S., "special aircraft jurisdiction of U.S." as including, 49 App. § 1301
Aircraft within U.S., "special aircraft jurisdiction of U.S." as including, 49 App. § 1301
Aircraft without U.S., "special aircraft jurisdiction of U.S." as including, 49 App. § 1301
Antiterrorism assistance. Terrorists and Terrorism, generally, this index
Attempt to commit,
  As within special aircraft jurisdiction of U.S., 49 App. § 1472
  As within special aircraft juris-

Death of another person resulting from commission or attempted commission of offense, penalty for, 49 App. § 1472
Death penalty, 49 App. § 1472
  Procedure in respect of, 49 App. § 1473
Defined, criminal penalties, Aviation Act of 1958, 49 App. § 1472
Establishment of security programs by airport operators to insure safety of persons from violence
Outside special aircraft jurisdiction of U.S., criminal penalties, 49 App. § 1472
Penalties, 49 App. §§ 1472, 1473
Presentence report, disclosure of material in to defendant or counsel, procedure in respect of death penalty, 49 App. § 1473
Procedures in respect of civil and criminal penalties, 49 App. § 1473
Screening procedures to assure security against, 49 App. § 1356
Sentence and punishment, 49 App. §§ 1472, 1473
  Guidelines and statutory index, 18 App.
Territorial applicability of provisions, 49 App. § 1472
Using illegal seizure of aircraft, etc., as instrument of policy, foreign nations aiding, suspension of air services, 49 App. § 1514
  Violations respecting, application for judicial enforcement, 49 App. § 1487
Venue and prosecution of offenses, 49 App. § 1473
When aircraft considered to be in flight,
  Commission of offense, 49 App. § 1472
  For purposes of definition of special aircraft within jurisdiction of U.S., 49 App. § 1301
When offense considered committed, 49 App. § 1472

AIRCRAFT SABOTAGE ACT

Washington, DC: Government Printing Office.

Figure 5-8: *United States Code* (1988 edition), Title 49, Appendix—Transportation

§ 1356. Screening procedures for passengers; promulgation and amendment of regulations by Administrator; reports to Congress; exempted air transportation operations

(a) The Administrator shall prescribe or continue in effect reasonable regulations requiring that all passengers and all property intended to be carried in the aircraft cabin in air transportation or intrastate air transportation be screened by weapon-detecting procedures or facilities employed or operated by employees or agents of the air carrier, intrastate air carrier, or foreign air carrier prior to boarding the aircraft for such transportation. One year after August 5, 1974, or after the effective date of such regulations, whichever is later, the Administrator may alter or amend such regulations, requiring a continuation of such screening only

. . . . scheduled passenger operations performed by air carriers engaging in interstate, overseas, or foreign air transportation under a certificate of public convenience and necessity issued by the Civil Aeronautics Board under section 1371 of this Appendix or under a foreign air carrier permit issued by the Board under section 1372 of this Appendix.

(Pub. L. 85-726, title III, § 315, as added Pub. L. 93-366, title II, § 202, Aug. 5, 1974, 88 Stat. 415, and amended Pub. L. 99-83, title V, § 551(b)(1), Aug. 8, 1985, 99 Stat. 225.)

AMENDMENTS

1985—Subsec. (a). Pub. L. 99-83 inserted provisions relating to information described in section 1515 of this Appendix.

TERMINATION OF CIVIL AERONAUTICS BOARD; TRANSFER OF FUNCTIONS; TERMINATION OF AUTHORITY

The Civil Aeronautics Board terminated on Jan. 1, 1985, and all functions, powers, and duties of the Board were terminated or transferred by section 1551 of this Appendix, effective in part on Dec. 31, 1981, in part on Jan. 1, 1983, and in part on Jan. 1, 1985.

RESEARCH AND DEVELOPMENT OF IMPROVED AIRPORT SECURITY SYSTEMS

Pub. L. 100-649, § 2(d), Nov. 10, 1988, 102 Stat. 3817, provided that: "The Administrator of the Federal Aviation Administration shall conduct such research and development as may be necessary to improve the effectiveness of airport security metal detectors and

airport security x-ray systems in detecting firearms that, during the 10-year period beginning on the effective date of this Act [see Effective Date of 1988 Amendment; Sunset Provision note set out under section 922 of Title 18, Crimes and Criminal Procedure], are subject to the prohibitions of section 922(p) of title 18, United States Code."

SECTION REFERRED TO IN OTHER SECTIONS

This section is referred to in sections 1356a, 1358, 1472, 1511, 1515 of this Appendix.

§ 1356a. Security measures in foreign air transportation

(a) Compensation of air carriers

The Secretary of Transportation shall compensate any air carrier certificated by the Civil Aeronautics Board under section 401 of the Federal Aviation Act of 1958 [49 App. U.S.C. . . . . such compensation for

fined in the Federal Aviation . . . App. U.S.C. 1301 et seq.] shall have the same meaning as such terms have in such Act.

(c) Authorization of appropriations; limitation on compensation

(1) There is authorized to be appropriated out of the Airport and Airway Trust Fund for amounts expended before the date specified in paragraph (2) of this subsection not to exceed $15,000,000. No such amounts shall be appropriated prior to September 30, 1981.

(2) No compensation shall be paid by the Secretary of Transportation under this section for amounts expended after the date which is 180 days after February 15, 1980.

(Pub. L. 94-353, title I, § 24, July 12, 1976, 90 Stat. 885; Pub. L. 97-248, title V, § 524(d), Sept. 3, 1982, 96 Stat. 697.)

REFERENCES IN TEXT

The Federal Aviation Act of 1958, referred to in subsec. (b), is Pub. L. 85-726, Aug. 23, 1958, 72 Stat. 731, as amended, which is classified principally to this chapter. For complete classification of this Act to the Code, see Short Title note set out under section 1301 of this Appendix and Tables.

CODIFICATION

Section was enacted as part of the Airport and Airway Development Act Amendments of 1976, and

Washington, DC: Government Printing Office.

subject searching the General Index, but in searching the Popular Name index you may locate directly the names of statutes that could be relevant to your topic. In searching the Popular Name index of the 1988 edition, we did not find any acts beginning with the words "Terrorism" or "Hijacking". However, further searching turned up "Air

Figure 5-9: *United States Code* (1988 edition), Acts Cited by Popular Name

ACTS CITED BY POPULAR NAME   Page 954

Federal-Aid Highway Act of 1987—Continued
Pub. L. 100–457, title III, § 352, Sept. 30, 1988, 102 Stat. 2157

Federal-Aid Highway Amendments of 1974
Pub. L. 93–643, Jan. 3, 1975, 88 Stat. 2281
Pub. L. 94–134, title I, Nov. 24, 1975, 89 Stat. 703
Pub. L. 94–280, title I, § 138, May 5, 1976, 90 Stat. 443
Pub. L. 95–599, title I, § 135, Nov. 6, 1978, 92 Stat. 2709
Pub. L. 100–17, title I, § 133(e)(2), Apr. 2, 1987, 101 Stat. 173

Federal Aid in Fish Restoration Act of 1950
See Fish Restoration and Management Projects Act

Federal Aid in Wildlife Restoration Act
See Wildlife Restoration Act

Federal Aid Road Act
See Federal Highway Act

Federal Aid to Wildlife Restoration Act
See Wildlife Restoration Act

Federal Arbitration Act
See Arbitration

Federal Aviation Act of 1958
Pub. L. 85–726, Aug. 23, 1958, 72 Stat. 731 (Title 49 App., § 1301 et seq.)
Pub. L. 86–81, July 8, 1959, 73 Stat. 180
Pub. L. 86–199, Aug. 25, 1959, 73 Stat. 427
Pub. L. 86–546, § 1, June 29, 1960, 74 Stat. 255
Pub. L. 86–627, July 12, 1960, 74 Stat. 445
Pub. L. 86–758, § 1, Sept. 13, 1960, 74 Stat. 901
Pub. L. 87–89, July 20, 1961, 75 Stat. 210
Pub. L. 87–197, Sept. 5, 1961, 75 Stat. 466
Pub. L. 87–225, § 2, Sept. 13, 1961, 75 Stat. 497
Pub. L. 87–255, § 9, Sept. 20, 1961, 75 Stat. 527
Pub. L. 87–367, title I, § 103(2), title II, § 205, Oct. 4, 1961, 75 Stat. 787, 791
Pub. L. 87–528, §§ 1–6, 12, 13, July 10, 1962, 76 Stat. 143–146, 149, 150
Pub. L. 87–793, § 1001(h), Oct. 11, 1962, 76 Stat. 864
Pub. L. 87–810, Oct. 15, 1962, 76 Stat. 921

Washington, DC: Government Printing Office.

Transportation Security Act of 1974" and the "Antihijacking Act of 1974", both of which may be relevant to our topic (see Figure 5-10).

Secondary Sources for Federal Statute Law

In order to place the information you gained from primary legal sources into a broader perspective, you can utilize secondary sources. Besides the various books, periodical articles, and government documents we have located so far, there are additional secondary sources that are particularly relevant to legal research. In the case of federal statute law, Congressional Quarterly Inc., an editorial research service and publishing company, produces several works focused directly upon Congress and its legislation. Most commonly available in college and university libraries are the *Congressional Quarterly Weekly Report*, the *CQ Almanac, Congress and the Nation, Congressional Quarterly's Guide to Congress, Congress A to Z*, and *Politics in America*. *Guide to Congress* is a massive handbook and research guide. *Congress A to Z* is a one-volume encyclopedia with thirty major essays and almost 250 shorter articles. *Politics in America* is an annual almanac and directory for members of Congress and their states and districts. A competing publication to the latter is *Almanac of American Politics*.

A primary use of the *Weekly Report* is to stay up-to-date on pending and recently enacted legislation. To illustrate this, we have selected the cumulated index to the 1989 volume of the *Weekly Report*. Here, in Figure 5-11, we find several entries under "Terrorism". Looking at one, "Airport security equipment", we see several page

Figure 5-10: *United States Code* (1988 edition), Acts Cited by Popular Name

---

Air Mail Acts—Continued
June 23, 1938, ch. 601, title IV, § 405(1), title
XI, § 1107(d), (k), 52 Stat. 997, 1027, 1029
July 6, 1945, ch. 274, § 16, 59 Stat. 451
Aug. 14, 1946, ch. 963, 60 Stat. 1062
June 23, 1948, ch. 607, 62 Stat. 576
1012 (Title 49 App., §§ 601, 602.)

Air Transport Labor Act
See Railroad Labor Act

Air Transportation Security Act of 1974
Pub. L. 93-366, title II, Aug. 5, 1974, 88 Stat.
415 (Title 49 App., §§ 1301, 1356, 1357,
1472, 1511, 1516)

Aircraft Contracts Act
Mar. 5, 1940, ch. 44, 54 Stat. 45

Aircraft Development Act
June 30, 1938, ch. 852, 52 Stat. 1255 (Title

Antihijacking Act of 1974
Pub. L. 93-366, title I, Aug. 5, 1974, 88 Stat.
409

Anti-Immunity Act (Trusts and Interstate Commerce)
June 30, 1906, ch. 3920, 34 Stat. 798 (Title
49 App., § 48)

Anti-Injunction Law
Mar. 23, 1932, ch. 90, 47 Stat. 70 (Title 29,
§ 101 et seq.)

Pub. L. 93-44, §§ 2-6, June 18, 1973, 87 Stat.
88-90
Pub. L. 94-353, title I, §§ 2-15, title II, § 201,
July 12, 1976, 90 Stat. 871-886
Pub. L. 95-504, § 41, Oct. 24, 1978, 92 Stat.
1748
Pub. L. 96-193, title I, § 103(b), title II,
Feb. 18, 1980, 94 Stat.
Pub. L. 97-248, title V, Sept. 3, 1982, 96 Stat.
671 (Title 49 App., § 2201 et seq.)
Pub. L. 97-276, § 167, Oct. 2, 1982, 96 Stat.
1204
Pub. L. 97-424, title IV, § 426(a)-(d), Jan. 6,
1983, 96 Stat. 2167
Pub. L. 100-223, title I, §§ 102(a)-(c), 103,
104, 105(a), (b)(1), (c)-(g), 106(a), (b),
107-116, Dec. 30, 1987, 101 Stat. 1487-1507
Pub. L. 100-591, § 7, Nov. 3, 1988, 102 Stat.
3014

Airport and Airway Revenue Act of 1970
title II, May 21, 1970, 84
July 3, 1946, ch. 537, 60 Stat. 420 (Title 29,
§ 17 note; See Title 18, § 1951; Title 29,
§§ 52, 101, 151 note)

Anti-Rebate Act (Railroads)
Feb. 19, 1903, ch. 708, 32 Stat. 847 (See Title
49, §§ 11703, 11902, 11903, 11915, 11916)
June 29, 1906, ch. 3591, § 2, 34 Stat. 587

Anti-Reviver Act (Repeals)
Feb. 25, 1871, ch. 71, § 3, 16 Stat. 431 (See
Title 1, § 108)

Washington, DC: Government Printing Office.

---

references. In the first, we see the beginning of a two-page article analyzing House committee approval of federal funding of airport security equipment. As with many *Weekly Report* articles, an inset box summarizes pertinent information concerning the subject of the article—in this case, bill HR 1659. The figure also illustrates CQ's practice of including cross-references to earlier, related *Weekly Report* articles.

If no cumulative index is available for the time period being searched, you can still rather quickly scan the issue indexes printed on the back cover of each *Weekly Report*. Figure 5-12 presents an issue index that directs us to an article covering final passage of the "Undetectable Firearms Act of 1988", which we previously examined in the slip laws (see Figure 5-5).

Depending upon the time frame and level of detail of your research, you may need to consult particular issues of CQ's *Almanac* and/or *Congress and the Nation*. In terms of level of detail, the most thorough day-to-day coverage of Congressional lawmaking is found in the *Weekly Report*. The *Almanac* surveys and summarizes a Congressional session with a broader perspective and the benefit of hindsight. The perspective of *Congress and the Nation* is a further step removed in time, analyzing the two Congresses that met in a particular presidential term. A unique and important feature of CQ's *Weekly Report, Almanac*, and *Congress and the Nation* is their tabulation of House and Senate roll call votes. Further information on these CQ vote tables is presented in Chapter 6, "Locating General Information".

In terms of time frame, each volume of *Congress and the Nation* is issued one year after the end of each four-year, presidential term. Each volume of the *Almanac* covers one session of Congress and is issued the following year. The *Weekly Report* obviously covers this most recent gap. All three publications date back to 1945. You should check your library's catalog or check with a reference librarian to determine your library's holdings of these three publications.

ADMINISTRATIVE LAW

Applying Montesquieu's principle of separation of powers, the Founding Fathers created an executive branch to carry out the laws and programs enacted by Congress. However, the Constitution gives limited information about the structure and functioning of the executive branch. Only the powers of the President (and, to a much lesser extent, the Vice-President) are addressed in any detail. The other members of the executive branch are referred to as "principal officers" of the executive departments, "other public ministers and consuls", and "inferior officers". The duties and organization of these departments and officers are left unspecified by the Constitution.

An Overview of the Administrative Process

Applying their own principle of overlapping powers, the Founding Fathers gave Congress the authority to approve the creation and reorganization of the executive branch bureaucracy. Over time, as increasingly complex national problems demanded attention, Congress added to the executive bureaucracy and delegated more authority to it. The most significant expansion of federal regulation of economic and social activities occurred during three eras: the post-Civil War industrial revolution, Franklin Roosevelt's New Deal response to the depression of the 1930s, and Lyndon Johnson's Great Society programs of the 1960s. An excellent overview of the history, techniques, achievements, and shortcomings of the federal regulatory process is presented in a 77-page essay at the beginning of Congressional Quarterly's *Federal Regulatory Directory* (5th ed., 1986).

As Congress created these regulatory agencies, it gave them quasi-legislative authority to make *administrative rules* (also called *administrative regulations*) that carry the force of law. Congress also gave administrative agencies quasi-judicial authority to conduct hearings and issue *administrative orders* (also called *administrative directives*) that carry the force of law in resolving disputes concerning administrative regulations. Thus, the general rules or regulations issued by federal agencies are enforced by orders that direct specific violators to come into compliance. As national problems have become more technically complex, practically all individuals and organizations are directly affected by administrative regulations.

Administrative agencies and departments that issue regulations are not the only executive branch officials with quasi-legislative authority. An *executive order* (EO) is a directive issued by a chief administrative officer—a president, governor, or mayor—that

Figure 5-11: *Congressional Quarterly Weekly Report*, Cumulative Index for 1989 and May 6, 1989 issue, page 1035

TRANSPORTATION

House Committee Authorizes Funding for Air Security

Republicans favor cost-sharing by airlines, but reluctantly back the measure

Despite resistance from the Bush administration, the House Public Works Committee May 4 approved a measure authorizing the federal government to pay the full cost of new security equipment to thwart terrorism against air travelers.

With reluctant support from Republicans wary of being branded soft on the issue, the committee adopted the bill (HR 1659) by voice vote. It authorizes a total of $270 million to airlines for a new generation of bomb-detection devices and to airports for improved security equipment.

Bush is moving on his own to require industry to upgrade security and to pay for the improvements. The White House views HR 1659 as unnec-

BOXSCORE

Bill: HR 1659 — aviation-security equipment authorization.

Latest action: Approval by House Public Works Committee by voice vote, May 4.

Next likely action: Markup in House Foreign Affairs Committee, as yet unscheduled.

Background: Bill is response to terrorists' bomb on Pan Am jet last December that killed 270 people.

Reference: Subcommittee dispute, Weekly Report p. 962.

ulations calling for tightened access to certain areas of the facilities.

Money for the airline and airport grants is to come from the Airport and Airway Trust Fund, which is financed primarily by an 8 percent tax on passenger tickets. The funding is offset by a rescission of $270 million worth of previously authorized but unspent trust-fund grants to airports for expansions and other construction projects. Although airports are objecting to this cut, Aviation Subcommittee Chairman James L. Oberstar, D-Minn., said it was unlikely that this money would ever be spent because of spending caps placed on the construction-grant program by appropriators.

The trust fund enjoyed a cash surplus of $5.8 billion at the end of fiscal 1988. Tax rates are slated to be cut in half on Jan. 1 due to a "trigger-tax" provision enacted by lawmakers in 1987 to force Congress either to accelerate trust-fund spending or to ease the tax burden. But because of the large surplus, the rate cut is not expected to have an immediate impact on aviation-program funding. *(Weekly Report p. 745)*

Republican Objections

Oberstar's panel May 2 approved

Figure 5-12: *Congressional Quarterly Weekly Report*, October 22, 1988 Table of Contents

Congressional Quarterly Weekly Report

October 22, 1988
Volume 46, No. 43
Pages 3029-3084

carries the force of law. The power of the president to issue executive orders, in part, comes from authority delegated in treaties and statutes (as is also the case with administrative regulations issued by executive departments and agencies). However, presidents also issue executive orders under powers broadly granted by constitutional provisions (e.g., as commander-in-chief and as chief executive) required to "take care that the laws be faithfully executed".

Executive orders deal with a wide range of subjects. Although most are simply delegations of presidential authority to lesser administrative offices, some executive orders have had broad applicability and landmark significance, especially in the area of civil rights, e.g., Franklin D. Roosevelt's outlawing of racial, religious, and ethnic discrimination in defense plants (EO 8802 (1941)), Harry S. Truman's racial integration of the U.S. armed services (EO 9981 (1948)), and Lyndon B. Johnson's requirement that federal government contractors adopt affirmative action programs (EO 11246 (1965)).

The president also issues proclamations that, unlike executive orders, do not carry the force of law. A *proclamation* (Proc) is an official, published declaration by a chief executive—president, governor, or mayor—that usually deals with matters of a symbolic or ceremonial nature, but sometimes announces a public policy of substantive significance (e.g., Lincoln's Emancipation Proclamation in 1862 and 1863).

A Codified Source for Federal Administrative Law:
Code of Federal Regulations

Because our research so far has not turned up any references to federal regulations or executive orders, we will need to apply decision rule 3(c) of Table 5-3—and subject search the appropriate code for any relevant citations before turning to the chronological sources to further update what we may find in the codes. As with our discussion of federal statute codes, this section will focus on the use of official regulatory codes and only mention the annotated regulatory code that is commercially published.

The *Code of Federal Regulations* (CFR) is the official codification of all currently in force federal administrative regulations issued by Executive departments and agencies. The CFR is divided into fifty titles, each dealing with a different, broad subject area—for example, Title 14, Aeronautics and Space. Each CFR title is divided into chapters, usually corresponding to the issuing agency (e.g., Title 14, Chapter I regulations are issued by the FAA). Each chapter is divided into parts, which cover specific regulatory areas (e.g., Title 14, Chapter I, Part 108 deals with airplane operator security). Within each CFR part are numbered sections (e.g., 14 CFR §108.9 is the section dealing with screening passengers and baggage for weapons and explosives). Because of the number of regulations included, many CFR titles are issued as several paperbound volumes. All titles and volumes are revised at least once each year with a new color binding so that the user can at a glance determine which volumes and titles were most recently revised.

Like all codes, the *Code of Federal Regulations* has a general index. However, regrettably, even experienced users find it lacking in adequate detail. Because of this shortcoming, at least two commercial publishers compile and issue a much more detailed general index to the CFR. R.R. Bowker publishes the *Code of Federal Regulations Index* annually with quarterly, cumulative supplements. Congressional Information Service, Inc. publishes its *Index to the Code of Federal Regulations* annually. If these are not shelved with the CFR, check with a reference librarian to see if your library subscribes to these publications.

Finding no headings for terrorism or hijacking, we turn to headings beginning with the word "Air" and find "Air carriers". Listed under this heading is an entry for "Airplane operator security" with a citation to 14 CFR §108 (see Figure 5-13). Locating title 14 of the CFR, and then the volume that contains part 108 (easily determined from title and part numbers listed on the spine), we find that these regulations were issued by the Federal Aviation Administration (see Figure 5-14). At the beginning of each CFR part is an outline of section headings contained therein. One of these, section 108.10, "Prevention and management of hijacking and sabotage attempts", is obviously relevant to our topic and is also shown in Figure 5-14. Other sections on passenger screening and bomb threats may also prove valuable.

Following the section outline at the beginning of Part 108 are two useful notations. The first notation cites the *U.S. Code* and public law citations to statutes delegating authority to the FAA for issuing these regulations. The second cites the *Federal Register* (FR) issue that first published Part 108 of the FAA regulations. Notice that a later FR citation is given for Section 108.10 illustrating the evolving nature of most federal regulations, which are frequently added to or amended. These changes are first reported in the FR, which is published each working day and is the chronological record of proposed and issued federal administrative regulations.

Figure 5-13:
Code of Federal Regulations,
1991 Index

Washington,
DC: Government
Printing Office.

Air carriers	CFR Index

Job opportunities and basic skills training program, 45 CFR 250

Medicaid

 Eligibility in Guam, Puerto Rico, and Virgin Islands, 42 CFR 436

 Eligibility in States, District of Columbia, Northern Mariana Islands, and American Samoa, 42 CFR 435

Public service employment demonstration projects, 45 CFR 282

Records and information, official, disclosure, 20 CFR 401

Transitional child care, 45 CFR 256

Work supplementation program, 45 CFR 239

Air carriers

See also Air rates and fares
  Air taxis
  Charter flights

Air carrier associations participation in aviation proceedings, 14 CFR 263

Aircraft accident liability insurance, 14 CFR 205

Aircraft loan guarantee program, 14 CFR 199

Airline deregulation, employee protection program, 14 CFR 314

Airline employee protection program, 29 CFR 220

Airline service quality performance reports, 14 CFR 234

Airplane operator security, 14 CFR 108

Alaskan air carriers, classification and exemption, 14 CFR 292

Audit reports submission, 14 CFR 248

Bumping procedures for subsidized air carriers from eligible points, 14 CFR

Scheduled air carriers with helicopters, 14 CFR 127

Compensation for losses incurred in continuing service under Transportation Department aviation proceedings order, 14 CFR 324

Computer reservation systems, carrier-owned, 14 CFR 255

 Joint operations display, 14 CFR 256

Consumer Credit Protection Act implementation with respect to air carriers and foreign air carriers, 14 CFR 374

Continuance of expired authorizations by operation of law pending final determination of applications for renewal thereof, 14 CFR 377

Contract of carriage, notice of terms, 14 CFR 253

Customs Service, air commerce regulations, 19 CFR 122

Data to support fitness determinations, 14 CFR 204

Domestic baggage liability, 14 CFR 254

Domestic cargo transportation, 14 CFR 291

Embargoes on air freight shipments, 14 CFR 228

Energy Policy and Conservation Act implementation, 14 CFR 313

Essential air transportation, guidelines for subsidizing air carriers providing, 14 CFR 271

Essential air transportation to Micronesia, Marshall Islands, and Palau (Freely Associated States), 14 CFR 272

Fair Labor Standards Act, miscellaneous exemptions, 29 CFR 786

Foreign air carrier or other foreign lease of aircraft with crew, 14

Two Chronological Sources for Federal Administrative Law

To bring your search of administrative law up-to-date since the last issue of the *Code of Federal Regulations*, you will need to find any newly issued regulations and/or executive orders in chronological sources. Such a search applies decision rule 3(g) in Table 5-3.

Since 1907, all executive orders have been consecutively numbered. By the beginning of the Bush administration, preceding presidents had issued more than 12,000 executive orders. Prior to 1936, all executive orders were issued in slip form by the Department of State and published after each session of Congress in the *U.S. Statutes at Large*. Since 1936, all executive orders are published first in the *Federal Register*. Since 1965, they are also compiled weekly in the *Weekly Compilation of Presidential Documents*. The

Weekly Compilation also includes addresses and remarks, appointments and nominations, bill signings and veto messages, transcripts of news conferences, and other presidential statements. All executive orders promulgated since 13 March 1936 are also compiled in Title 3 of the *Code of Federal Regulations*.

Federal Register (FR). There are at least two reasons to search the FR. First, as mentioned above, you can use the FR issues published since the latest revision of the *Code of Federal Regulations* to determine whether any additional regulations or executive orders have been issued. Second, after finding a regulation in the *Code of Federal Regulations*, it is a good idea to locate the original announcement of a regulation's issuance in the FR because extensive background information is sometimes provided in addition to the text of the regulation—and only the latter appears in the CFR. Due to the huge amount of shelf space necessary to accommodate the FR in paper copy, many libraries do not keep issues once the CFR is updated. However, FR is also issued in microfiche, so more libraries keep back issues in this form.

Unless you know the date an executive order was promulgated or when a federal regulation was proposed or issued, you can save yourself time by looking in available FR indexes. These indexes are issued monthly and are cumulative for the year to date. There is usually a six- to eight-week publication delay, so if you are searching for information more current than that in FR, you will need to look at each issue's table of contents. There are two online databases that provide solutions to this indexing delay. *Federal Register Abstracts* is updated weekly and provides current, detailed indexing to FR from 1977 to date. The second database, the *Federal Register*, includes the full text of FR. See Chapter 7, "Computer Database Searching", for more information about this search method.

To use the FR index successfully to locate regulations, you need to know which department or agency is likely to have proposed or issued the regulation you seek. The FR index is alpha-ordered by department and agency and then subdivided by rules, proposed rules, notices, and other announcements. In Figure 5-15, we see an entry under "FAA Rules" concerning airport security. The starting page number is given but not the date. Therefore you need to turn to the end of the index, where you will find a tabulation of inclusive pages, dates, and issue numbers (see Figure 5-16). Now we know that we need the issue for 6 January 1989. Turning to this issue (see Figure 5-17), we find several pages of background information concerning the airport security access control system, followed by the full text of the regulation issued as Section 107.14.

Weekly Compilation of Presidential Documents. Whereas the *Federal Register* is a chronological source for administrative law issued by the entire executive branch, the *Weekly Compilation of Presidential Documents* provides chronological access to presidential documents only. Each issue has a name index as well as a subject index. Cumulative indexes are issued quarterly, semiannually, and annually.

Applying decision rule 3(d) of Table 5-3, we search the indexes to *Weekly Compilation* and find several entries under "Terrorism" in the third quarter index to 1989 (see Figure 5-18). The fourth page reference under "Antiterrorism efforts" directs us to page 1209, on which we find Executive Order 12686, "President's Commission on

(1) A record is made of each law enforcement action taken in furtherance of this part;

(2) The record is maintained for a minimum of 90 days; and

(3) It is made available to the administrator upon request.

Jan. 10, 1986]

PART 108—AIRPLANE OPERATOR SECURITY

where security conducted;

(3) Make these documents available for inspection upon request of any Civil Aviation Security Inspector;

(4) Restrict the availability of information contained in the security program to those persons with an operational need-to-know; and

(5) Refer requests for such information by other persons to the Director of Civil Aviation Security of the FAA.

[Doc. No. 108, 46 FR 3786, Jan. 15, 1981, as amended by Amdt. 108-3, 50 FR 28893, July 16, 1985; Amdt. 108-7, 54 FR 36946, Sept. 5, 1989]

§ 108.9 Screening of passengers and property.

(a) Each certificate holder required to conduct screening under a security program shall use the procedures included, and the facilities and equipment described, in its approved security program to prevent or deter the carriage aboard airplanes of any explosive, incendiary, or a deadly or dangerous weapon on or about each individual's person or accessible property, and the carriage of any explosive or incendiary in checked baggage.

(b) Each certificate holder required to conduct screening under a security ... to transport—

AUTHORITY: 49 U.S.C. 1354, 1356, 1357, 1421, 1424, and 1511; 49 U.S.C. 106(g) (revised, Pub. L. 97-449, January 12, 1983).

SOURCE: Docket No. 108, 46 FR 3786, Jan. 15, 1981, unless otherwise noted.

§ 108.1 Applicability.

(a) This part prescribes aviation security.

tion Security.

(b) This part does not apply to helicopter or to all-cargo operations.

[Doc. No. 24883, Amdt. 108-4, 51 FR 1352, Jan. 10, 1986, as amended by Amdt. 108-6, 54 FR 28984, July 10, 1989]

§ 108.3 Definitions.

The following are definitions of terms used in this part: (a) *Certificate holder* means a person holding an FAA operating certificate when that person engages in scheduled passenger or public charter passenger operations or both.

(b) *Passenger seating configuration* means the total number of seats for which the aircraft is type certificated that can be made available for passenger use aboard a flight and includes that seat in certain airplanes which may be used by a representative of the Administrator to conduct flight checks but is available for revenue purposes on other occasions.

Private charter means any char-

10, 1986; Amdt. 108-5, 52 FR 48509, Dec. 22, 1987]

§ 108.10 Prevention and management of hijackings and sabotage attempts.

(a) Each certificate holder shall—

(1) Provide and use a Security Coordinator on the ground and in flight for each international and domestic flight, as required by its approved security program; and

(2) Designate the pilot in command as the inflight Security Coordinator for each flight, as required by its approved security program.

(b) *Ground Security Coordinator.* Each ground Security Coordinator shall carry out the ground Security Coordinator duties specified in the certificate holder's approved security program.

(c) *Inflight Security Coordinator.* The pilot in command of each flight shall carry out the inflight Security Coordinator duties specified in the certificate holder's approved security program.

[Doc. No. 24719, 50 FR 28893, July 16, 1985]

§ 108.11 Carriage of weapons.

(a) No certificate holder required to ... screening under a security

---

Figure 5-14:
Code of Federal Regulations, Title 14, Federal Aviation Administration, DOT

Washington, DC: Government Printing Office.

Aviation Security and Terrorism". This EO establishes an investigatory body to "...review and evaluate policy options in connection with aviation security...."

Secondary Sources for Federal Administrative Law:
United States Government Manual, Federal Regulatory Directory, Government Agencies, and *National Journal*

As Table 5-2 indicates, there are at least four useful secondary sources for background information, analysis, and interpretation of federal administrative law. Two are directories, one is a handbook, and one is a weekly professional magazine of government and politics. The directories and handbook discuss the structure and function of the federal regulatory agencies. The magazine provides week-to-week coverage of ongoing regulatory controversies.

The *United States Government Manual* is the official handbook of the federal government and is published annually by the Office of the Federal Register. It provides directory information on official and quasi-official agencies of all three branches of the federal government. A typical entry includes principal officials, mission statement, major activities and programs, brief history (including sources of legal authority), and sources of information concerning the agency.

Congressional Quarterly Inc. publishes the *Federal Regulatory Directory*. The fifth edition begins with an excellent, 77-page essay on the regulatory process. The rest of the directory provides detailed profiles of the hundred-plus federal regulatory agencies, both independent and those located within cabinet departments. An additional feature of the *Federal Regulatory Directory* is an appendix on how to use the *Federal Register* and *Code of Federal Regulations*. The profiles are grouped into the 13 major agencies followed by the 90 other regulatory agencies. Among the latter, under the Department of Transportation, is the FAA. Its profile, like each of the others, describes the mission, history, directory of major personnel, information sources, authorizing legislation, and regional offices (where applicable). Figure 5-19 shows a portion of the FAA profile.

Government Agencies is one in a series of volumes that constitute the Greenwood Encyclopedia of American Institutions. It offers authoritative but dated summaries (1983) on a wide array of executive departments and agencies. Each essay discusses the history of the government entity, its administrative structure, and its program successes and failures. A brief annotated bibliography (including sources of primary information) follows each essay. Figure 5-20 shows a portion of the seven-page FAA entry in *Government Agencies*.

The *National Journal* is similar in nature to the *Congressional Quarterly Weekly Report*; however, whereas the *Weekly Report* focuses on Congressional politics, the *National Journal* emphasizes administrative politics and is thus a good source for up-to-date interpretation of regulatory decisions and controversies. *National Journal* is indexed in *PAIS International in Print*, which is covered in Chapter 3.

Figure 5-15: *Federal Register Index*, January-December 1989

FAA

Servicing and collections—
Administrative offset, 34773
Community facilities loan and grant
programs, 9217
Interest, penalties, and administrative
~~costs, 3610~~

~~Organization, functions~~
delegations:
State Directors; debt settlements and liability
releases approval, 43840

Federal Aviation Administration

RULES

Air carrier certification and operations:
Anti-drug program for personnel in specified
aviation activities, 15148
Compliance date delayed, 53282
Correction, 1288, 15072
Cargo or baggage compartment; fire
protection requirements, 7384
Cockpit voice and flight recorders, 28769
Correction, 29892
Foreign air carriers and operators written
security program, 11116
Grand Canyon National Park; flight rules in
vicinity; (SFAR No. 50), 11926
Implementation policy, 25551
Passenger-carrying and cargo air operations
for compensation or hire (SFAR No.
38), 23864
Protective breathing equipment, 22270
~~Smoking aboard aircraft, 22872~~

Explosives detection systems for checked
baggage, 36938
Flight restrictions in vicinity; Prince William
Sound, AK (SFAR No. 55), 13810
Grand Canyon National Park; flight rules in
vicinity; (SFAR No. 50), 11926
High pressure weather conditions instrument
approaches and visual flight rules;
restrictions (SFAR No. 54), 5580

High traffic density airports; air carrier and
commuter operator slots, allocation and
transfer methods, 34904, 39843
Correction, 37303
National Airspace System; air traffic control
radar beacon system and Mode S

reporting capability requirements; policy
statement, 27836
Transport category airplanes—
Passenger emergency exit locations, 26688
Airmen certification:
Airmen medical certificate applications
falsification; drug convictions, drug-and-
alcohol-related traffic convictions
records, 15144
Anti-drug program for personnel in specified
aviation activities, 15148
Correction, 1288, 15072
Recreational pilots and annual flight review
requirements, etc., 13028
Flight time clarification, etc., 41234
Airplane operator security:
Security directives and information circulars,
28982
Airport radar service areas, 9028, 9406, 12532,
13053, 13455, 39167, 47662
Airport security; access to secured areas, 582
Airspace:
Airspace overlying waters between 3 and 12
nautical miles from U.S. coast;
applicability, 264
Warning areas establishment (SFAR No.

13875, 14206, 14639-14643, 15741,
18275, 19874, 19875, 20118, 21414,
21932, 21933, 22583, 23643, 24161,
25709, 25710, 26019, 26021-26023,
27157, 27629, 28023, 28025, 29008,
29529-29534, 30007, 30009, 30720,
30721, 31507, 31509, 31653, 31803,
34500, 36282, 36283, 38209, 38210,

39163, 39342, 40632, 40633, 40635-
40637, 41053, 41821, 41958, 42289,
43046, 43579, 43801, 43802, 46366-
46370, 47511, 48080, 48856, 49964,
50346, 50488, 51191-51195, 51876,
51972, 53046
~~Boeing et al., 10276, 34762~~

~~Davis Aircraft~~
Dornier, 4764, 5928
EMBRAER, 4264, 28026, 39162, 42621,
43047, 43805
Enstrom, 6391
Facet, 6514
Fairchild, 10139, 31804
Fokker, 3432, 3433, 4769, 6642, 11171, 11939,
11940, 21598, 31808, 38212, 39165,
49275, 49276
Garrett, 3433, 11368, 29009, 39344
General Electric Co., 22883, 31324, 38814,
51015, 52873
Goodyear, 1342, 47200
GQ Parachutes, Ltd., 25445, 28554
Grob Werke GmbH & Co., 12898
Gulfstream, 1343, 11165, 11166, 13874,
15744, 34971
Hamilton Standard Hydromatic, 31010
Honeywell, Inc., 1344, 38213, 39345
Israel Aircraft Industrie, 24163
Learjet, 22879
Lockheed, 26370, 29535, 31652, 34501,
34972, 39347, 41959
McDonnell Douglas, 104, 105, 1675, 4265,
~~8527, 10622, 10624, 11167, 11168, 11170,~~

Sikorsky, 107, 598, 6512, 12986, 12987,
31505, 40639, 48582
SOCATA, 22584
Switlik Parachute Co., Inc., 9026
Teledyne Continental Motors, 36287, 46726,
46727
Textron Lycoming, 21418, 32437, 46880,
46885

Washington, DC: Government Printing Office.

Figure 5-16: *Federal Register Index*, January-December 1989

FEDERAL REGISTER PAGES AND DATES—JANUARY-DECEMBER 1989

Pages	Date	(Issue No.)	Pages	Date	(Issue No.)	Pages	Date	(Issue No.)
1-96	Jan. 3	(1)	18873-19152	3	(84)	35867-36024	30	(167)
97-270	4	(2)	19153-19342	4	(85)	36025-36274	31	(168)
271-386	5	(3)	19343-19536	5	(86)	36275-36750	Sept. 1	(169)
387-594	6	(4)	19537-19806	8	(87)	36751-36954	5	(170)
595-786	9	(5)	19807-20112	9	(88)	36955-37088	6	(171)
787-960	10	(6)	20113-20366	10	(89)	37089-37286	7	(172)
961-1142	11	(7)	20367-20500	11	(90)	37287-37448	8	(173)
1143-1324	12	(8)	20501-20782	12	(91)	37449-37634	11	(174)
1325-1674	13	(9)	20783-21042	15	(92)	37635-37780	12	(175)
1675-1922	17	(10)	21043-21186	16	(93)	37781-37926	13	(176)
1923-2080	18	(11)	21187-21396	17	(94)	37927-38190	14	(177)
2081-2964	19	(12)	21397-21586	18	(95)	38191-38368	15	(178)
2965-3404	23	(13)	21587-21930	19	(96)	38369-38506	18	(179)
3405-3576	24	(14)	21931-22272	22	(97)	38507-38642	19	(180)
3577-3768	25	(15)	22273-22404	23	(98)	38643-38812	20	(181)
3769-3978	26	(16)	22405-22574	24	(99)	38813-38960	21	(182)
3979-4248	27	(17)	22575-22736	25	(100)	38961-39154	22	(183)
4249-4748	30	(18)	22737-22874	26	(101)	39155-39332	25	(184)
4749-5070	31	(19)	22875-23192	30	(102)	39333-39516	26	(185)
5071-5206	Feb. 1	(20)	23193-23448	31	(103)	39517-39720	27	(186)
5207-5404	2	(21)	23449-23630	June 1	(104)	39721-39974	28	(187)
5405-5582	3	(22)	23631-23948	2	(105)	39975-40368	29	(188)
5583-5920	6	(23)	23949-24130	5	(106)	40369-40626	Oct. 2	(189)
		(24)	24131-24312	6	(107)	40627-40856	3	(190)
					(108)	40857-41038	4	(191)
							5	(192)

Washington, DC: Government Printing Office.

Figure 5-17: *Federal Register*, Volume 54, No. 4, January 6, 1989

DEPARTMENT OF TRANSPORTATION

Federal Aviation Administration

14 CFR Part 107

[Docket No. 25568; Amdt. No. 107-4]

RIN 2120-AC69

Access to Secured Areas of Airports

AGENCY: Federal Aviation Administration (FAA), DOT.
ACTION: Final rule.

SUMMARY: This rule establishes a requirement for certain airport operators to submit to the Director of Civil Aviation Security, for approval and inclusion in their approved security programs, amendments to ensure that only those persons authorized to have access to secured areas of an airport are able to obtain that access and, also, to ensure that such access is denied immediately to individuals whose authority to have access changes. The rule provides for the installation and use of a system, method, or procedure that meets certain performance standards, or the use of an approved alternative system, method, or procedure for controlling access to secured areas of airports. This rule is needed to improve control of the locations that provide access to secured areas of airports. It is intended to enhance airport security by precluding access to these areas by

for approval were approved by the Office of Management and Budget (OMB) under Control No. 2120-0075. Pursuant to this final rule, the FAA forwarded an amendment to Control No. 2120-0075 to OMB in accordance with the Paperwork Reduction Act of 1980 (Pub. L. 96-511). OMB approved the FAA's amendment of Control No. 2120-0075 on January 3, 1989.

Federalism Implications

The FAA believes that airport operators and sponsors will not be unduly burdened by the requirements of the final rule based on (1) the availability of AIP funding; (2) potential lower costs associated with alternative systems, methods, or procedures; and (3) the extended implementation schedule providing amortization of installations costs. On these bases, the FAA has determined that this regulation will not have a substantial direct effect on the States, on the relationship between the National Government and the States, or on the distribution of power and responsibilities among the various levels of government. Therefore, in accordance with Executive Order 12612, preparation of a Federalism assessment is not warranted.

Conclusion

For the reasons discussed in the

restricted area. The FAA is concerned that these procedures could allow an individual using forged, stolen, or noncurrent identification to compromise the secured areas. The FAA is also concerned that former employees could use their familiarity with airline and airport procedures to succeed in entering a secured area and possibly commit a criminal act on board an aircraft.

The December 7, 1987, tragedy involving Pacific Southwest Airlines (PSA) Flight 1771, in which 38 passengers and 5 crewmembers were killed after departing Los Angeles International Airport, highlighted FAA's interest in improving the control of access to secured areas of an airport. An airport area where access to aircraft and airport facilities is possible should be accessible only to an individual who is authorized to be in that area. These areas should be controlled carefully to prevent tampering with aircraft and airport facilities and to preclude tragic consequences.

The FAA accelerated its efforts to head off the type of situation potentially reflected by the crash of PSA Flight 1771 and to improve the level of security generally. This acceleration resulted in the promulgation of an emergency final rule amending the preboarding screening procedures contained in Parts 108 and 129 of the Federal Aviation Regulations (52 FR 48508; December 22, 1987). To complement the procedures

Aviation Regulations (14 CFR Part 107) is amended as follows:

PART 107—AIRPORT SECURITY

1. The authority citation for Part 107 continues to read as follows:

Authority: 49 U.S.C. 1354, 1356, 1357, 1358, and 1421; 49 U.S.C. 106(g) (Revised, Pub. L. 97-449; January 12, 1983).

2. By adding a new § 107.14 to read as follows:

§ 107.14   Access control system.

(a) Except as provided in paragraph (b) of this section, each operator of an airport regularly serving scheduled passenger operations conducted in airplanes having a passenger seating configuration (as defined in § 108.3 of this chapter) of more than 60 seats shall submit to the Director of Civil Aviation Security, for approval and inclusion in its approved security program, an amendment to provide for a system, method, or procedure which meets the requirements specified in this paragraph for controlling access to secured areas of the airport. The system, method, or procedure shall ensure that only those persons authorized to have access to secured areas by the airport operator's security program are able to obtain that access and shall specifically provide a that such access is

allowed to install alternative systems which, in the Administrator's judgment, would have the same capabilities as the computer-card system and would provide an equivalent level of security.

Additionally, Notice No. 88-6 specifically stated that the proposal would supplement, not replace, the existing photo identification system required by an airport operator's approved security program. The continuous display of the individual identification in secured areas is necessary so that unauthorized individuals can be challenged in accordance with § 107.13. However, the notice proposed that the airport operator be given the option of integrating the system proposed by Notice No. 88-6 with the photo identification system and issuing a single credential.

The anticipated capabilities of a computer-controlled card access system were discussed in Notice No. 88-6. In addition to being able to monitor each location where access to the secured area is permitted by means of a "card reader" linked to the control computer, the system would be designed to provide for unique coding for each card. The system would also be capable of performing other functions that can improve an airport's security profile including the ability to cause an alert when access is denied to a person who attempts to use an invalid card and to establish a log of the system's activity. The notice intentionally did not address designated as the actual locations

Aviation Security. The amendment shall specify that the system, method, or procedure must be fully operational within 18 months after the date on which an airport operator's amendment to its approved security program is approved by the Director of Civil Aviation Security.

(2) By August 8, 1989, or by 6 months after becoming subject to this section, whichever is later, for airports where more than 2 million persons are screened annually. The amendment shall specify that the system, method, or procedure must be fully operational within 24 months after the date on which an airport operator's amendment to its approved security program is approved by the Director of Civil Aviation Security.

(3) By February 8, 1990, or by 12 months after becoming subject to this section, whichever is later, for airports where at least 500,000 but not more than 2 million persons are screened annually. The amendment shall specify that the system, method, or procedure must be fully operational within 30 months after the date on which an airport operator's amendment to its approved security program is approved by the Director of Civil Aviation Security.

(4) By February 8, 1990, or by 12 months after becoming subject to this section, whichever is later, for airports

Washington, DC: Government Printing Office.

Figure 5-18: *Weekly Compilation of Presidential Documents*, **1989**

Administration of George Bush, 1989

Taiwan
    Administration policies—239
    Relations with China—239, 247
    Relations with U.S.—247
    Take Pride in America Awards—1148

Telecommunication Union, ...
Telecommunications Advisory Committee, President's National Security—1473, 1655, 1711, 1970
Television. *See* Communications
Tennessee
    Governor—1816
    President's visit—1816
Tennessee, University of—586, 1804
Terrorism
    See also specific country or region
    Administration policies—1942, 1961
    Antiterrorism efforts—162, 439, 440, 1209, 1210, 1274, 1289
    Bombing incidents in U.S. *See specific State*
    President's views—218, 295, 368, 378, 1185, 1400, 1402, 1439, 1880, 1921, 1922
Teton Science School—890
Texas
    Corpus Christi, mayor—1994
    Dallas, mayor—1731
    Economy—621

Texas National Research Laboratory Commission—621
Texas Vietnam Veterans Memorial Fund—1731
Textiles—1659, 1660
Thailand
    Prime Minister—241

Transportation, ...
    Airline labor dispute, role—279, 290
    Assistant Secretaries—372, 373
    Aviation Administration, Federal—290, 374, 1688
    Aviation safety, role. *See* Aviation
    Aviation security commission, role. *See* Aviation Security and Terrorism, President's Commission on
    Budget—1490, 1614, 1809
    Coast Guard, U.S.—434, 435, 450, 454, 500, 501, 505, 537, 623, 626, 627, 766, 1271, 1323, 1402, 1416, 1786, 1789
    Deputy Secretary—211
    General Counsel—374
    Highway Administration, Federal—556, 885, 1614
    Highway Traffic Safety Administration, National—388, 1637
    Maritime Administration—1211
    President's views—162
    Federal—367

Administration of George Bush, 1989 / Aug. 4

Prior to this, he was Assistant Secretary of Defense for Research and Technology, 1986, and Director of the Defense Advanced Research Projects Agency, 1985.

Dr. Duncan graduated from the U.S. Naval Academy (B.S., 1945; B.S., 1953) and the Massachusetts Institute of Technology (M.S., 1954; Ph.D., 1961). He served in the U.S. Navy from 1945 to 1960. Dr. Duncan was born November 21, 1923, in Jonesville, VA. He is married, has four children, and resides in Washington, DC.

Executive Order 12686—President's Commission on Aviation Security and Terrorism
August 4, 1989

By the authority vested in me as President by the Constitution and laws of the United States of America, and in order to establish a Commission on Aviation Security and Terrorism, it is hereby ordered as follows:

Section 1. Establishment. (a) There is established the President's Commission on Aviation Security and Terrorism to review and evaluate policy options in connection with aviation security, with particular refer-

December 21

Washington, DC: Government Printing Office.

Federal
Aviation
Administration

800 Independence Ave. S.W., Washington, D.C. 20591

The Federal Aviation Administration (FAA) establishes and enforces rules and regulations for safety standards covering all aspects of civil aviation. Major areas under FAA regulatory control are the manufacture, maintenance and operation of aircraft; the training and certification of air personnel (pilots, flight engineers, navigators, aviation mechanics, air traffic controllers, parachute riggers and aircraft dispatchers); security measures at airports; domestic and international air traffic; and noise and exhaust emissions from aircraft (in cooperation with the Environmental Protection Agency). The FAA also develops air traffic rules and regulations and allocates the

training of foreign ... of information with foreign governments. It provides technical representation at conferences, including participation in the International Civil Aviation Organization and other international organizations.

The FAA administers the Civil Aviation Security Program to prevent criminal acts such as air piracy, hijacking, sabotage and extortion. The administration requires all airports to maintain security systems to screen airline passengers. It also investigates selected aviation accidents in cooperation with the Na-

The FAA publi... and financial reports as well as economic studies on domestic and international air traffic activity, the aviation industry, aviation safety and air personnel. Publications are described in and may be ordered through the *Guide to Federal Aviation Administration Publications*, available from the Public Inquiry Center.

Publications

Public Inquiry Center
Federal Aviation Administration
800 Independence Ave. S.W.
Washington, D.C. 20591
(202) 426-8058
Tina Mallory, acting chief

The FAA annually publishes the *Guide to Federal Aviation Administration Publications*. The guide lists and describes materials published by the FAA as well as information on materials published by other agencies related to the work of the FAA. The guide is available from the FAA Public Inquiry Center.

Information materials listed in the guide include the agency charter, rulemaking materials, federal aviation regulations, *Code of Federal Regulations* materials, enforcement activities, type certifications, airworthiness

tional Transportation Safety Board (NTSB) *(p. 510)* to determine their causes.

The FAA came under criticism in August 1985 when the House Public Works and Transportation Committee released a report saying that the margin of safety for air travelers had decreased since the 1981 air traffic controllers' strike, in which approximately 16,000 controllers had walked off the job. The same month, Transportation Secretary Elizabeth Hanford Dole released an unrelated internal report acknowledging that the administration had been less than proficient in ensuring that safety regulations had been enforced. The report faulted the FAA for not carrying out actions promptly, lacking uniform ... ...ards for ... ...ulations and and called for better communication within the administration.

In addition the secretary in 1985 proposed to increase the civil penalty limit for safety violations by airlines and other commercial operators. New FAA rules were issued concerning the length of time pilots are permitted to fly and how much rest they are permitted between trips. And legislation was introduced in 1985 requiring the DOT to assess security standards at foreign airports and to notify

....
written by the staff of the Flight Standards Service, available on a subscription basis.

Legislation

The FAA is responsible for the administration of parts of several statutes, most of which are related to aviation safety. The FAA carries out its responsibilities under:

Federal Aviation Act of 1958 (72 Stat. 737, 49 U.S.C. 1301). Signed by the president Aug. 23, 1958. Created the Federal Aviation Agency and gave the agency authority to regulate aviation safety standards, to control the nation's navigable airspace, to operate air navigation facilities, to formulate air traffic rules and regulations, to issue certificates of standards for air personnel and aircraft, to establish grant programs for the construction and improvement of airports, to require registration of aircraft and to establish security provisions for aircraft and airports.

Department of Transportation Act (80 Stat. 931, 49 U.S.C. 1651). Signed by the president Oct. 15, 1966. Created the Cabinet-level Department of Transportation; placed the functions, powers and authorities of the Federal Aviation Agency in one of the three ... ...ministrations within the Transpor-

in helping the rural poor ended. It has received mixed reviews, generally being praised by liberal ideologists but criticized by conservatives.

In retrospect, the FSA was a symbol of America's agricultural ills in the twentieth century. It symbolized the pathos of the rural poor, bringing attention to the long decline of agriculture in the United States and the painful transition of those people caught in the change. In this respect, the FSA was admired for its work, being regarded as a sincere attempt by the federal government to *New Deal Comm.......* ~~~~~~~~~~~~~trodden. Yet, the FSA symbolized the difficulty program. A valuable source of technical information ..... ~~~~~~~~~ ~~~~~~~~~~~ible for to the FSA is *Farm Security Administration Hearings*, Select Committee of the House Committee on Agriculture to Investigate the Activities of the Farm Security Administration, 78th Cong., 1st Sess., H. Resolution 119, May 11 to 28, 1943.

D. CLAYTON BROWN

FEDERAL AVIATION ADMINISTRATION (FAA). Since 1926, the Aeronautics Branch in the Department of Commerce* and its successors have overseen the development and regulation of commercial aviation, promoting airmail, passenger, and cargo services. The original thrust stressed the licensing of all flight personnel, the establishment of safety rules, and Civil Air Regulations for the crews, aircraft manufacturers, airport operators, and other ground employees. Moreover, the branch certified the airworthiness of each aircraft and mandated periodic subsequent inspections of the craft and personnel. These chores initially proved to be rather vexing because seasoned, private aviators looked with utter disdain at the notion of showing their skills to federal inspectors, who, in turn, sometimes displayed their own arrogance of power. A number of years elapsed which ... ~~~~~~~~~~~~~lators finally caught several unwilling pilots. controllers' strike ended in their dism......~ ~~~~~~~ ~~~ backing, enthusiasm and other problems remain to confront us in the 1980s.

FOR ADDITIONAL INFORMATION: For primary sources, the researcher should examine the FAA files, Record Group 237, and the older materials from predecessor agencies in the National Archives,* particularly Record Group 40, Department of Commerce. The presidential libraries hold valuable records. One comprehensive scholarly account, Donald R. Whitnah, *Safer Skyways: Federal Control of Aviation, 1926-1966* (1966), covers developments and controversies for both the FAA and predecessors and primarily the accident chores of the CAB for this period. The FAA sponsored a four-book series on its history. Nick A. Komons, *Bonfires to Beacons: Federal Civil Aviation Policy Under the Air Commerce Act, 1926-1938* (1978), is especially sound on the cutthroat aviation competition without regulation before 1938 and the political infighting. John R.M. Wilson, *Turbulence Aloft: The Civil Aeronautics Administration Amid Wars and Rumors of Wars, 1938-1953* (1979), stresses the airport programs and research developments. Stuart I. Rochester, *Takeoff at Mid-Century: Federal Civil Aviation Policy in the Eisenhower Years, 1953-1961* (1976), describes in detail the feuding between the CAA and Commerce and the battles of General Quesada as administrator. Richard J. Kent, *Safe, Separated, and Soaring: A History of Federal Civil Aviation Policy, 1961-1972* (1980), concentrates on the Halaby-McKee administrations, the scrapping of the SST program, the rise of the DOT, and unsuccessful attempts to place the FAA under the military. The reader should also consult the various aviation journals which nearly always reflect the biases of their individual constituents, for example, pilots, owners, general aviation, or the military.

DONALD R. WHITNAH

~~~~~~TIGATION (FBI).** The Attorney General
~~ ~~~~ time.

CASE LAW

An Overview of the Judicial Process

The United States has one of the most complex legal systems in the world. Most geographically large nations with a federal system have only a few regional courts from which cases may be appealed to one national court. In the United States, each of the fifty states has a separate court system composed of trial, intermediate appellate, and supreme courts. There is some variation across states in how courts are structured and named (*Book of the States 1988-89 Edition*, pp. 157-160).

In addition, we have a federal court system of trial, intermediate appellate, and supreme courts. There are presently almost one hundred federal trial courts (called District Courts) with at least one in every state, the District of Columbia (DC), and the territories of Guam, Puerto Rico, the Northern Marianas, and the U.S. Virgin Islands. There are presently twelve federal intermediate appellate courts (called Courts of Appeal—prior to 1948, they were known as Circuit Courts), one located in DC and the others divided across the fifty states. Congress, in 1982, also created a Court of Appeals for the Federal Circuit that has nationwide original and appellate jurisdiction based on selected types of subject matter rather than geographic location.

Both state and federal court systems also have specialized courts of limited jurisdiction—at the state level, examples are juvenile, probate, small claims, and traffic courts; at the federal level, examples include international trade, military appeals, and tax courts.

Courts at the same level in either the federal or state court structure perform basically the same function. *Trial courts* are where most criminal and civil cases begin. There are two parties to each trial court case: 1) the *plaintiff* (the individual or government that brought a civil complaint) or the *prosecution* (the government that brought a criminal charge), and 2) the *defendant* (against whom the complaint or charge was brought).

The title of most trial court cases takes the form of plaintiff or prosecution v. defendant. Hence, Smith v. Jones would be a civil case in which Smith brought a complaint against Jones. N.C. v. Smith or U.S. v. Jones could be either civil or criminal cases but in either case the individual is the defendant. However, not all court cases involve adversary parties (e.g., bankruptcy, probate, or guardianship cases). The title of such cases take the form, *In re* Smith, meaning in the matter of or concerning Smith.

Trial court judges (and—often but not always—juries) listen to witnesses, see evidence presented, and consider legal arguments before reaching a verdict. It is at the trial court level that verdicts are handed down, and sentences imposed. Most legal disputes end at the trial court level.

However, *appellate courts* exist in both state and federal court systems to hear appeals of trial court decisions presented by the losing party. The title of an appellate court case involving adversarial parties lists first the name of the party appealing the adverse judgment of the lower court (called the *petitioner* or *appellant*) followed by the name of the party against whom the appeal is taken, who was usually the winner in the lower court case (called the *respondent* or *appellee*). Hence, if in a trial court case, Smith (plaintiff) v. Jones (defendant), Smith wins; and if Jones appeals that adverse judgement; the appellate court case would become Jones (petitioner) v. Smith (respondent).

Appellate courts, composed of judges but not juries, are usually limited to reviewing points of law rather than questions of fact or evidence. Appellate courts function to insure that the procedural rights of the losing party were respected at the trial court level but not to review or re-evaluate questions of fact or evidence. Hence, the appellate court's decision in a criminal case is not between guilt or innocence, but whether to affirm or reverse the lower court's decision. Sometimes the appellate court decision is to remand (i.e., to return) the case back to the lower court for retrial with instructions concerning how the lower court should differently interpret a point of law or follow a legal procedure.

At both the intermediate appellate and supreme court levels, courts usually but not always accompany their decision with one or more written opinions. The *opinion of the Court* states the reasoning accepted by the majority of the justices joining in the Court's decision. Sometimes called a *majority opinion*, opinions of the Court are announced (or signed) by one member of the majority. In contrast, a *per curiam opinion* (by the court) is the Court's decision although not signed or announced by any member of the Court (for example, announcing that a lower court judgment is affirmed because the Court is equally divided). A *memorandum opinion* is a unanimous decision by the Court not accompanied by an opinion.

There may also be concurring and dissenting opinions. *Concurring opinions* express the reasoning of justices who agree with the court's decision but on differing grounds. *Dissenting opinions* present the arguments of justices who disagree with both the decision and the opinion of the court.

In all state court systems as well as in the federal court system, there is a "court of last resort" or *supreme court* to give a final review to appeals of adverse decisions handed down by lower courts. At either the state or federal level, such supreme courts accept for review relatively few appeals from lower court decisions. The losing party can, under certain conditions, petition a higher court to grant a writ of certiorari. A *writ* is a written court order requiring that some action be taken or be prohibited. A writ of *certiorari* is an order from a higher court to a lower court requiring that the record of a case be sent up for review. Most cases reach the U.S. Supreme Court on a writ of certiorari. Such a writ is granted by the U.S. Supreme Court when four or more justices agree that the Court should review a case. When any higher court denies a petition for writ of certiorari, the decision of the lower court stands.

State or federal supreme court decisions in the relatively few cases accepted for review can have tremendous importance. They are binding on all lower courts and often involve constitutional or statutory interpretations of broad impact.

Chronological Case Law Sources: Court Reporters, Slip Opinions,
United States Reports, United States Supreme Court Reports, **and** *Supreme Court Reporter*

Court reporters are compilations of court decisions and opinions arranged by date of decision. The official court reporter for the U.S. Supreme Court is *United States Reports*. Until 1874, cases in *U.S. Reports* were cited by the last name of the editor (e.g., Dred Scott v. Sandford was cited as 19 Howard 393 (1857)). In 1875 the first 90 volumes of *U.S. Reports* (Dallas through Wallace) were renumbered consecutively and both earlier and later cases began to be referred to by their *U.S. Reports* citations (however, citations to pre-1875 cases still frequently use the earlier form). All following volumes have continued the *U.S. Reports* numbering sequence initiated in 1875 (e.g., Plessy v. Ferguson, 163 US 537 (1896)).

As the Court decides each case, that decision and its accompanying opinion(s) are first issued by the U.S. Government Printing Office as a separate *slip opinion*. To provide even quicker access to current Supreme Court decisions, your library may subscribe to either *United States Law Week* or *Commerce Clearinghouse Supreme Court Bulletin*. Both mail to subscribers copies of all slip opinions within a week of release by the Court. Slip opinions are subsequently compiled into paperbound volumes (also called *advance sheets* or *preliminary prints*). These, in turn, are replaced with hardbound volumes after the end of each *October term* (which ends the following June or July).

The slip opinions are usually published within two to three weeks of their decision date. After each term of the Court, a multi-volume, paperbound preliminary print of *U.S. Reports* is published. The paperbound preliminary print offers, in addition to the case reports, a subject index, a table of cases reported that is alphabetized by the names of both parties (except U.S.), and court orders.

Court orders are notices or directives issued by a court. For our purposes, the most significant types of orders are those granting or denying petitions for writs of certiorari and motions to file *amicus curiae* (friend of the court) briefs. If allowed to submit an amicus curiae brief, a person or organization—that is not a direct party to a case—is allowed to present to the court written arguments concerning resolution of the issues in dispute.

Unlike the slip opinions, the preliminary prints give the volume and pagination information used in case citations. After a time lag of about two years from the end of a term, the final version of *U.S. Reports* is published in hardbound volumes. These have the same additional sections as the preliminary prints. The bound volumes also contain both a "Table of Cases Cited" (in the cases reported) and a section listing orders announced by the Court.

Besides *U.S. Reports*, your library may have one or both of the two commercially published, annotated court reporters. *United States Supreme Court Reports*, published by the Lawyers Cooperative Publishing, is cited with the abbreviation LEd or LEd 2d. The first LEd series contains all of the opinions in 1-349 US. Volume one of LEd 2d, the second series, starts with opinions in 350 US. *Supreme Court Reporter*, published by the West Publishing Company, is cited SCt. The first volume of this series begins with opinions reported in 106 US (1882).

U.S. Supreme Court Reports (LEd) and *Supreme Court Reporter (SCt)*, in addition to reprinting the Court's opinions that appear in *U.S. Reports*, also present annotations and headnotes which precede each opinion. *Annotations* are brief essays that summarize and interpret the Court's opinion. *Headnotes* are numbered, short paragraphs that each analyze a separate point of law covered in an opinion. Annotations and headnotes offer the reader an overview of the legal issues decided in the case. Cases reported in both *U.S. Supreme Court Reports (LEd)* and *Supreme Court Reporter (SCt)* provide cross references to the corresponding volume and page for that case in *U.S. Reports*. Like the official reporter, the two commercial reporters provide advance sheets prior to publication of hardbound volumes at the end of each October term.

One recent case, that at time of writing was not available in either hard- or paperbound volumes of *U.S. Reports*, involves the terrorist hijacking of the cruise ship *Achille Lauro*.[1] We found this slip opinion by applying decision rule 3(g) (i.e., by thumbing through the slip opinions, scanning the titles and introductory materials). This case is only marginally relevant to prevention of aircraft hijacking. It relates to the terrorist hijacking of a cruise liner rather than an airliner and the point of law at dispute is right of appeal rather than prevention techniques. However, as we will see later, few cases involving aircraft hijacking have been decided by the U.S. Supreme Court.

The *syllabus* at the beginning of the slip opinion is an unofficial but extremely useful synopsis of the case (see Figure 5-21). The title, Lauro Lines S.R.L. v. Chasser et al., tells us that Lauro Lines is petitioning for relief from an adverse decision at a lower court level and that Chasser and others are the respondents. The line below the title tells us that this case was ordered up for review from the U.S. Court of Appeals for the Second Circuit. The docket number, No. 88-23, tells us that this case was the twenty-third case accepted for review by the Supreme Court in its October 1988 term. The volumes of court reporters are labelled with the October term year. Hence, the Lauro v. Chasser decision and opinions will be published in an October 1988 term volume of *U.S. Reports* even though that case was decided in 1989.

The next section of the syllabus summarizes the history of the case followed by a summary of the holding (opinion) of the Court. At the end of the syllabus is the decision or judgment of the Court—in this case affirming the Court of Appeals decision. Finally, the syllabus indicates who delivered the Court's opinion (Brennan) and who authored any concurring (Scalia) and/or dissenting opinions (in this case there was none).

Secondary Sources for U.S. Supreme Court Decisions
Preview, Court Digests, Legal Encyclopedias, and Indexes

There are at least two characteristics of secondary sources that are useful when researching case law—they provide interpretative material to help you understand the cause, nature, and consequence of case law on your topic and they also offer finding aids to help you more thoroughly search the primary sources for relevant cases.

Some secondary sources for legal research might also be considered a primary source for other research purposes. An example is *Landmark Briefs and Arguments of the Supreme Court of the United States*. This multi-volume series reprints petitions, motions, written briefs, and oral arguments from selected, historically important cases decided by the U.S. Supreme Court. To a legal researcher, such material is not considered primary because (unlike the Court's decisions and opinions) it does not carry the force of law. However, to a political scientist researching the judicial process, this same material might well be considered a primary source because it is original information coming directly from the source unaltered by second party analysis or interpretation.

An excellent secondary source for keeping up-to-date on cases pending before the U.S. Supreme Court is the periodical, *Preview of United States Supreme Court Cases*,

---

[1]This case has now been issued in a volume and can be cited as 490 US 495.

**Figure 5-21:
Slip Opinion for
*Lauro Lines S.R.L.
v. Chasser et al.***

**Washington, DC:
Government
Printing Office.**

(Slip Opinion)

> NOTE: Where it is feasible, a syllabus (headnote) will be released, as is being done in connection with this case, at the time the opinion is issued. The syllabus constitutes no part of the opinion of the Court but has been prepared by the Reporter of Decisions for the convenience of the reader. See *United States* v. *Detroit Lumber Co.*, 200 U. S. 321, 337.

SUPREME COURT OF THE UNITED STATES

Syllabus

LAURO LINES S.R.L. *v.* CHASSER ET AL.

CERTIORARI TO THE UNITED STATES COURT OF APPEALS FOR THE SECOND CIRCUIT

No. 88–23.   Argued April 17, 1989—Decided May 22, 1989

Respondents—passengers and representatives of the estates of passengers on a cruise ship hijacked by terrorists—filed suit in the District Court against petitioner, the ship's owner, to recover damages for personal injuries and for the wrongful death of one passenger.   Before trial, petitioner moved to dismiss the actions, citing the forum-selection clause printed on each passenger ticket, which purported to obligate passengers to institute any suit in connection with the contract in Italy and to renounce the right to sue elsewhere.   The District Court denied the motions, holding that the ticket did not give passengers reasonable notice that they were waiving the opportunity to sue in a domestic forum.   The Court of Appeals dismissed petitioner's appeal on the ground that the District Court's dismissal orders were interlocutory and not appealable under 28 U. S. C. § 1291, holding that the orders did not fall within the exception to the rule of nonappealability carved out by the collateral order doctrine.

Held: An interlocutory order denying a defendant's motion to dismiss a damages action on the basis of a contractual forum-selection clause is not immediately appealable under § 1291.   Such an order is not final in the ~~litigation on~~ the merits but, on the lihood of eventual success on the merits.   P. ~~~~

844 F. 2d 50, affirmed.

BRENNAN, J., delivered the opinion for a unanimous Court.   SCALIA, J., filed a concurring opinion, *post*, p. 502.

---

published by the American Bar Association's Public Education Division.[2] Its articles are good examples of *case briefs*. Such a brief is an abstract of a case that usually includes a synopsis of the issue(s), facts, background and significance, and oral arguments. Figure 5-22 shows excerpts of the *Preview* article briefing the Lauro v. Chasser case

---

[2]For a subscription to *Preview of United States Supreme Court Cases*, write Order Fulfillment, American Bar Association, 750 N. Lake Shore Dr., Chicago, IL 60611 ($120/yr.).

while it was still pending before the Court. Because we knew the case name and term of the Court from looking at its slip opinion, we were able to find this article quickly by using *Preview*'s case name index, which cumulates for the term with each issue. If, instead of the case title, you know the major issue or point of law at dispute in the case, you can search *Preview*'s subject index.

While *Preview* briefs cases pending before the U.S. Supreme Court, two other basic types of legal secondary sources—case digests and legal encyclopedias—analyze decisions after they are announced by the Court. A fundamental difference between Supreme Court digests and legal encyclopedias is that the former analyze only cases decided by the U.S. Supreme Court, whereas the latter refer to decisions of lower level courts as well.

A *case digest* can be described as an index that subject classifies reported case decisions and presents a brief abstract for each decision. Thus, each case is analyzed to identify all specific findings and general principles which may serve as precedent in future cases. These various points are then subject-arranged and indexed in a multi-volume set updated by pocket-parts. As with court reporters, there are digests for all levels of federal courts and for major state courts as well. As Table 5-2 indicates, the major case digests for the U.S. Supreme Court are *United States Supreme Court Digest*, published by West Publishing Company, and *United States Supreme Court Reports Digest*, published by Lawyers Cooperative Publishing.

A portion of the "Word Index" to *U.S. Supreme Court Digest* is shown in Figure 5-23. Under the subject heading "Piracy", we see an entry for "Aircraft piracy" referring to section 1 of the *Digest*'s topic entitled "Aeronautics". Turning to that topic in the *Digest*, we find that the topic title has been changed to "Aeronautics and Space" (see Figure 5-24). The "Parallel Reference (Transfer) Table" at the beginning of each volume lists all such changes in topic titles. Under section 1 of "Aeronautics and Space", two types of references are listed—research and cross-references. The research references are to a variety of primary and secondary sources (e.g., legal encyclopedias, *U.S. Code, U.S. Statutes at Large, U.S. Code Service*, and so on). The cross-references are to other topic titles within the *Digest* as well as relevant U.S. Supreme Court cases. One case that we find cited here clearly deals with an incident of aircraft piracy (U.S. v. Healy, 376 US 75, 84 SCt 553, 11 LEd 2d 527). This search illustrates decision rule 3(e) in Table 5-3.

A *legal encyclopedia* presents introductory-level summary articles on hundreds of legal topics. As decision rule 3(a) from Table 5-3 points out, they are a good place to go for information about both case and statute law when you know relatively little about a legal topic. Since they—like the case digests—cite cases, the topical articles in these encyclopedias can identify relevant cases from which you will want to read decisions and opinions. Doing so will also put your research within a broader perspective.

The two major legal encyclopedias are *American Jurisprudence 2d* (Am Jur 2d) and *Corpus Juris Secundum* (CJS). The "2d" in Am Jur and "secundum" in CJS refer to second edition, not second series as found in court reporters. Like more generalized encyclopedias, both *American Jurisprudence 2d* and *Corpus Juris Secundum* are multi-volume works that present hundreds of articles written in narrative form that are arranged alphabetically by topic title. Both use extensive footnotes to cite federal and state court decisions relevant to the article's topic. Both are updated by pocket parts and replacement volumes to reflect the current law in force.

Is a trial court's decision not to enforce a forum selection clause immediately appealable?

by Linda S. Mullenix

Lauro Lines, s.r.l.

v.

Sophie Chasser, et al.
(Docket No. 88-23)

Argument Date: April 17, 1989

In what is now becoming a staple of the annual Supreme Court diet, the Court once again this term will consider the immediate appealability of a trial court's order concerning an aspect of trial procedure. To keep trials from bogging down with numerous interruptions (so-called "piecemeal litiga-

events surrounding the hijack.......

Lauro and the death of passenger Leon Klinghoffer.

ISSUE

The issue in *Lauro Lines* is whether a federal district court's order, denying enforcement of a contractual clause that specified a foreign forum for adjudication of any legal disputes, is immediately appealable as an exception to the final judgment rule under the "collateral order" doctrine.

FACTS

In one of the most gripping terrorist incidents in recent years, the cruise ship *Achille Lauro* was hijacked in October 1985 by terrorists of the Palestine Liberation Organization as it was cruising in the Mediterranean Sea. While most of the world watched in horror, the ship's passengers were held hostage, and one elderly and infirm passenger, Leon Klinghoffer, was murdered and thrown overboard.

.... number of Ameri-

selection clause. Since Lauro Lines does not want to have to litigate the passengers' claims in the United States, it petitioned the Supreme Court to overturn the 2d Circuit ruling on the issue of whether an immediate appeal may be had from an adverse ruling on forum selection clause enforceability.

BACKGROUND AND SIGNIFICANCE

The *Lauro Lines* case combines two issues that have recently engaged the Supreme Court's attention: forum se-
.... clauses and interlocutory appeals. Just last term the
....

ARGUMENTS

For Lauro Lines, s.r.l. *(Counsel of Record, Raymond A. Connell, 29 Broadway, New York, NY 10006; telephone (212) 943-3980):*

1. Although there is a strong federal policy limiting appeals to final decisions, the Supreme Court has recognized exceptions to this final judgment rule for certain kinds of collateral orders.
2. The New York trial judge's refusal to enforce the forum selection clause specifying Naples as the place of trial for any dispute arising from the cruise, falls into the collateral order exception to the final judgment rule.
3. The trial judge's order refusing to enforce the forum selection clause conclusively determined the disputed question, resolved an important issue completely separate from the merits of the action; and would be effectively unreviewable on appeal from a final judgment.

can passengers who had been held captive and terrorized by the hijackers brought suit in federal district court in New York City against the joint venture *Lauro Lines* and other organizations that had chartered the ship and promoted the cruise. The various actions were to recover damages for physical and psychological injuries resulting from the incident and for the wrongful death of Leon Klinghoffer.

The *Achille Lauro* was chartered to a joint venture of Italian partners located in Naples, Italy. The joint venture, which sold tickets for its cruises worldwide, retained Chandris Inc. in New York City to promote bookings for the ship and to distribute cruise tickets to travel agencies. Chandris distributed tickets to Crown Travel Service, a New York agency, which sold the tickets to New York residents and
.... the plaintiffs in
of the passengers had org..
provision at the end of the ticket.

The American passengers brought their various lawsuits in the federal district court in New York City in November 1985. Lauro Lines responded by filing a motion to dismiss the lawsuits on the grounds that the court in New York did not have personal jurisdiction over it, that the New York court was an inconvenient forum, and that the ticket required that any lawsuits be brought in Naples, Italy.

In October 1987, the district court judge in New York heard arguments on the motion to dismiss the case. After argument, the judge rendered an oral ruling from the bench finding that "the ticket does not give fair warning to the American citizen passenger that he or she is renouncing and waiving his or her opportunity to sue in a domestic forum over a contract made and delivered in the United States."

Calling the question a close one upon which reasonable jurists, lawyers, and laymen might differ, the judge nonethe-
.... "whether the ticket

Lines to an immediate review of that decision. ....
court. The parties all agree that the judge's order meets the first two requirements of the collateral order exception. They dispute, however, whether the third requirement is satisfied: that the judge's ruling would be effectively unreviewable on appeal from a final judgment.

Thus, Sophie Chasser and the other passengers contend that the lawsuit must now proceed in New York federal court and that any review of the trial judge's decision on the forum selection clause must await the end of the entire trial. Lauro Lines, on the contrary, argues that it must have immediate
.... clause because

tively reviewable on appeal. This order .....
judge's order denying a motion to dismiss for improper venue or *forum non conveniens.*

5. The 3rd Circuit's view that a refusal to enforce a forum selection clause is unreviewable on appeal is based on an obscure statutory provision (28 U.S.C. § 2105), and is misconceived and inconsistent with current appellate practice.
6. An erroneous ruling on a forum selection clause may be reversed on appeal, and the right to secure trial in a particular court will not be forfeited simply because enforcement is postponed.

AMICUS BRIEFS

In Support of Lauro Lines

Chandris Cruise Lines and Chandris (Italy) Inc.

Figure 5-23:
United States Supreme Court Reports Digest, Lawyers Edition, Volume 16D, General Index, 1990

Reprinted by permission of Lawyers Cooperative Publishing, a division of Thomson Legal Publishing, Inc.

U. S. SUPREME COURT INDEX

PIPES AND PIPELINES—Cont'd
Taxes—Cont'd
– user fees, legislation authorizing Transportation Secretary to establish schedule of pipeline safety user ...
Valuation data, 91 L Ed 22, 329 US 29, 67 S Ct 1

PIRACY
For general treatment, see L Ed Digest topic **Piracy**

PIRACY—Cont'd
Airline piracy, 11 L Ed 2d 527, 376 US 75, 84 S Ct 553; L Ed Digest, **Aeronautics** § 1
Alien's suit in admiralty against state for ... of captured slaves, 8 L Ed 808,
Automobile dealerships, stay pending appeal of injunction against enforcement of statute governing location, 54 L Ed 2d 439, 434 US 1345, 98 S Ct 359

Consult POCKET PART for most current materials.

246

There are some important differences between *American Jurisprudence 2d* and *Corpus Juris Secundum. Corpus Juris Secundum* is more comprehensive than *American Jurisprudence 2d* in its case citations. *Corpus Juris Secundum,* since it is issued by West Publishing Company, uses the West "Key Number" system which directs you to topics in West case digests. *American Jurisprudence 2d,* a Lawyers Cooperative publication, cross-references to other Lawyers Cooperative publications and to law review articles. *American Jurisprudence 2d* also has a "Desk Book" that in essence is a legal almanac—containing directory and statistical information, abbreviations of legal sources, and texts of major legal documents.

Legal encyclopedias offer both a general index for the entire multi-volume set and volume indexes that are more detailed for the topic(s) covered within a specific volume. Turning to the general index in *American Jurisprudence,* we find that "Hijacking" sends us to "Piracy" (see Figure 5-25). Under "Piracy", an entry for "Aircraft, piracy of" sends us to "Aviation". When we look under "Aviation", there is a subheading for "Hijacking" and within that an entry for "prevention". This entry lists two topics that cover this subject.

Turning to the first of these, Aviation—section 51, we find an *American Jurisprudence* section heading, "Security measures; screening of passengers" (see Figure 5-26). The following several-page article summarizes statute, regulatory, and case law on this subject. Footnotes to *American Jurisprudence* articles provide citations to primary legal sources as well as to secondary legal sources, such as law review articles and *American Law Reports* (another Lawyers Cooperative source). For example, Figure 5-26 includes footnote references to *U.S. Code Service, Code of Federal Regulations, Fordham Law Review,* and other *American Jurisprudence* articles.

If your library has *American Law Reports* (ALR), you should make use of its unique features. ALR is a hybrid legal source, combining features of a legal encyclopedia with those of a court reporter. Hence, like a reporter it reprints decisions (of selected appellate court cases); but like a legal encyclopedia it adds summary articles that link the reported case to all important related cases with commentary and synthesis.

Before leaving case law, we should mention a useful finding aid that will help you locate secondary sources on U.S. Supreme Court decisions. *United States Supreme Court Decisions* (1983) is an index to excerpts, reprints, and discussions about selected,

AERONAUTICS AND SPACE

Scope of Topic: This topic covers aircraft and aeronautics, and facilities therefor, generally; including questions of ownership and operation; public regulation and control; licenses and permits; taxation specifically applicable to aircraft; property rights; relative rights in the airspace; and tortious acts and injuries. The topic also includes principles of carriers pertaining to aircraft; public regulation thereof; and functions, powers, and practices of administrative agencies relative thereto.

Treated elsewhere are questions as to insurance (see INSURANCE); general property taxation (see TAXES); and criminal offenses not peculiarly applicable to aviation and aircraft (see CRIMINAL LAW). Matters of procedure and proof in judicial proceedings are treated in such topics as EVIDENCE; PLEADING; TRIAL; etc.)

[For fact-word approach see Word Index to this Digest]

I. IN GENERAL.
     § 1   Generally.
     § 2   Public regulation and control.

II. AIR CARRIERS.
     § 3   Generally.
     § 4   Public regulation and control.
     § 5   Administrative control and proceedings.
     § 6   —judicial relief, review, or enforcement.

I. IN GENERAL

§ 1 Generally.

Research References

8 Am Jur 2d, Aviation §§ 1, 2

ALR Digests: Aeroplanes and Aeronautics, §§ 1–47

Construction and application of § 902(i-l) of Federal Aviation Act of 1958, as amended (49 USC § 1472(i-l)) punishing aircraft pi-

later history and annotation references through the Auto-Cite computer research system.

Cross References

Flight of, over land, as taking for which landowners must be compensated, see EMINENT DOMAIN § 103.

The transportation of an airplane knowing it to have been stolen, is not a violation of the National Motor Vehicle Theft Act of October 29, 1919, 41 Stat at L 324, chap 89, USC title 18, § 408, imposing a penalty upon anyone who shall transport, or cause to be transported, in interstate or foreign commerce, a motor vehicle knowing it to have been stolen, and providing that "the term 'motor vehicle' shall include an automobile, . . . motorcycle, or any other self-propelled vehicle not designed for running on rails." McBoyle v United States, 283 US 25, 51 S Ct 340,

75 L Ed 816

One of the purposes of the aircraft piracy amendment to the Federal Aviation Act (94 USC § 1472(i)) is to provide a solution to the jurisdictional problems involved in fixing a locus for a crime committed in transit and in arresting a deplaning passenger who may have engaged in criminal activity over the territory of a different state, and such problems are as pertinent to acts committed aboard private aircraft as to acts committed aboard commercial airliners. United States v Healy, 376 US 75, 84 S Ct 553,

11 L Ed 2d 527

Under the aircraft piracy amendment to

p) of Federal Aviation Act 1958, as amended (49 USCS § 1472(a–p)). 39 ALR Fed 851.

Liability of United States for negligence or air traffic controller. 46 ALR Fed 24.

Liability of United States for negligence of person other than air traffic controller in connection with aviation control operations. 47 ALR Fed 85.

Warsaw Convention (49 Stat 3000 et seq.) as creating cause of action. 51 ALR Fed 949.

. . . . . . or flight of aircraft as

§ 2 Public regulation . . .

Research References

8 Am Jur 2d, Aviation §§ 9–19

ALR Digests: Aeroplanes and Aeronautics, §§ 3–21

Validity, under commerce clause of Federal Constitution, of state tolls or taxes on, or affecting, interstate or foreign air carriers or passengers. 31 L Ed 2d 975.

Validity, under Federal Constitution, of preflight procedures used at airports to prevent hijacking of aircraft. 14 ALR Fed 286.

Regulation of air travel clubs, charter flights, and the like, by the civil aeronautics board. 27 ALR Fed 154.

What is proper venue under 49 USCS § 1473(a) for trial of crimes, including air piracy, committed in violation of § 902(a–p) of Federal Aviation Act 1958, as amended (49 USCS § 1472(a–p)). 39 ALR Fed 851.

Aerial observation or surveillance as violative of Fourth Amendment guaranty against unreasonable search and seizure. 56 ALR Fed 772.

Validity of Federal Aviation Administration regulations (14 CFR §§ 67.13, 67.15, 67.17) prescribing standards for issuance of medical certificates to airmen. 59 ALR Fed 682.

Construction and effect of 49 US Code § 1403, governing recordation of ownership, conveyances, and encumbrances on aircraft. 22 ALR3d 1270.

Aircraft operated wholly within state as subject to Federal regulation. 9 ALR2d 485.

Figure 5-24:
United States Supreme Court Reports Digest, Lawyers Edition, Volume 1, 1984

Reprinted by permission of Lawyers Cooperative Publishing, a division of Thomson Legal Publishing, Inc.

historically significant cases decided by that court. Included are references to more than six hundred books and three hundred periodicals "...generally accessible to undergraduate students...." (Guenther, p. v). Each entry includes the *U.S. Reports* citation and decision date so *U.S. Supreme Court Decisions* is also useful as a sort of popular names table for selected cases decided by that court. This work also provides a case name index and a limited subject index. A search using this index would apply decision rule 2(b) in Table 5-3.

INTERNATIONAL LAW

An Overview of the Diplomatic Process

Diplomacy is the process of negotiation between independent states as each attempts to achieve its foreign policy goals. Diplomatic negotiations exist within and contribute to a system of international law. International law is the set of rules and principles that defines the rights and obligations of sovereign states and their citizens in their mutual relations in the international arena. The purpose of diplomacy and international law, like domestic politics and law within states, is to substitute negotiation and the rule of law for the use of force in resolving disputes.

Sources of international law include treaties and other international agreements, enactments of international organizations, decisions of international courts, and custom. The latter was most important during the initial development of international law as it evolved with the European nation-state system in the early 1600s. With the increasing interdependency of sovereign states in the 20th century, the role of international organizations and courts in shaping international law has increased. However, the primary source of international law still remains the treaty or other international agreement.

A *treaty* is a formal agreement negotiated and accepted by two or more sovereign states that specifies their mutual rights and obligations concerning a particular subject. Article II, Section 2 of the U.S. Constitution specifies that the President "...shall have power, by and with the advice and consent of the Senate, to make treaties, provided two thirds of the Senators present concur...." In practice, this means that the U.S. end of treaty negotiations is usually conducted by Foreign Service diplomats within the State Department under the direction of the President with some members of the Senate occasionally participating. Once a treaty document has been hammered out through diplomatic negotiation, it still must be presented to the U.S. Senate for its advice (and possible modification) and consent (approval by a two-thirds vote of members present). If the Senate votes to approve and if the President accepts changes they may have made, then the President formally ratifies the treaty and it carries the force of law. During the Carter administration, Senator Barry Goldwater challenged President Carter's power to abrogate a treaty without seeking Senate advice and consent. A divided U.S. Supreme Court dismissed Goldwater's case without hearing argument, thus leaving in place the president's authority to unilaterally terminate treaties (Goldwater v. Carter, 44 US 996 (1979)).

Figure 5-25: *American Jurisprudence 2d*, General Index, 1991

AMERICAN JURISPRUDENCE 2d

HIGHWAYS, STREETS, AND BRIDGES —Cont'd

Violation of statutes or ordinance—Cont'd
- **Automobiles and Highway Traffic** (this index)
- [illegible] negligence, Highways §§ 560-569
- drawbridges, Highways §§ 553, 554
- excavations, Highways §§ 397, 405, 497, 500, 529, 591
- independent contractors, Highways §§ 409, 432, 500
- judicial notice, Highways § 591
- lights, Highways §§ 397, 405, 406, 409, 492
- obstructions, generally, Highways §§ 290, 491-495
- openings in sidewalks, Highways §§ 497, 505
- overhead obstructions, Highways § 453
- slippery conditions, Highways § 463
- temporary obstructions, Highways § 452
- toll bridges, Highways § 629

Washington, D.C. **District of Columbia** (this index)

Striking pipeline, Pipe [illegible]

Structure. Buildings or structures, supra

Subpoenas, National Transportation Safety Board hearings, Pipe § 19

Subrogation, Trans-Alaska Pipeline Authorization Act, Pipe § 41

Supreme Court of United States as reviewing decision ordering removal of hazard, Pipe § 12

Surface, Pipe §§ 37, 41-43

Suspension of right of way, Pipe § 24

Taxation (this index)

Telegraph or telephone report of accident, Pipe § 14

Temporary injury to land, measure of damages for, Pipe § 41

Temporary permits, construction of pipelines upon grant of, Pipe § 25

Termination of right of way, Pipe § 24

Test failure while testing gas or other test medium, report on, Pipe § 14

Third persons, Pipe §§ 53, 54

Time and date
- construction of additional pipelines as affected by rule against perpetuities, Pipe § 32
- [illegible] damage, payment of specified damages

HIGHWAYS, STREETS, AND BRIDGES —Cont'd

Waters—Cont'd
- border or extension of highway on water, Waters § 434
- bridges, supra
- [illegible] (this index)

Weeds obstructing view, Highways [illegible], Mun Tort Liab § 641

Weighing scales as obstructions, Highways §§ 276, 289, 474

Weight limitations
- generally, Highways §§ 440, 605
- access rights of abutting owners affected by, Highways § 179
- **Automobiles and Highway Traffic** (this index)
- bridges, Highways §§ 551, 605

Welfare laws, eligibility of person injured in highway accident, Welf L § 57

Wells, Highways § 166

Wetness causing slippery conditions, Highways §§ 463, 465, 467

Wharves (this index)

[illegible] thrown from vehicles, injuries caused
- generally, Workm C § 127
- laying water or sewer lines, Workm C § 138

Writing, report of accident concerning failures in pipeline system by, Pipe § 18

→ **PIRACY**

Abandonment of crew on foreign shore, Piracy § 5

Acts constituting piracy, Piracy §§ 6-8

Aircraft, piracy of. **Aviation** (this index)

Arms and weapons
- statute designed to prevent hijacking of commercial airliner, Weap §§ 27, 28
- vessels, seizure of armed, Piracy § 11

Authority of federal officials, Piracy § 4

Autrefois acquit, plea of, Piracy § 1

Aviation (this index)

Belligerents, acts of, Piracy § 7

Breaking or entering vessel with intent to commit felony, Piracy § 5

Capital punishment, Piracy § 9

Captures animo furandi, Piracy §§ 1, 2

Captures jure belli, Piracy § 2

Cargo, confiscation of, Piracy § 11

Carriers, loss due to acts of pirates, Carriers § 523

HIGHWAYS, STREETS, AND BRIDGES —Cont'd

Width
- generally, Highways §§ 51-53
- access of abutting owners, Highways § 178
- alleys, Highways § 5
- dedication, Highways §§ 51, 61
- [illegible] Highways § 156
- Workers [illegible]

Written notice of defects or dangers, Highways §§ 415, 588

Zoning and Planning (this index)

HIGH WINDS

Weather (this index)

HIJACKING

Piracy (this index)

HIKING

Premises liability, Prem Liab §§ 125, 127-130

HILLS

Mountains or Hills (this index)

HILLSIDE

Intoxicating liquor, hillside as public place within drunkenness statute, Intox L § 36

[illegible] CLAUSES

Liability [illegible]

Libel and slander, charge of piracy, Lib & Sl § 35

Lienholder, attempt to prejudice rights of, Piracy § 5

Life imprisonment, Piracy §§ 3, 9

Lights, Piracy § 5

Location of act, Piracy § 8

Loss of or injury to goods caused by pirates, Carriers § 523

Master, overthrow of, Piracy §§ 3, 6

Merchant vessels, Piracy §§ 6, 11

Mistake as defense, Piracy §§ 6, 11

Moorings, malicious destruction of, Piracy § 5

Murder, Piracy §§ 1, 4

Mutiny, inciting or participating in, Piracy §§ 5, 6

Nationality, Piracy §§ 4, 6

Outfitting and sailing of privateer as crime, Piracy § 5

Ownership and title, Piracy §§ 11, 12

Place of act, Piracy § 8

Plundering, Piracy §§ 5, 6

President's power to protect merchant vessels, Piracy § 11

Privateering, generally, Piracy § 2

AMERICAN JURISPRUDENCE 2d

AVIATION—Cont'd

Federal Tort Claims Act—Cont'd
- military or other authorized personnel use, Avi §§ 92, 127; Fed Tort § 58
- National Guard member as employee of government, Fed Tort § 58
- property of servicemen, injury to, Fed Tort § 78
- questions of law and fact, Fed Tort § 139
- res ipsa loquitur, Fed Tort § 90
- respondeat superior doctrine, Fed Tort §§ 63, 65, 66
- scope of office or employment, employee

AVIATION—Cont'd

Foreign citizen or country—Cont'd
- offenses and penalties—Cont'd
- – remission or mitigation of fines and assessments, Aliens §§ 1796-1798
- – unlawfully bringing in aliens, Aliens §§ 1770, 1775-1777, 1780, 1783
- pilots, Aliens §§ 15, 2094
- ports of entry, regulation of civil aircraft in, Avi § 10
- registration of aircraft, Aliens § 2099; Avi § 22
- searches and seizures, Aliens §§ 20, 37, 741, 1935-1958

AVIATION—Cont'd

Highway, movement of aircraft upon, Avi § 28

Hijacking
- generally, Avi § 162
- accidents and injuries related to, Avi § 132
- false imprisonment, False Imp § 9
- mental injury as covered by Warsaw Convention, Avi § 118
- prevention, Avi § 51; Weap §§ 27, 28
- **Searches and Seizures** (this index)
- venue of action, Avi § 167
- Warsaw Convention, Avi §§ 116, 118

Hire
- bailment, supra

Reprinted by permission of Lawyers Cooperative Publishing, a division of Thomson Legal Publishing, Inc.

Figure 5-26:
American Jurisprudence 2d, Volume 8, 1980

Reprinted by permission of Lawyers Cooperative Publishing, a division of Thomson Legal Publishing, Inc.

While the practice of "overbooking" does not per se give rise to an actionable violation of the prohibition against preferences or discrimination, violation by the carrier of its own boarding priority rules does give rise to such a cause of action.[48] Also, it has been held that a common-law tort action for fraudulent misrepresentation arising from an air carrier's alleged failure to inform prospective passengers in advance of its deliberate overbooking practices could be maintained consistent with the Federal Aviation Act, and the plaintiff's misrepresentation action did not have to be stayed pending reference to the Civil Aeronautics Board.[49]

§ 51. Security measures; screening of passengers.

The Federal Aviation Act provides that the Federal Aviation Administrator shall prescribe or continue in effect reasonable regulations requiring that all passengers and all property intended to be carried in the aircraft cabin in air transportation or intrastate air transportation be screened by weapon-detecting procedures or facilities employed or operated by employees or agents of the

uled flight as a result of the unjustified refusal of the airline to allow him to use his ticket, since she was not personally denied access to airline services and facilities, and derivative claims are not actionable under the antidiscrimination clause of 49 USCS § 1374; additionally no private damage remedy could be implied under § 1374 for the airline's failure to ... for absence of

modations provided to other members of the tour at lesser cost. Polansky v Trans World Airlines, Inc. (CA3 NJ) 523 F2d 332.

No claim existed under 49 USCS § 1374(b) for unjust discrimination in a suit against an airlines by a passenger who was requested to disembark at an intermediate stop on his flight, treated as a stand-by passenger, and rerouted ... his destination approximately 2

certain instances, to withhold, revoke, or ... authority of airlines of a nation which fails to meet agreed security standards relating to transportation of persons or property or mail in foreign air transportation.[60]

An antihijacking system which includes such preflight procedures as "profile" selection, magnetometer detection, and frisking, has been held to be constitutional.[61] It is provided that the Federal Aviation Administrator shall, by

50. 49 USCS § 1356(a), which also empowers the Administrator to alter or amend such regulations, requiring a continuation of such screening only to the extent deemed necessary to assure security against acts of criminal violence and aircraft piracy in air transportation and intrastate air transportation.

For FAA regulations dealing with aircraft security, see 14 CFR §§ 121.538, 121.538a. McGinley & Downs, Airport Searches and Seizures—A Reasonable Approach. 41 Fordham L Rev 293, Dec. 1972

As to constitutional validity of preflight procedures to prevent hijacking of aircraft, see 68 Am Jur 2d, SEARCHES AND SEIZURES § 59.

51. 49 USCS § 1356(b).

52. 49 USCS § 1356a.

53. 49 USCS § 1357(a)(1).

54. 49 USCS § 1357(b).

55. 49 USCS § 1357(c).

56. 49 USCS § 1357(d)(1).

57. 49 USCS § 1357(e).

58. 49 USCS § 1358.

59. 49 USCS § 1514.

60. 49 USCS § 1515.

61. See 68 Am Jur 2d, SEARCHES AND SEIZURES § 59.

407

Other forms of international agreement include less formal documents—such as the *aide memoire, entente, modus vivendi,* and protocol—which are types of diplomatic correspondence that clarify the terms and objectives of negotiations in progress. However, for the United States, there is one other type of international agreement that has great and increasing significance—the *executive agreement*. This is a negotiated formal agreement between the U.S. and one or more nation-states that does not require Senate consent.

Although the Constitution does not mention executive agreements, Congress has delegated authority to Presidents to use them (primarily in the area of international trade). In addition, Presidents have expanded the use of executive agreements on the basis of claims to inherent powers related to their roles in foreign relations and as commander in chief. Although the large majority of executive agreements are negotiated under authority specifically delegated by Congress, the remaining class of executive agreements—made on the basis of the constitutional authority of the president—are sometimes the source of controversy. Examples of the latter include the lend-lease agreement negotiated between President F.D. Roosevelt and Prime Minister Winston Churchill in 1940 and more recent arms sales to Middle Eastern countries by Presidents Ford, Carter, and Reagan.

In 1937 the Supreme Court ruled that executive agreements—like treaties—are the supreme law of the land (U.S. v. Belmont, 301 US 324). This Court ruling did not end the controversy over executive agreements. In the early 1950s, a proposed constitutional amendment (the Bricker Amendment) that would have sharply limited executive agreements came within one vote of passage in the Senate. In 1972 Congress reacted to the Nixon administration's use of secret executive agreements by passing the Case Act (PL 92-403, 86 STAT 619, 1 USC 112b) requiring the President to inform Congress within sixty days after such agreements are entered into force (agreements involving national security secrets go only to the foreign relations committee of each chamber). The Case Act does not require Congressional approval for executive agreements.

Topics of treaties and executive agreements include all aspects of international relations—including commerce, mutual defense alliances, peace, and territorial boundary definitions. A general rule proposed by Congress (that has important exceptions imposed by Presidents) is that treaties should be used for politically controversial topics while executive agreements are reserved for largely technical and non-controversial subjects. Treaties and executive agreements between two states are termed bilateral; those among more than two states are multilateral.

Chronological Sources for International Law:
Slip Treaties (TIAS) and *United States Treaties and Other International Agreements* (UST)

The publication sequence for treaties and international agreements includes four different types of publications. As we saw above, when treaties have been negotiated by the President and the Department of State, they are sent to the U.S. Senate for "advice and consent" prior to presidential ratification. At this stage, you can locate a pending treaty published as a Senate Executive Document by using the finding aids and search strategies discussed in Chapter 4, "Locating U.S. Government Documents". After ratification, the full text (or a summary of more lengthy treaties) is published in the *Department of State Bulletin* (1939-1989) or the *U.S. Department of State Dispatch* (1990-date).

The publications mentioned above provide unofficial but timely access to texts of treaties and other international agreements. After a considerable publication delay (currently about five years), the official text of U.S. treaties and other international agreements is made available first in slip treaties (entitled *Treaties and Other International Acts Series* (TIAS)). Then, approximately two years later, the full text is published in hardbound volumes entitled *United States Treaties and Other International Agreements* (UST). UST has been published since 1950. Prior U.S. treaties and other international agreements are published in *Treaties and Other International Agreements of the United States of America, 1776-1949*. This series is commonly cited by the compiler's last name (Charles I. Bevans). As with slip laws and slip opinions, slip treaties are issued without an index; however—like *U.S. Statutes at Large* and *U.S. Reports*—*U.S. Treaties and Other International Agreements* is published with an index in each volume.

One of the earliest multilateral treaties dealing with the prevention of aircraft hijacking was signed at Tokyo on 14 September 1963. Figure 5-27 shows portions of this treaty. Beneath the title is printed the treaty's equivalent of a statute's legislative history. In this case, although the treaty was signed in 1963, the U.S. Senate did not give its advice and consent to ratification until six years later. Hence, it was compiled with all other treaties and other international agreements finalized in 1969 and published in the 1969 volumes of *U.S. Treaties and Other International Agreements* (UST). Following the treaty's history is a presidential proclamation giving the full text of the treaty in English, French, and Spanish. Depending upon the signatories, the text of the treaty may appear in various languages besides English. Besides the UST citation at the top of the page, the *Treaties and Other International Acts Series* (TIAS) citation is also given at the bottom of the page. In this case, the Tokyo Convention was the six thousand, seven hundred, and sixty-eighth treaty or other international agreement entered into force by the United States.

Secondary Sources for International Law:
Treaties in Force, American Foreign Policy
Current Documents*, and *Digest of United States
Practice in International Law

As with statute, administrative, and case law, there are subject-arranged finding aids for locating treaties, other international agreements, and other foreign policy documents. However, as with case law, there is no official codification of U.S. treaties and other international agreements.

Treaties in Force serves as an index to U.S. treaties and other international agreements currently in force. This index has been published by the Department of State annually since 1958 and irregularly back to 1929. The Tokyo Convention that we discussed above was located by using *Treaties in Force*. Our initial search under "Hijacking" referred us to "Aviation" (see Figure 5-28). Scanning all the entries under "Aviation" we found several entries for relevant treaties, of which two are shown. The entry tells us the UST, TIAS, and UNTS (*United Nations Treaty Series*) citations. Each entry lists the states which are parties as well as notes indicating any special provisions or reservations respective to each. This search illustrates decision rule 3(f) in Table 5-3.

Up to this point, we have searched for the text to specific treaties and other international agreements. However, if your purpose is to view the broader context of American foreign policy, then there are two series of subject-arranged guides to foreign

Figure 5-27:
United States Treaties and Other International Agreements, Volume 20, Part 3, 1969

Washington, DC: Government Printing Office.

MULTILATERAL

Aviation: Offenses and Certain Other Acts Committed on Board Aircraft

Convention done at Tokyo September 14, 1963;
Ratification advised by the Senate of the United States of America May 13, 1969;
Ratified by the President of the United States of America June 30, 1969;
Ratification of the United States of America deposited with the International Civil Aviation Organization September 5, 1969;
Proclaimed by the President of the United States of America October 1, 1969;
Entered into force December 4, 1969.

By the President of the United States of America

A PROCLAMATION

WHEREAS the Convention on Offences and Certain Other Acts Committed on Board Aircraft was signed at Tokyo on September 14, 1963;

WHEREAS the text of the Convention, in the English, French and Spanish languages as certified by the Legal Bureau of the Inter- .... word for word as follows:

CONVENTION ON OFFENCES AND CERTAIN OTHER ACTS COMMITTED ON BOARD AIRCRAFT	CONVENTION RELATIVE AUX INFRACTIONS ET A CERTAINS AUTRES ACTES SURVENANT A BORD DES AERONEFS	CONVENIO SOBRE LAS INFRACCIONES Y CIERTOS OTROS ACTOS COMETIDOS A BORDO DE LAS AERONAVES
THE STATES Parties to this Convention HAVE AGREED as follows:	LES ETATS Parties à la présente Convention SONT CONVENUS des dispositions suivantes:	LOS ESTADOS Partes en el presente Convenio HAN ACORDADO lo siguiente:
Chapter I—Scope of the Convention	**Titre 1er—Champ d'application de la Convention**	**Capítulo I—Campo de aplicación del Convenio**
Article 1	*Article 1er*	*Artículo 1*
1. This Convention shall apply in respect of:	1. La présente Convention s'applique:	1. El presente Convenio se aplicará a:
a) offences against penal law;	a) aux infractions aux lois pénales;	a) las infracciones a las leyes penales;
b) acts which, whether or not they are offences, may or do jeopardize the safety of the aircraft or of persons or property therein or which jeopardize good order and discipline on board.	b) aux actes qui, constituant ou non des infractions, peuvent compromettre ou compromettent la sécurité de l'aéronef ou de personnes ou de biens à bord, ou compromettent le bon ordre et la discipline à bord.	b) los actos que, sean o no infracciones, puedan poner o pongan en peligro la seguridad de la aeronave o de las personas o bienes en la misma, o que pongan en peligro el buen orden y la disciplina a bordo.
2. Except as provided in Chapter III, this Convention shall apply in respect of offences committed or acts done by a person on board any aircraft registered in a Contracting State, while that aircraft is in flight or on the surface of the high seas or of any ...	2. Sous réserve des dispositions du Titre III, la présente Convention s'applique aux infractions commises ou actes accomplis par une personne à bord d'un aéronef immatriculé dans un Etat contractant pendant que cet aéronef se trouve, soit en vol, soit à la surface de la haute mer ou d'une région ne faisant	2. A reserva de lo dispuesto en el Capítulo III, este Convenio se aplicará a las infracciones cometidas y a los actos ejecutados por una persona a bordo de cualquier aeronave matriculada en un Estado Contratante mientras se halle en vuelo, en la superficie de alta mar o en la de cualquier otra zona situada ... del territorio de un Estado.

TIAS 6768

Figure 5-28: *Treaties in Force*, 1990

---

288   TREATIES IN FORCE

AUTOMOTIVE TRAFFIC (Cont'd)

Amendment:
June 6, 1967 (19 UST 4684; TIAS 6461; 596 UNTS 542).

NOTES:
 [1] With reservation.
 [2] See under country heading in the bilat-

Iraq
Italy
Kuwait
Laos
Lebanon
Libya
Luxembourg
Madagascar
Mali
Mauritania
Mexico[2]
Netherlands[2][3]
Niger
Norway
Pakistan
Paraguay
Philippines
Portugal
Rwanda
Seychelles
Sweden
Switzerland
Thailand

Bahamas, The
Bahrain[2]
Bangladesh
Barbados
Belgium
Benin
Bhutan
Bolivia
Botswana
Brazil[2]
Brunei
Bulgaria[2]
Burkina Faso
Byelorussian Soviet Socialist Rep.[2]
Cameroon
Canada
Cape Verde
Chad
Chile
China[1][2][3]

Jordan
Luxembourg
Malaysia
Mali
Malta
Mauritius
Mexico[1]
Morocco
Nepal
Netherlands[4]
New Zealand[*]
Nigeria

NOTES:
 [*] Applied provisionally from January 1, 1983, except for article 9.
 [1] Subject to the availability of funds.

→ Convention on offenses and certain other acts committed on board aircraft. Done at Tokyo September 14, 1963; entered into force December 4, 1969.
20 UST 2941; TIAS 6768; 704 UNTS 219.
States which are parties:
Afghanistan
Antigua & Barbuda
Argentina
Australia
Austria
Bahamas, The
Bahrain[1]
Bangladesh
Barbados
Belgium

Mauritius
Mexico
Monaco
Mongolia[2]
Morocco[2]
Nauru
Nepal
Netherlands[7]
New Zealand
Nicaragua
Niger
Nigeria
Norway
Oman
Pakistan
Panama
Papua New Guinea[2]
Paraguay
Peru[2]
Philippines

→ AVIATION

(See also INTERNATIONAL CIVIL AVIATION ORGANIZATION)

Convention for the unification of certain rules relating to international transportation by air, with additional protocol. Concluded at Warsaw October 12, 1929; entered into

Kuwait
Laos
Lebanon
Lesotho
Libya
Luxembourg
Madagascar
Malawi
Malaysia
Maldives
Mali
Marshall Is.
Mauritania
Mauritius
Mexico
Monaco
Morocco[2]
Nauru
Nepal
Netherlands[4]
New Zealand
Nicaragua

 [*] Extended to all territories under the territorial sovereignty of the United Kingdom.

→ Convention for the suppression of unlawful acts against the safety of civil aviation. (Sabotage) Done at Montreal September 23, 1971; entered into force January 26, 1973.
24 UST 564; TIAS 7570.
States which are parties:
Afghanistan[1]
Antigua & Barbuda
Argentina
Australia
Austria
Bahamas, The
Bahrain[1]
Bangladesh
Barbados
Belgium

Washington, DC: Government Printing Office.

policy documents. *American Foreign Policy Current Documents* and *Digest of United States Practice in International Law* are published by the U.S. Department of State. Under various titles, *Current Documents* provides excerpts of principal public foreign

CHAPTER 5: LEGAL RESEARCH   121

policy messages, addresses, statements, interviews, press briefings, and congressional testimony dating (at time of writing) from 1941 to 1987. The *Digest* contains essays written by State Department and other U.S. government officials discussing various aspects of international law affecting U.S. interests. The *Digest* is published in annual volumes that (at time of writing) cover issues dating from 1973 to 1980. While different in content—the first series focusing on source documents and the second series on interpretive analysis—both series are useful in gaining a broader perspective to place into context your narrow research topic.

SUMMARY

1. Because of the constitutional division of power across levels of American government, you may need to research laws at the local, state, or federal level. In this chapter, we limit our focus to legal research at the federal level, including treaties and other international agreements. However, the search skills and strategies appropriate to legal research at the federal level apply equally well to researching state and local laws.

2. As with other forms of library research, legal research requires locating and using both primary and secondary sources.

   a) Primary legal sources are those publications that present the law itself—the actual text of constitutions, statutes, regulations, executive orders and proclamations, court decisions, or treaties and other international agreements.

   b) Secondary sources are those publications that provide finding aids to or analysis and interpretation of the laws. Secondary sources help you locate and place into perspective the information gained from primary sources.

3. Primary legal sources fall into two basic types of publications.

   a) Chronological series compile the full text of the law in the order in which it was adopted. There are separate, official chronological series for statutes, regulations, presidential orders, administrative regulations, court cases, and treaties and other international agreements.

   b) Codes collect or arrange the law according to topics or subjects. There are separate, official codes for federal statute and regulatory laws but not for federal case law or treaties and other international agreements.

4. Citations to all primary legal sources (chronological series or code) follow a common pattern within each type.

    a) At a minimum, a citation to an entry in a legal chronological series should contain three elements:

        1) the short title or popular name of the statute, regulation, case, or treaty or other international agreement;

        2) the facts of publication (volume number, followed by an abbreviation of the main title of the chronological series, followed by the starting page number); and

        3) the year in which the statute, regulation, case, or treaty or other international agreement was put in force.

    b) At a minimum, citations to entries in legal codes contain just two elements:

        1) the facts of publication (the title number, followed by an abbreviation of the code's title, followed by the section number); and

        2) the year of the code's edition or supplement that is cited.

5. While there are more than two dozen primary and secondary sources discussed in this chapter, Table 5-3 summarizes a set of decision rules to help you decide where to start. That, in turn, depends upon the breadth and depth of the information you wish to locate and the nature of the information you already know.

CHAPTER 6

LOCATING GENERAL INFORMATION: BIOGRAPHIES, STATISTICS, AND FACTS

This chapter is organized into three parts, which address, in turn, the special information sources relevant to finding biographical, statistical, and factual information. When looking for these three special types of information you can apply the searching and evaluating skills we have discussed in other contexts. There are, however, several additional sources as well as new ways of thinking about your topic that you need to be aware of as you search for biographical, statistical, and factual information.

First, you may find it necessary to get background information about persons involved with your topic. These people may be thinkers or doers or both. In our research about terrorism, one cannot go far before encountering the name of Muammar al-Qaddafi, head of state of Libya. Qaddafi has admitted that his country is a haven and even provides training for Palestinian terrorists, but he does not accept responsibility for loss of life caused by terrorist acts. Another name we have seen several times in previous chapters of this guide is Richard Clutterbuck, who we have learned is an expert on counter-terrorism. These men represent different viewpoints of the terrorism issue. By examining their backgrounds and beliefs, we may better understand the larger issue.

A second, special type of information you may need is statistics. Statistics are commonly used to quantify phenomena. Measuring the extent of a characteristic, opinion, or occurrence of an event and comparing it with similar measurements over time, place, or season makes it easier for legislators and other policy makers to monitor trends, take intelligent action, and allocate limited resources. Anyone who wishes to inform or persuade will find that using statistics is a convincing way to prove a point. For our research about prevention of aircraft hijacking, we can compare the number of hijacking incidents before and after programs of increased airport security have been instituted to determine if these additional precautions have been beneficial.

The final category of information needs addressed in this chapter is that of finding general factual information such as current events summaries and background information about political entities (e.g., cities, states, regions, countries, international organizations). With so much information available about aircraft hijacking, finding summaries of specific incidents and how they were handled may be helpful. And, learning more about the physical setting, history, and political situation in countries which have been accused of sponsoring terrorist acts or harboring terrorists will be important in determining what laws and policies can be enacted to prevent future hijacking incidents.

FINDING BIOGRAPHICAL INFORMATION

There are hundreds of specialized biographical encyclopedias, each with its own scope or inclusion criteria, and of course there are tens of thousands of magazine, newspaper, and journal articles about people. When searching for biographical information, as with practically any type of research, the materials you need to examine can be sorted into two types: finding aids and actual sources.

Three Biographical Finding Aids:
Biography Index, Biography and Genealogy Master Index (or *Biobase*),
and *Biography Almanac*

The finding aids, or indexes, are time-saving devices to tell you exactly where to look for a specific person's biography. While no index is ever complete, they do take a lot of guess-work out of the search process. There are three finding aids to biographical material commonly found in college and university libraries (and many public libraries).

Biography Index is an index to books and articles in periodicals and *The New York Times*. While most of the entries are for periodical articles, the book entries are especially helpful because *Biography Index* gives citations to sections of books as well as references to entire books about a person. This is a great service because, as we discussed in Chapter 2, a library's catalog only describes the general subject of the entire book and does not provide detailed contents indexing. The list under Qaddafi's name in Volume 15 of *Biography Index* includes references to twenty sources, one of which is a book (see Figure 6-1). Notice that on this page, Qaddafi's name is spelled nine different ways! This is an extreme case of a not unusual occurrence when words are transliterated from one alphabet to another.

The first entry in Figure 6-1 is an article in *Middle East Journal*, followed by two articles from *Macleans*. Now look at the fourth entry. It does not have the "volume number: page number, issue date" configuration we have become accustomed to seeing in periodical indexes. This entry is for a 230-page book by David Blundy and Andrew Lycett, entitled *Qaddafi and the Libyan Revolution*, published by Little, Brown in 1987. The list of citations in Figure 6-1, covering September 1986 to August 1988, does not include any citations to portions of books.

The second finding aid you should be aware of is *Biography and Genealogy Master Index*, or its microfiche version *Biobase*, or its online version *Biography Master Index*. It serves as a cumulated index to about 500 biographical dictionaries, encyclopedias, and indexes. (For this discussion, the 1990 Master Cumulation of *Biobase* was used.) Figure 6-2 shows entries for Qaddafi. Here, again, Qaddafi's name is spelled in more than a half-dozen different ways! Unlike *Biography Index, Biobase* makes no effort to standardize forms of personal names; the name is simply printed as it appears in the original source, including cross-reference names. For example, Qaddafi's name is also listed in *Biobase* under "Gaddafi".

Figure 6-1: *Biography Index*, **page 615, 1986-1988, Volume 15**

Pushkin, Aleksandr Sergeevich, 1799-1837, Russian poet
The Penguin encyclopedia of horror and the supernatural; edited by Jack Sullivan; with an introduction by Jacques Barzun. Viking 1986 p340 bibl il pors facsims

Putnam, Brenda, 1890-1975, sculptor
Nickerson, R. A vanguard of American women sculptors. il por *Sculpt Rev* 35:16-24+ Wint '86-'87

Putnam, Donald H., 1925-1987, electronics executive
Obituary
   N Y Times pD-18 My 26 '87
   N Y Times Biogr Serv 18:515 My '87

Putnam, Herbert, 1861-1955, librarian
ALA world encyclopedia of library and information services. 2nd ed American Lib. Assn. 1986 p687-8 bibl il pors

Putnam, Pat, sportswriter
Barr, D. J. Letter from the publisher. il por *Sports Illus* 64:4 Ap 28 '86

Puttnam, David, 1941-, English motion picture producer
Dougherty, M. He rode into Hollywood on a Chariot of fire, but David Puttnam's job at Columbia went up in smoke. il pors *People Wkly* 28:125-6+ N 16 '87

Egan, J. Felled in Hollywood's 'killing fields'. por *U S News World Rep* 103:82 S 28 '87

MacCabe, C. Puttnam's new mission [interview] *Am Film* 12:39-41+ O '86

Reese, M. and Foote, J. A Hollywood outsider's exit. il por *Newsweek* 110:65 S 28 '87

Rudolph, B. Mr. Puttnam goes to Hollywood. por *Time* 128:52 S 8 '86

Skrzycki, C. 5 power players worth watching. il por *U S News World Rep* 101:69-71 D 29 '86/Ja 5 '87

Putzer, Murray, d. 1987, optical engineer
Obituary
   N Y Times por pD-12 Jl 20 '87
   N Y Times Biogr Serv por 18:707-8 Jl '87

Puzo, Mario, 1920-, author
Giordano, Joseph. The Italian-American catalog. Doubleday 1986 p134-5 bibl il pors map facsims

Pyburn, Wes, automobile racer
Getting the jump on adults at 13, Wes Pyburn guns for racing's top. il por *People Wkly* 26:119 N 24 '86

Pye, A. Kenneth, university president
Lederman, D. Southern Methodist U.'s new president: near-perfect fit, but no 'S' on his chest. por *Chron Higher Educ* 33:35-6 Je 10 '87

Pyfer, Jean, physical educator
Young, D. Making a difference. il pors *South Living* 22:98+ Je '87

Pyle, Ernie, 1900-1945, journalist
Pyle, Ernie. Ernie's war; the best of Ernie Pyle's World War II dispatches. Random House 1986 432p bibl il

Skow, J. Worm's eye. por *Time* 128:96 S 15 '86

Pyle, Howard, 1853-1911, author and illustrator
Contemporary graphic artists, v2; a biographical, bibliographical, and critical guide to current illustrators, animators, cartoonists, designers, and other graphic artists; Maurice Horn, editor. Gale Res. 1987 p204-8 bibl il pors

May, Jill P. Howard Pyle. (In Dictionary of literary biography, v42. Gale Res. 1985 p295-308) bibl il pors autog

Pyne, Schuyler Neilson, d. 1987, admiral
Obituary
   N Y Times pB-13 Je 18 '87
   N Y Times Biogr Serv 18:589 Je '87

Pyrnelle, Louise-Clarke, 1850-1907, author
Miller, Susan E. Louise-Clarke Pyrnelle. (In Dictionary of literary biography, v42. Gale Res. 1985 p308-11) bibl il

Pytka, Joe, television advertising executive
Miller, A. It's positively Pytka. por *Newsweek* 110:59 S 14 '87

Q

Q, Stacey, singer
Rock wrap up. il por *Teen* 31:58 Mr '87

Qaddafi, Muammar al-, 1942-, Libyan head of state
Anderson, L. Qadhdhafi and his opposition. *Middle East J* 40:225-37 Spr '86

Barber, J. A master manipulator. il por *Macleans* 99:16 Ap 7 '86

Bilski, A. Khadafy's visions. il por *Macleans* 99:15 Ja 13 '86

Blundy, David, and Lycett, Andrew. Qaddafi and the Libyan revolution. Little, Brown 1987 230p

Breslau, A. Demonizing Qaddafy. *Afr Rep* 32:46-7 Mr/Ap '87

Chesnoff, R. Z. Qadhafi magic: turning defeat to verbal victory. il por *U S News World Rep* 102:31 Ap 13 '87

Chesnoff, R. Z. and Victor, B. 'I am a mixture of Washington and Lincoln' [interview] il por *U S News World Rep* 101:31-2 N 10 '86

Cockburn, A. Superfiend. *Nation* 242:576-7 Ap 26 '86

Crozier, B. Moscow's Libyan tool. *Natl Rev* 38:26 Je 6 '86

Davis, J. Hydrocarbon prince. por *New Statesman* 113:14-15 Ja 2 '87

Dickey, C. A Kaddafi comeback? il por *Newsweek* 111:30+ F 22 '88

Gaddafi's world. il por *World Press Rev* 33:25-7 Mr '86

Grogan, D. A jackal at bay. il pors *People Wkly* 25:42-5 My 5 '86

Henderson, G. Gadafy's very own revolution. por *New Statesman* 111:17-18 My 2 '86

Hersh, S. M. Target Qaddafi. il *N Y Times Mag* p16-22+ F 22 '87

Marshall, R. Waiting for Muammar. por *Newsweek* 108:42 N 10 '86

Miller, J. and Colvin, M. Qaddafi on the edge. il pors *Roll Stone* p38-40+ Ag 14 '86

Shell-shocked. por *Time* 127:54 Je 23 '86

St John, R. B. The ideology of Muammar al-Qadhdhafi: theory and practice. *Int J Middle East Stud* 15:471-90 N '83

St John, R. B. Whatever's happened to Qaddafi? *World Today* 43 :58-9 Ap '87

Qianlong *See* Ch'ien-lung, Emperor of China, 1711-1799

Qiao Shi, Chinese communist leader
The four rising stars in China's inner circle. *N Y Times Biogr Serv* 18:1143 N '87
           Beijing Rev 30:22-3 N

Figure 6-2: *Biobase Master Cumulation*, 1990

LAST NAME, FIRST NAME, MIDDLE	BIRTH DATE*	DEATH DATE*	SOURCE BOOK	LAST NAME, FIRST NAME, MIDDLE	BIRTH DATE*	DEATH DATE*	SOURCE BOOK
Caboos Bin Said	1940		IntWW 81	Qader, Yahia Hasan Abd Al-			IntWW 77
Caboos Bin Said	1940		IntWW 82	Qader, Yahia Hasan Abd Al-			IntWW 78
Caboos Bin Said	1940		IntWW 83	Qader, Yahia Hasan Abd Al-			IntWW 79
Caboos Bin Said	1940		MidE 78	Qader, Yahia Hasan Abd Al-			IntWW 80
Caboos Bin Said	1940		MidE 79	Qader, Yahia Hasan Abd Al-			IntWW 81
Caboos Bin Said	1940		MidE 80	Qadhafi, Mo'ammar Mohammed El-			BioIn 9
Caboos Bin Said	1940		MidE 81	Qadhafi, Mo'ammar Mohammed El-			BioIn 10
Caboos Bin Said	1940		MidE 82	Qadhafi, Mo'ammar Mohammed El-			BioIn 11
Caboos Bin Said	1940		WhoWor 80	Qadhafi, Mo'ammar Mohammed El-			BioIn 12
Caboos Bin Said	1940		WhoWor 82	Qadhafi, Mo'ammar Mohammed El-			BioIn 13
Caboos Bin Said	1940		WhoWor 84	Qadhafi, Mu'ammar, Al-			BioIn 10
Caboos Bin Said	1940		WhoWor 87	Qadhafi, Mu'ammar, Al-			BioIn 11
Caboos Bin Said	1940		WhoWor 89	Qadhafi, Mu'ammar Al-			IntWW 81
Caboos Bin Said, Sultan Of Muscat & Oman	1940		BioIn 10	Qadhafi, Mu'ammar Al-			IntWW 82
Caboos Bin Said, Sultan Of Muscat & Oman	1940		BioIn 11	Qadhafi, Mu'ammar Al-			IntWW 83
Caboos Bin Said, Sultan Of Muscat & Oman	1940		BioIn 13	Qadi Qadan Of Sehwan		D1551	DcOrL 2
Caboos Bin Said Al Bu Said			BusPN	Qadi, Abdul Rahman Ibrahim, Al-	1931		WhoArab 76
Caboos ibn Sa'id	1940		EncWB	Qadi, Abdul Rahman Ibrahim Al-	1931		WhoArab 81
Cabus Bin Said	1940		CurBio 78	Qadi, Abdullah Fadlallah	1939		WhoArab 81
Qadar, Basheer			ComAu X	Qadi, Abdullah Fadlallah	1939		WhoSauA 76
Qaddafi, El-	1942		WorAl	Qadi, Mounir Al-			WhoArab 81
Qaddafi, Hana al-	1985	1986	BioIn 14	Qadi Zada Al-Rumi	1364?1436?		DcScB
Qaddafi, Moamar Al-			IntWW 74	Qadir Yar			DcOrL 2
Qaddafi, Moamar Al-			IntWW 75	Qadir, Sir Abdul	1874		WhEEEA
Qaddafi, Muammar, Al-			BioIn 9	Qadir, Chaudry Abdul	1909		WhoWor 89
Qaddafi, Muammar, Al-			BioIn 11	Qadir, Ghulam	1947		WhoEmL 87
Qaddafi, Muammar Al-			BioIn 12	Qadir, Ghulam	1947		WhoMW 86
Qaddafi, Muammar Al-			BioIn 13	Qadir, Ghulam	1947		WhoMW 88
Qaddafi, Mu'ammar Al-			IntWW 76	Qadir, Isma'il Bin Abd Al-			BioIn 11
Qaddafi, Mu'ammar Al-			IntWW 77	Qadir, Syed Muhammad Abdul	1943		WhoSSW 78
Qaddafi, Mu'ammar Al-			IntWW 78	Qadir, Syed Muhammad Abdul	1943		WhoSSW 80
Qaddafi, Mu'ammar Al-			IntWW 79	Qadir, Syed Muhammad Abdul	1943		WhoSSW 82
Qaddafi, Mu'ammar Al-			IntWW 80	Qadir, Syed Muhammad Abdul	1943		WhoSSW 84
Qaddafi, Mu'ammar Al-			IntWW 81	Qadir, Zain Al-Abdin Mohammed Ahmed A	1940		WhoWor 74
Qaddafi, Mu'ammar Al-			IntWW 82	Qadir, Zain Al-Abdin Mohammed Ahmed A	1940		IntWW 74
Qaddafi, Mu'ammar Al-			IntWW 83	Qadir, Zayn Al-Abidin Mohamed Ahmed A	1940		WhoArab 81
Qaddafi, Muammar Al-			MidE 79	Qadiri, Abdullo			DcOrL 3
Qaddafi, Muammar Al-			MidE 80	Qadiriy, Abdullah	1894	1940	EncWL 2
Qaddafi, Muammar Al-			MidE 81	Qadmani, Bashir Sobhi Al-	1914		WhoArab 81
Qaddafi, Muammar al-			MidE 82	Qadri, Munammad Said			WhoArab 81
Qaddafi, Muammar al-	1942		BioIn 14	Qadri, Shane Haider	1948		WhoMW 78
Qaddafi, Muammar al-	1942		BioIn 15	Qadri, Shane Haider	1948		WhoMW 80
Qaddafi, Muammar El-	1938		WorDW	Qadri, Sohan	1936		DcCIWLA
Qaddafi, Muammar El-	1942		CurBio 73	Qadri, Syed M Hussain	1942		AmMWSc 73P
Qaddafi, Muammar Muhammed			WhoWor 87	Qadri, Syed M Hussain	1942		AmMWSc 76P
Qaddafi, Muammar Muhammed			WhoWor 89	Qadri, Syed M Hussain	1942		AmMWSc 79P
Qaddafi, Muammar Muhammed Al-	1942		WhoWor 82	Qadri, Syed M Hussain	1942		AmMWSc 82P
Qaddafi, Muammar Muhammed Al-	1942		WhoWor 84	Qadri, Syed M Hussain	1942		AmMWSc 86P
Qaddama, Ahmad Muhammad Sadeqi	1918		WhoArab 81	Qadri, Syed M Hussain	1942		AmMWSc 89P
Qaddifi, Muammar Al-			MidE 78	Qadus, Mohamad Ahmad Abdel Hamid	1930		WhoArab 81
Qaddoura, Abdurrazzaq			WhoArab 81	Qady, Abdul Rahman Ibrahim, Al-	1931		WhoSauA 78
Qaddouri, Fakhri Yasin	1932		WhoArab 81	Qady, Abdullah Fadlallah			WhoSauA 75
Qaddurah, Ahmad Sadaqah	1938		WhoSauA 76	Qady, Hamad Abdullah, Al-	1950		WhoSauA 78
Qadurah, Mohamad Ibrahim	1930		WhoArab 81	Qady, Sobhi Abdul Hafiz	1944		WhoSauA 78
Qadurah, Mohamad Ibrahim	1930		WhoSauA 76	Qafisheh, Hamdi Ahmad	1935		DrAS 78F
Qadurah, Mohamad Ibrahim	1930		WhoSauA 78	Qafisheh, Hamdi Ahmad	1935		DrAS 78F
Qader, Sheikh Abdul	1940		BiDrAPA 77	Qafisheh, Hamdi Ahmad	1935		DrAS 82F
Qader, Shaik Abdul	1932		AmMWSc 73P	Qannor, Abdullo	1907		DcOrL 3
Qader, Yahia Hasan Abd Al-			IntWW 74	Qahimi, Abdulaziz Ali Al-	1918		WhoArab 81
Qader, Yahia Hasan Abd Al-			IntWW 75	Qanimi, Ahmad			WhoArab 81
Qader, Yahia Hasan Abd Al-			IntWW 76	Qantani, Mohamad Said Abdul Rahman, Al-	1940		WhoSauA 76

* NOTE: BIRTH/DEATH CODES ARE AS FOLLOWS: A = AD; B = BC; D = DEATH DATE; U = ?BC; X = ?AD

To find out what the source abbreviations used in *Biobase* stand for, look in the "Bibliographic Key" (a separate booklet accompanying *Biobase*). There are several entries under Qaddafi for "BioIn", which the key tells us is *Biography Index* (see Figure 6-3). Qaddafi (and Qadhafi) is included in Volumes 9 through 15. Knowing this before using *Biography Index* saves you the time it would take to search Volumes 1 through 8. However, since this part of *Biobase*, the 1990 Master Cumulation, only includes indexing for Volumes 1 through 15 of *Biography Index*, this does **not** tell you if Qaddafi is included in any subsequent volumes. Supplements to *Biobase* are issued on an irregular basis, but there will always be a time lag between the publication of source material and the index to that material.

If your library does not own *Biobase* or *Biography and Genealogy Master Index*, another similar, but more selective source may be available to you—*Biography Almanac*. This index includes references to "24,000 famous and infamous newsmakers from Biblical times to the present" (title page). Although it uses the same sources as *Biobase*, it does not index every name in each source, but, rather, only those considered

Figure 6-3:
*Biobase Master Cumulation
Bibliographic Key*, **1990**

BioIn
Biography Index. A cumulative index to biographical material in books and magazines. New York: H.W. Wilson Co., 1949-1988.

BioIn 1	Volume 1: January, 1946-July, 1949; 1949
BioIn 2	Volume 2: August, 1949-August, 1952; 1953
BioIn 3	Volume 3: September, 1952-August, 1955; 1956
BioIn 4	Volume 4: September, 1955-August, 1958; 1960
BioIn 5	Volume 5: September, 1958-August, 1961; 1962
BioIn 6	Volume 6: September, 1961-August, 1964; 1965
BioIn 7	Volume 7: September, 1964-August, 1967; 1968
BioIn 8	Volume 8: September, 1967-August, 1970; 1971
BioIn 9	Volume 9: September, 1970-August, 1973; 1974
BioIn 10	Volume 10: September, 1973-August, 1976; 1977
BioIn 11	Volume 11: September, 1976-August, 1979; 1980
BioIn 12	Volume 12: September, 1979-August, 1982; 1983
BioIn 13	Volume 13: September, 1982-August, 1984; 1984
BioIn 14	Volume 14: September, 1984-August, 1986; 1986
BioIn 15	Volume 15: September, 1986-August, 1988; 1988

newsworthy. This time Qaddafi's name is spelled "Khadafy". In Figure 6-4 *Biography Almanac* lists abbreviations that identify five different sources of biographical information about Qaddafi. We will return to two of these sources when we distinguish between encyclopedic narrative and abbreviated abstract biographical reference sources.

Biographical Sources

Just as we have found with other information searches throughout this guide, biographical information will be found in books, reference sources, periodicals, newspapers, and in some cases even government documents. Entire books may be available about the person for whom you are seeking information, and he or she may also be included in a chapter or essay in a book. There may be an article in a general or specialized encyclopedia, periodical, or newspaper about the person. Since you may not have time to read an entire book, and since a periodical article is likely to cover just the current phase of a person's activities, it is usually a good idea to start with a biographical encyclopedia or directory to get a brief but long-term overview of the person's life.

Figure 6-4:
Biography Almanac, Volume 1, 3d edition, edited by Susan L. Stetler

---

Biography Almanac • 3rd Edition   **KHAIKIN**

Key, Valdimer Orlando, Jr.
American. Political Scientist, Author
Wrote *Public Opinion and American Democracy,* 1961.
b. Mar 13, 1908 in Austin, Texas
d. Oct 4, 1963

Source: *BioIn 10*

Keylor, Arthur W
American. Publisher
Publishes *Life, Fortune;* helped launch *People,* 1974; *Discovery,* 1980.
b. 1920
d. Aug 17, 1981 in Manchester, Vermont
Source: *ConAu 104; Dun&B 79; WhoF&I 74*

Keynes, John Maynard, Baron
English. Economist, Journalist
Best known for *The General Theory of Employment, Interest, and Money,* 1936; theories of unbalanced budgets.
b. Jun 5, 1883 in Cambridge, England
d. Apr 21, 1946 in London, England
Source: *DcLEL; EvLB; LongCTC; NewC; ObitOF 79; OxEng; PseudN 82; REn; TwCA, SUP; WebE&AL; WhDW; WhAm 2; WorAl*

Keys, Ancel Benjamin
American. Physiologist, Author
Nutrition expert; developed WW II K-rations; researched diet, heart disease.
b. Jan 26, 1904 in Colorado Springs, Colorado
Source: *AmM&WS 76P, 79P; BioIn 5, 7;*

d. May 1, 1978 in Moscow, U.S.S.R.
Source: *CurBio 48; DcCM; DcFM; IntWW 74; WhoMus 72*

Khadafy, Moammar
[Moamar al-Gaddafi; Mu'ammar al-Qadhafi]
Liberian. Political Leader
Led military coup against monarchy, 1969; pres., Mar 1977--.
b. 1942 in Misurata, Libya
Source: *CurBio 73; IntWW 80, 81; IntYB 80, 81; MidE 80; WhoGov 72*

Khaikin, Boris
Russian. Conductor
b. 1905
d. May 11, 1978 in Moscow, U.S.S.R.
Source: *BioIn 11; WhoSocC 78*

927

Two Styles of Biographical Reference Sources

In this section we discuss examples of two of the most common styles of presenting biographical information in reference sources—the encyclopedic narrative style typified by *Current Biography* and the abbreviated abstract style like that used in various *Who's Who* publications.

Encyclopedic narrative. The first source cited in *Biography Almanac* (see Figure 6-4) under Khadafy is *Current Biography*, a monthly collection of biographical essays about persons in the news. The monthly issues are cumulated annually as *Current Biography Yearbook*. The essays are in alphabetical order by the subject's last name. A cumulative index covering 1940-85 is helpful in locating an individual's biographical essay since once included in a yearbook they are seldom updated in a later volume. Additionally, each yearbook contains an index covering the essays published in *Current Biography* during that decade. For example, the 1989 yearbook offers an index to 1981-89 essays.

The *Current Biography Yearbook 1973* contains a three-page essay about Qaddafi's background and activities (see Figure 6-5), beginning with birth date, position, and address. The article includes a photograph (not shown in Figure 6-5), and ends with references to additional sources of information. Think of *Current Biography* as a specialized encyclopedia in which all of the entries are for contemporary figures active from 1940 to the present.

Abbreviated abstract. The entry in *International Who's Who* (see Figure 6-6) is an abbreviated, highly structured biography, which is a characteristic of most "Who's Who"

Figure 6-5: *Current Biography Yearbook 1973*

he was born and raised a ▪▪▪▪▪▪ maintains no religious affiliation as an adult. Unmarried, he was selected in August 1972 as one of the "Ten Outstanding Single Men" by *Ebony* magazine.

References

Ebony 27:90+ Ag '72 por
Biographical Directory of Fellows and Members of the American Psychiatric Association, 1968
Metcalf, George R. Up from Within: Today's New Black Leaders (1971)
Who's Who in America, 1972-73
Who's Who in the East, 1972-73

→ QADDAFI, MUAMMAR EL-

1942- Chairman of the Revolutionary Command Council of the Libyan Arab Republic
Address: Revolutionary Command Council, Tripoli, Libyan Arab Republic

The chairman of the Revolutionary Command Council of the Libyan Arab Republic, Colonel Muammar el-Qaddafi, is widely regarded as heir to the mantle of late Egyptian President Gamal Abdel Nasser as leader of the Arab world. On September 1, 1969 Qaddafi, then a twenty-seven-year-old signal corps captain, led a military coup deposing the aged King Idris Senussi I, who had reigned over the former Italian colony of Libya ever since it obtained independence under United Nations auspices in December 1951. Through the vast wealth in oil revenues—about $2.4 billion in 1972—that he commands, and through the force of his own personality, Qaddafi has emerged as one of the world's leading power ▪▪▪▪▪ champion of Arab unity, and ▪▪▪▪▪▪▪▪▪

References

N Y Times p2 D 21 '70 por; p6 My 26 '73 por
N Y Times Mag p10+ F 6 '72 pors
Time 101:23+ Ap 2 '73 por
Haddad, George M. Revolutions and Military Rule in the Middle East vol 3 (1973)
International Who's Who, 1972-73
Who's Who in the Arab World, 1971-72

RABE, DAVID (rāb)

Mar. 10, 1940- Playwright
Address: b. c/o Theatre Department, Villanova University, Villanova, Pa. 19085

Hailed by some critics as the most promising young dramatist to appear in a decade, David Rabe made a shattering impact on the American theatre with his *The Basic Training of Pavlo Hummel* and *Sticks and Bones*. He wrote both plays in 1967-68 as a graduate student at Villanova University after his return from military service in Vietnam. The first, which earned Off-Broadway's coveted Obie award, canvasses the effects of war on combatants and victims, while the second, which received a Tony award as the best Broadway play of 1971-72, indicts the "Middle American" family for refusing to allow tragedy to deflect it from its shallow materialism. A third play by Rabe, *The Orphan,* in which he deals with contemporary problems within a framework of classical myth, was less successful. Although the controversial nature of his plays has given them a topical importance that tends to obscure their artistic value, Rabe insists that he is not a conventional antiwar polemicist. "All ▪▪▪▪▪▪▪ "is define the event

publications. Each entry follows a strict format, giving the person's current position, birth date and place, parents' names, marriage date and spouse's name (Gaddafi's wife's name is not given here), number and sex of children, a chronological list of positions held, publications, and address. Only the information that fits into this structure is provided.

To decide in which sources to look for the person you are researching, it is important to know that most biographical sources have very specific inclusion criteria—for instance, the person may be required to be of a particular nationality or profession. Some of these sources only include persons who are dead; others include only those who are living (at the time of publication). The *Dictionary of American Biography* (encyclopedic narrative style) requires both that the subject be dead and that he or she "lived in the territory now known as the United States" (Introduction, p.v.). In contrast, *Who's Who in America*

Figure 6-6: *International Who's Who*, 47th ed. 1983

G

GABALLAH EL-SAYED, Sayed; Egyptian politician; ed. Cairo and Wisconsin Univs.; Teacher, Cairo Univ., Head Agric. Econ. Section; Under-Sec. of State for Planning 1963–71; Minister for Planning 1971–74. *Address:* c/o Ministry of Planning, Cairo, Egypt.

GABRE-SELLASSIE, Zewde, PH.D.; Ethiopian diplomatist; b. 12 Oct. 1926, Metcha, Shoa; ed. Haile Sellassie I Secondary School, Coll. des Frères and St. George School, Jerusalem, Coll. des Frères and American Mission, Cairo, Univ. of Exeter, Oxford Univ. and Lincoln's Inn, London; Econ. Attaché, later Head of Press, Information and Admin. Div., Ministry of Foreign Affairs 1951–53; Dir.-Gen. Maritime Affairs 1953–55; Deputy Minister, Ministry of Public Works, Transport and Civil Aviation 1955–57; Mayor and Gov. of Addis Ababa 1957–59; Amb. to Somalia 1959–60; Minister of Justice 1961–63; Senior mem. St. Antony's Coll., Oxford 1963–71; Perm. Rep. to the UN 1972–74; Minister of Interior March-May 1974, of Foreign Affairs May-Dec. 1974; Deputy Prime Minister July-Sept. 1974; Visiting lecturer, Univ. of Calif., U.S.A. 1965; Vice-Pres. ECOSCO 1974; Officer of Menelik II (Ethiopia), Grand Cross, Order of Phoenix (Greece), of Istiqlal (Jordan), Grand Officer Flag of Yugoslavia, Order of Merit (Fed. Repub. of Germany), Commdr. Order of St. Olav (Norway), of Orange-Nassau (Netherlands).

GABRIEL, Ralph Henry, PH.D., LITT.D.; American historian; b. 29 April 1890, Reading, N.Y.; s. of Cleveland and Alta Monroe Gabriel; m. Christine Davis 1917; two s. one d.; ed. Yale Univ.; on staff Yale Univ. 1915, Prof. 1928–58; mem. staff U.S. War Dept. School of Mil. Govt. 1943–46; mem. American Historical Asscn.; mem. Newcomen Society; Visiting Prof. Sydney Univ. Australia 1946; Prof. American History, Cambridge Univ. 1951–52; Prof. of American Civilisation, American Univ. 1958–64; Visiting Prof. Tokyo Univ. 1964, George Washington Univ. 1965; U.S. Del. at Tenth Session of UNESCO 1958; mem. of U.S. Nat. Comm. for UNESCO 1958–63; Ed. Pageant of America (15 vols.) 1924–29; Joint-Ed. The American Mind 1937; Ed. Library of Congress Series in American Civilisation. *Publications:* Evolution of Long Island

Castellini 1939; one s.; ed. Pavia Univ.; Novelist and journalist; Italian Literary Prizewinner 1930, Bagutta Prize for Literature for La Paura 1971. *Publications:* L'Entusiastica Estate 1924, Liuba 1926, Verdemare 1927, Mozzo 1930, A Gonfie Vele 1931, Gagliarda 1932, Orchidea 1934, Festa da Ballo 1937, Nuvola 1938, Moti del Cuore 1940, Vocazione Mediterranea 1940, Incomparabile Italia 1947, Beati Regni 1954, Vita e melodie di Giacomo Puccini 1955, Adamira 1956, Vanterie Adolescenti 1960, Cinema e civiltà 1960, Cinema e Giustizia 1961, Cinema e Sesso 1962, Cinema e Libertà 1963, La Milano dei Navigli 1965, Cinema e Società 1965, La Brianza 1966, La Paura 1970, Confessioni di Carlo Emilio Gadda 1974, Concerto d'Autunno 1976; plays: La Veste d'Oro 1924, Dulcinea 1927. *Address:* Piazza Castello 20, Milan, Italy. *Telephone:* 873-771, 80-33-58.

GADDAFI, Col. Mu'ammar Muhammad al-; Libyan army officer and political leader; b. 1942, Serte; s. of Mohamed Abdulsalam Abuminiar and Aisha Ben Niran; m. 1970; four s. one d.; ed. Univ. of Libya, Benghazi; served with Libyan Army 1965–; Chair. Revolutionary Command Council 1969–77; C.-in-C. of Armed Forces Sept. 1969–; Prime Minister 1970–72; Minister of Defence 1970–72; Pres. of Libya March 1977–; Sec.-Gen. of Gen. Secretariat of Gen. People's Congress 1977–79; Chair. OAU 1982–83; mem. Pres. Council, Fed. of Arab Republics 1971–; rank of Maj.-Gen. Jan. 1976, still keeping title of Col. *Publications:* The Green Book (3 vols.), Military Strategy and Mobilisation, The Story of the Revolution. *Address:* Office of the President, Tripoli, Libya.

GADDAFI, Wanis; Libyan politician; Head of Exec. Council in Cyrenaican Prov. Govt. 1952–62; Fed. Minister of Foreign Affairs 1962–63, of Interior 1963–64, of Labour 1964; Amb. to Fed. Repub. of Germany 1964–65; Minister of Planning and Devt. 1966–68, of Foreign Affairs 1968; Prime Minister 1968–69; imprisoned for two years Nov. 1971. *Address:* Tripoli, Libya.

GADSDEN, Sir Peter Drury Haggerston, G.B.E., M.A., D.SC., F.ENG., F.I.M.M., F.INST.M.; British business executive; b. 28 June 1929, Mannville, Alberta, Canada; s. of late Rev. Basil C. and Mabel F.

(abbreviated abstract style) requires that the person be living at the time the information for the entry is collected. To be included in *Who's Who in American Politics* (abbreviated abstract style), a person must be a living American involved in some aspect of politics or government. Using even more specialized criteria, each edition of the *Official Congressional Directory* (abbreviated abstract style) includes biographies only for those persons currently serving in either house of the U.S. Congress. When you search for a biography, it is important to consider the scope of a source so you can choose the most appropriate publication.

With biographical research, it is especially important to note dates—dates on which momentous things happened to the person. It is on these dates (and anniversaries of them) that information is most likely to be published. For instance, if you are looking for information about Muammar el-Qaddafi, you may expect to find more information during 1986. During this year, Qaddafi was accused of supporting Abu Nidal in the December 1985 attack at the Rome and Vienna airports and the April 1986 bombing of TWA Flight 840. Also happening in the year 1986 were U.S.-Libyan confrontations in the Gulf of Sidra and the U.S. aircraft bombing raid on Qaddafi's headquarters near Tripoli. The background information you find in biographical encyclopedias (if they are current enough) will alert you to these important dates.

Hundreds of Other Sources of Biographical Information

When finding aids like *Biography Index, Biobase*, and *Biography Almanac* are available, they are a great, time-saving place to start searching for biographical information. Using encyclopedic narrative biographical sources, such as *Current Biography*, or abbreviated abstract biographical sources, such as the various "Who's Who" publications, gives you a lot of information in a few words. You should not, however, neglect to search your library's catalog and the periodical and government document indexes for the person's name. In some cases, these additional searches will yield the latest information available on your subject.

When searching for books by or about your biographical subject in the library's catalog you may need to specify if you are searching for the person's name as an author or as a subject. If there is any chance that the person for whom you are searching has ever written a book, it is a good idea to perform two searches, one for the person as author, another for the person as subject. Ask a reference librarian if your library's catalog is set up to find books by and about a person at the same time (as in dictionary card catalogs which file author, title, and subject cards in one alphabet) or if it is necessary to do two searches (as with some online systems which require that you select the type of search to be performed).

For some searches, you may be looking for someone not well-known enough (or not well-known long enough) to be in the standard biographical reference sources. Searching the periodical indexes discussed in Chapter 3 may provide the information you need. Using these sources can also update the information found in biographical reference sources. For instance, a search for information about Abu Nidal in *Biobase* turns up only four references (in the 1990 Master Cumulation), but a search in *General Periodicals Index: Academic Library Edition* finds several articles about this alleged terrorist, as well as book reviews, alerting you to look in your library catalog for this recently-published book (see Figure 6-7).

Because there are so many biographical finding aids and sources, because (as discussed above) some present particular problems, and because some of the titles discussed in this chapter may not be available in your library, it is—as always—a good idea to consult with a reference librarian.

FINDING STATISTICAL INFORMATION

Usefulness of Statistics

Biographical research shows a microcosm by presenting an individual's experience or point of view. Statistical research analyzes a macrocosm by examining phenomena from a larger perspective. Statistical analysis involves collecting information from a defined population and observing trends, the distribution of certain characteristics of the population, and even proposing theories about cause and effect. By quantifying or assigning a numeric value to a phenomenon, it becomes easier to make generalizations about the phenomenon, to make comparisons among different populations or across a span of time, or to predict the results of a proposed change.

Figure 6-7: *General Periodicals Index—Academic Libraries Edition*™

```
┌─────────────────────────────────────────────────────────────────────────┐
│ ┌──────────────┐                                                          │
│ │ Infotrac EF  │   General Periodicals Index-A        Brief Citations     │
│ └──────────────┘                                                          │
│  ┌──────────────────────────────────────┐                                │
│  │ Key Words:  abu nidal ◄──             │        Journal Available       │
│  └──────────────────────────────────────┘        Press F5 for details    │
│ ─────────────────────────────────────────────────────────────────────────│
│                            ─────1 of 11─────                              │
│ 1          Terrorist´s aide shot dead. (Palestinian Abu Nidal´s aide, Khalil│
│    Abul-Hana of the Fatah Revolutionary Council, killed in Lebanon)       │
│    (International Pages) The New York Times, July 10, 1992 v141 pA4(N)     │
│    1 col in.                                                              │
│ 2          Set up to make a killing: how Abu Nidal is expanding his terror│
│    franchise, with new sponsors and new targets. Douglas Waller.         │
│    Newsweek, April 6, 1992 v119 n14 p31(2).                              │
│ 3          Abu Nidal: a Gun for Hire. (book reviews) Amos Perlmutter.     │
│    National Review, March 30, 1992 v44 n4 p40(2). IAC Coll. 63M0219.     │
│ 4          Abu Nidal: a Gun for Hire. (book reviews) The Economist, Feb 15,│
│    1992 v322 n7746 p103(1).                                              │
│ 5          Terrorist with a gold card. (Abu Nidal) (Brief Article) Janice │
│    Castro. Time, Dec 9, 1991 v138 n23 p21(1). IAC Coll. 6201410 and      │
│    62G1088.                                                              │
│ ─────────────────────────────────────────────────────────────────────────│
│ Display  Narrow  Explore        Esc Return to prior subject list   F3 Print│
│                                 F1 Help   F2 Start over   F4 Mark         │
│ Display full record             F9 View backfile citations               │
└─────────────────────────────────────────────────────────────────────────┘
```

Selection and Interpretation Problems

Statistics are powerful arguments. Be sure to use authoritative statistics and to interpret them carefully. When using statistics, it is important to compare numbers in a logical manner. If you are comparing from year to year, you must be sure the numbers were collected and counted in the same manner and for the same subject population. For instance, if you are comparing the number of aircraft hijacking incidents from one year to the next, be sure the same criteria are applied in both years. Do not compare hijackings of just U.S.-registered aircraft for one year with *all* hijackings for the next. Similarly, do not confuse statistics on attempted hijackings with those for successful incidents. Table or figure titles, headings, and notes should clarify the exact definition of the statistic(s) being reported or displayed.

Another common error in using statistics is to fail to carefully read the table or figure title, headings, and notes to correctly identify the units of measure used to report or display the statistics in the table or figure. For example, in order to save space, many tables report entries in units of hundreds, thousands, millions, or even billions. Other entries may be reported in percent or as a ratio. Some entries may be in English measures (inch, foot, yard, etc.) other entries may be in metric measures (millimeter, centimeter, meter, etc.).

Reliability and Validity Problems

"There are three kinds of lies—lies, damned lies, and statistics". This quote has been attributed to Benjamin Disraeli, Mark Twain, and several others, but whoever said it had a good point.[1] Some governments and private organizations have hidden agendas and may intentionally misrepresent data and results by omission as well as distortion. You must be very careful that statistical measures are valid and reliable. Statistics are also frequently misused to support cause and effect assertions. It is common to hear politicians claim credit for certain improvements that have occurred during their time in office, improvements that may in fact have very little to do with their actions.

Relying on statistics that were unintentionally skewed during collection and interpretation can also be dangerous. Statistics when applied illogically—or collected from too small a sample or an improperly selected sample—can lead to some very wrong conclusions. You should also be aware that unknown variables may have had an influence on the results of otherwise reputable surveys, censuses, or experiments.

For research in political science, there are many sources of statistical information in which the data are collected, summarized, and interpreted for the user. You will see and hear statistics reported daily in print and broadcast media. Statistics are also compiled and distributed in many formats (print, microform, CD-ROM, and online) by governmental and international agencies as well as trade, professional, and research organizations. Examples of such agencies and organizations are the U.S. Bureau of the Census, the United Nations, the National Safety Council, the Rand Corporation, and the Institute for Studies in International Terrorism. There are also guides and indexes to help you find specific statistics in these myriad sources. In research at the undergraduate level, you may find that you can often use these published statistics in lieu of compiling the data yourself.

---

[1]See *Respectfully Quoted: A Dictionary of Quotations Requested for the Congressional Research Service.* Washington, DC: Library of Congress, 1989.

Four Statistical Finding Aids:
Data Map, American Statistics Index,
Statistical Reference Index, and
Index to International Statistics

With statistics, as with biographical sources, you can save time and do a more thorough search by referring to indexes that identify which sources contain the information you want. Two are discussed here: *Data Map: Index of Published Tables of Statistical Data (Data Map)* and *American Statistics Index: A Comprehensive Guide to the Statistical Publications of the U.S. Government* (ASI). Both index sources of statistics that are highly respected. Most of the sources indexed in *Data Map* are collections of statistics gathered from governmental, international, and commercial sources. ASI cites both U.S. government statistical compendiums and other U.S. government documents which are not primarily statistical (e.g., congressional hearings, prints, and reports).

Data Map includes hundreds of references to statistical information in more than two dozen statistical sources published by the United States government, the United Nations, and several commercial publishers. It was published annually, but apparently ceased in 1990. Each issue includes three sections. The key to using *Data Map* is to start with Section III: "Subject Index", then work backwards to Section II: "Listing of Tables", and finally turn to Section I: "Listing of Sources".

Figure 6-8 shows a portion of the subject index of *Data Map 1989*. Under "Hijackers" we are told to see "Terrorists" instead. In contrast, under "Hijackings" we are told to see also "Crimes" and "Terrorism" in addition to the two entries listed here. The first entry is a cumulative table of statistics about aircraft hijackings, by location and outcome. The entry number "CJS0284" is the link to Section II: "Listing of Tables".

Figure 6-9 shows page 39 from Section II that includes this sequential entry number. Here we find two things. First, at the top of the page, the title of the source is identified, in this case, *Sourcebook of Criminal Justice Statistics 1986* with its abbreviation (CJS). Second, in the body of the page, we find our sequential entry number (CJS0284) followed by the full title of the statistical table, years reported, and source page number(s) on which this table is found. For a complete bibliographic reference to the source, turn to Section I: "Listing of Sources".

The *American Statistics Index* includes tens of thousands of references to statistical information published in approximately five thousand U.S. government documents. This guide is published monthly with an annual cumulation. Also currently available are two multiple-year cumulative indexes, one for 1980-84 and another for 1985-88.

ASI is issued in two parts. Part one is an index (arranged alphabetically by subjects and names) to U.S. government documents that include statistical information. Part two gives an abstract for each U.S. government document indexed. Each abstract includes the following: 1) a general description of the publication, 2) bibliographic reference information, and 3) where in the publication you can find specific statistical data.

Figure 6-8: *Data Map*, Subject Index. Reprinted from *Data Map 1989*, by Allison Ondrasik

474 / Higher Education

Higher Education *(continued)*
Research and Development *(Expenditures/ Total/and/Percentage/by Field/by Country).* USY0052
Research and Development *(Scientists/and/ Engineers/by Field/by Country).* USY0046
Statistics *(Errors/by Variable).* PES0027

Highway Trust Fund
See also Trust Funds
Federal Grants *(Total/and/Per Capita/by State).* SA0991

Speeding *(Percentage/by Speed/by .... by State).* SMA0099
State Funds *(Disbursements/by State/by Year).* SA0990
Vehicle-Miles *(Number/and/Percentage Change/by Region/by State).* SMA0099
Vehicle-Miles *(Urban/and/Rural/by Type/by Year/and/Percentage Change).* NTS0003
Vehicle-Miles *(by Year).* NTS0018

Hijackers
See Terrorists

Hijackings
See also Crimes, Terrorism
Aircraft *(by Location/by Outcome/ Cumulative).* CJS0284
Civil Aviation *(by Flag of Carrier/by Year).* SA1032

Hiking
See Hobbies

Hindu
See Religion(s)

Hispanic(s)
See also Ethnicity, Spanish-Americans
....Percentage

H.M.O.s
See Health Maintenance Organizations

Hobbies
See also Fishing, Gardening, Hunting, Leisure Activities, Photography, Skiing, Sports
Children *(Parents/Emphasis/Public Opinion).* POI1076
Participation *(Personal Action(s)/Public Opinion/in/Japan).* POI1709

Satisfaction with *(Public Opinion/by Year).* POI2096

Hobbs Act
See also Legislation
Violations *(by Type/by State/by Year).* CJS0257

Hockey
See National Hockey League, Sports

Hogs
See also Livestock, Pigs, Sows
Breeding *(by Year).* AS0405
Breeding *(by Year/by Quarter).* CY0323
Corn *(Price Ratio(s)/by Year).* AS0414
.... Year/by Month)
AS0401
Slaughters *(Federal Inspection/by Year/by Month).* CY0330
Slaughters *(Federal Inspection/by Year/by Week).* CY0324
Slaughters *(Total/and/Federal Inspection/by Year).* AS0411
Slaughters *(Value/by State).* AS0410
Slaughters *(Value/by Year).* AS0408
Slaughters *(by State).* AS0410, AS0412

Figure 6-9: *Data Map*, Listing of Tables. Reprinted from *Data Map 1989*, by Allison Ondraski

Sourcebook of Criminal Justice Statistics 1986 (CJS) / 39

CJS0255	Percent distribution of burglaries known to police, By place and time of occurrence, United States, 1976-85, p. 268
CJS0256	Percent distribution of larceny-thefts known to police, By type of target, United States, 1973-85, p. 268
CJS0257	Violations of the Federal Bank Robbery and Incidental Crimes Statute and of the Hobbs Act. By type of violation and jurisdiction, ... and type of weapon used, ...
CJS0261	Law enforcement officers killed, By circumstances at scene of incident and type of assignment, United States, 1976-85 (aggregate), p. 272
CJS0262	Law enforcement officers killed, By circumstances at scene of incident and type of assignment, United States, 1985, p. 273
CJS0263	Percent distribution of law enforcement officers killed, By selected characteristics of officers, United States, 1978-85, p. 274
CJS0264	Persons identified in the killing of law enforcement officers, By demographic characteristics and prior record, United States, 1976-85 (aggregate) and 1985, p. 274

CJS0275	Deaths, injuries, and property damage resulting from criminal bombings and accidental explosions, Reported to the Bureau of Alcohol, Tobacco and Firearms, United States, 1976-85, p. 282
CJS0276	Estimated number of fires, civilian fire deaths, and value of property loss due to incendiary or suspicious structure fires, United States, 1985, p. 282
CJS0277	Arson. By type of target, 1985, p. 283
CJS0282	International terrorist incidents involving U.S. citizens or property, By type of incident, 1979-84, p. 284
CJS0283	Regional distribution of international terrorist incidents involving U.S. citizens or property, By type of incident, 1984, p. 284
CJS0284	Reported aircraft hijackings in and outside the United States, By outcome, 1931-67 (aggregate), 1968-85, p. 285
CJS0285	Criminal acts involving U.S. civil aviation, By type of act, 1961-67 (aggregate), 1968-86, p. 285
CJS0286	Results of airline passenger screening, United States, 1976-85, p. 286
CJS0287	Percent distribution of fatally-injured motor .... by level of blood alcohol

Figure 6-10: *American Statistics Index*, 1987 Annual, Index of Subjects and Names

Index by Subjects and Names — **Hispanic Americans**

Govt employment and payroll, by function, level of govt, and jurisdiction, 1985, annual rpt series, 2466–1
Govt finances, by level of govt, State, and for large cities and counties, FY85-86, annual rpt series, 2466–2
Govt finances, tax systems and revenue, and fiscal structure, by level of govt and State, selected years 1929-89, annual rpt, 10044–1.3; 10044–1.10; 10044–1.11
Hwy Statistics, summary data by State, 1985-86, annual rpt, 7554–24
Hwy Statistics, summary data with trends

see National Guard
Air navigation
see Aeronautical navigation
Air piracy
Airport security operations to prevent hijacking, screening results, enforcement actions, and hijacking attempts, 1st half 1987, semiannual rpt, 7502–5
Airport security operations to prevent hijacking, screening test results, 1986, GAO rpt, 26113–296
Hijacking attempts on US and foreign aircraft, summary data, 1971-81, annual rpt, 7304–1
Hijackings, other crimes against aviation, and airport screening results, 1960s-86, annual rpt, 6064–6.3
Public opinion on crime and severity of offense, by offense, respondent characteristics, and location, 1977 survey, 6068–207
Sentences for Federal offenses, guidelines by offense and circumstances, 1987 rpt,

Hijacking of aircraft
see Air piracy
Hijikata, Heidi
"U.S. Trade Deficit with Japan: Impact of Savings-Investment Imbalances", 2048–128
Hilgert, Cecelia
"Nonprofit Charitable Organizations, 1983", 8302–2.712
Hill, Christopher T.
"Nobel-Prize Awards in Science As a Measure of National Strength in Science", 21708–120
"Science Policy Study Background Report

Carbon dioxide in atmosphere, environmental and other effects, and research activities and needs, series, 3006–10
Carbon dioxide in atmosphere, measurement, methodology, and research results, series, 3006–11
Coal-fired power plants air pollutant emissions and control technology costs, 1970s-85, and R&D funding by source, projected to 1992, 3008–117
Coastal environmental conditions, use, and socioeconomic data, for individual areas, series, 5506–4
Electric power plants coal and oil deliveries by sulfur content and location, and sulfur removal capacity use by plant, 1986, annual rpt, 3164–42
Electric power plants coal and oil receipts and average cost by sulfur content and State, quarterly rpt, 3162–39
Electric utilities privately owned, pollution abatement outlays by type of pollutant ... and firm, 1985, annual

Hirsch, Marilyn B.
"Users of Reproductive Health Clinic Services in a School Pregnancy Prevention Program", 4042–3.730
Hirschhorn, Eric
"Informational Content of Bank Examination Ratings", 9292–3.704
Hirst, Eric
"Cooperation and Community Conservation", 3226–2.7
"Electricity Use and Savings in the Hood River Conservation Project", 3226–2.6
Hirtle, Beverly
"Growth of the Financial Guarantee Market", 9385–1.708

air, emissions sources, and environmental and health effects, literature review, 1986 rpt, 9198–88
R&D funding and employment of industry, by firm size and industry group, 1956-84, annual rpt, 9627–21
Radionuclide concentrations in environment and food after Chernobyl reactor accident, monitoring results by US and foreign site, 1986 rpt, 9198–116
Radon indoor air pollution levels, by State and selected city, 1987 rpt, 3008–119
Radon indoor air pollution levels, measurement and remedial activities, and State programs, 1986/87 survey, 9198–117
Radon indoor air pollution R&D funding of Fed Govt, and remedial action standards of intl agency and foreign govts, 1986 hearing, 21708–121
Respiratory diseases from occupational hazards, epidemiology, diagnosis, and treatment, 1960s-85, 4248–85

Upon consulting the 1987 index part of ASI under "Hijacking of aircraft", we were told to see instead "Air piracy".[2] Figure 6-10 shows portions of those index pages. Under "Air piracy" we find seven entries. Since we have narrowed our topic to prevention of aircraft hijackings, a reading of the seven entries shows us that at least five appear to deal with prevention measures. Taking the first entry as an example, we need to use the entry number "7502-5" to look up the document description in the abstract part of ASI.

A portion of the abstract page describing the document cited in the index is shown in Figure 6-11. Here we find that the document is a semiannual report from the FAA to Congress concerning their Civil Aviation Security Program instituted to prevent aircraft hijackings and related crimes. This document includes five charts and three tables of statistical information on our topic. The Superintendent of Documents (SUDOC)

[2]Note that ASI uses the same subject headings as *CIS/Index*, which is discussed in Chapter 4. Both are published by Congressional Information Service.

Figure 6-11: *American Statistics Index*, 1987 Annual, Abstracts of Statistical Publications

---

2A-2B. Total losses [by] type of vessel, by age of vessel. (p. 194)

3. Summary of commercial vessels not involved in a total loss by vessel size [and type]. (p. 195)

4A-4B. Vessels not involved in a total loss [by] type of vessel, by age of vessel. (p. 198)

5A-5C. Summary of commercial vessel casualties by [detailed personnel, environment, and material related] cause. (p. 199-200)

6-7. Deaths/injuries resulting from total loss of commercial vessels and from a commercial vessel not involved in a total loss [by vessel type]. (p. 200-201)

8. Other deaths/injuries onboard commercial vessels (not related to a vessel casualty) [by cause and vessel type]. (p. 201)

[9]-[10]. Repeat tables 6-7 for 1984 (revised). (p. 202-203)

7502
FEDERAL AVIATION ADMINISTRATION
Current Periodicals

7502–5   SEMIANNUAL REPORT TO CONGRESS ON THE EFFECTIVENESS OF THE CIVIL AVIATION SECURITY PROGRAM, Jan. 1-June 30, 1987
Semiannual. Nov. 1987.
ii+16+8 p. † ASI/MF/3
TD4.810:987.

Twenty-sixth semiannual report to Congress on the Civil Aviation Security Program, and the operation of airport passenger and baggage screening procedures, Jan.-June 1987. Procedures were instituted to prevent aircraft hijackings and related crimes.

Includes 5 charts and 3 tables showing:

a. U.S. scheduled air carrier hijackings and hijacking attempts, and U.S. general aviation and foreign aircraft hijackings, annually 1978-86 and Jan.-June 1987; and date, airline flight, aircraft type, number aboard, hijacker's boarding point and objective, and outcome, for each U.S. and foreign aircraft hijacking, Jan.-June 1987.

b. Airline passengers screened and arrested, and weapons detected, by type; for U.S. airports, semiannually 1981-86.

c. Compliance and enforcement actions of FAA against U.S. and foreign air carriers, airports, and individuals, aggregate 1973-80, annually 1981-86, and Jan.-June 1987.

Previous report, for July-Dec. 1986, was received in July 1987 and is also available on ASI microfiche under this number [May 1987. ii+14+8 p. TD4.810:986-2. † ASI/MF/3].

7502–13   AIR CARRIER AIRCRAFT UTILIZATION AND PROPULSION RELIABILITY REPORT
Monthly. Approx. 30 p.
•Item 431-A-44. †
ASI/MF/3 TD4.59:(date).

Report has been issued since 1964.
Issues covered during 1987: Oct. 1986-Sept./ Oct. 1987 (P). Filmed quarterly.

7502–14   AIRPORT GRANT ALLOCATIONS
Quarterly. Approx. 60 p.
FAA (nos.-yr.) † ASI/MF/3

Quarterly press release on airport planning and development grants awarded under FAA's Airport Improvement Program and financed by user tax payments from the Aviation Trust Fund. Release is issued approximately 2 months after quarter of coverage.

Includes 1 table showing allocations; and list of grant awards, showing city, name of sponsor and airport, type of airport, grant amount, and project description, for each project; all by State and outlying area.

Issues covered during 1987: 1st Qtr.-3rd Qtr. FY87 (D).

7504
FEDERAL AVIATION ADMINISTRATION
Annuals and Biennials

7504–1   FAA STATISTICAL HANDBOOK OF AVIATION, 1985
Annual. 1987. xxiii+198 p.
•Item 431-C-14.
GPO $11.00; NTIS, price not given. ASI/MF/5
S/N 005-007-00747-7.
TD4.20:985.   LC 73-609572.

Annual report for 1985 presenting detailed and comprehensive data on all phases of aviation-related activity regulated by the FAA, with trends from 1976. Includes statistics on the National Airspace System operations, airports and aviation activity, air carrier operations, aircraft, personnel, and aircraft accidents, for airlines and general aviation; and aircraft production and trade.

Data are derived from a variety of FAA and

Classification Number is provided for locating the document in library collections which use the SUDOC Classification Scheme (see Figure 6-11).

Unfortunately, no U.S. depository item number is given in the abstract for the particular document. This indicates that the document was not automatically distributed to depository libraries (see Chapter 4 for a discussion of the depository library system). The publisher of ASI, Congressional Information Service, sells microfiche copies of every U.S. government document that they index. If your library subscribes to this service, locating this document should be no problem. Otherwise, search your library's catalog or ask a reference librarian or documents librarian to help you determine if your library acquired this document.

In addition to ASI, Congressional Information Service publishes two indexes to statistical sources other than those issued by the federal government. *Statistical Reference Index* (SRI) is an index to nongovernmental statistical sources. Statistical sources issued by international intergovernmental organizations are indexed in *Index to International Statistics* (IIS). As with ASI, the sources in SRI and IIS are available on microfiche from Congressional Information Service. Once again, it is a good idea to call upon a reference librarian's familiarity with your library's collection as you search for this information.

Statistical Compilations

Whether or not *Data Map* and ASI are available to you, you will find a variety of standard reference books which are compendiums of statistical information on an amazing range of subjects. Many of these compendiums limit their coverage to statistics about a particular level of government or political entity—international, national, state, or local. Table 6-1 lists some of the more useful compendiums commonly available in undergraduate libraries. Complete bibliographic information for these sources can be found in Appendix I.

Two subfields of political science are particularly oriented towards statistical analysis—public opinion and elections. There are several finding aids and compendiums included in Table 6-1 that focus upon these subfields. For example, subject indexes to public opinion data that are commonly found in undergraduate libraries include: *The Gallup Poll, American Public Opinion Index*, and the *Index to International Public Opinion*. These finding aids are also very useful in survey design—especially selection of questions and how to word them. Subject indexes to U.S. election data listed in Table 6-1 include: *America Votes, America at the Polls*, and *Congressional Quarterly's Guide to U.S. Elections*.

Because there are so many statistical sources, you need a few rules of thumb to help you locate those which are available in your library. We offer five guidelines. First of all, because both locating and interpreting statistics are complex endeavors, you will often need to consult a reference librarian for guidance. Second, search your library's catalog, paying special attention to headings that use "Statistics" as a subdivision (e.g., "United States—Statistics"). Third, as discussed in the previous section, specialized indexes like *Data Map* and ASI are very useful in identifying statistical sources. Fourth, remember that many statistical publications are government documents and may be cataloged and shelved separately in your library and may even have separate reference staff to assist you. Finally, pay attention to publication cycles noted in the catalog or index entry. Some statistics are collected and published annually (e.g., *Uniform Crime Reports*). Other statistical compilations appear every five years (e.g., *County and City Databook*). Still others like the *Census of Population and Housing* are issued once every ten years. And, some statistical compilations are issued irregularly or only once.

One of the most respected statistical compendiums is *The Statistical Abstract of the United States*, which is indexed in both *Data Map* and ASI. It is published annually by the U.S. Department of Commerce and contains statistics on a wide variety of topics relating to the United States and the world. Most of the figures reported in the *Statistical*

Table 6-1: Selected Statistical Sources

Level of Government	Type of Statistical Source	
	General	Special
International	• *European Historical Statistics* • *Statesman's Yearbook* • *Statistical Yearbook*	• *Demographic Yearbook* • *Index to International Public Opinion* • *International Almanac of Electoral History* • *World Military and Social Expenditures*
United States National	• *Historical Statistics of the United States* • *Statistical Abstract of the United States*	• *America at the Polls* • *America Votes* • *American Public Opinion Index* • *Business Statistics* • *Census of Population* • *CQ's Guide to U.S. Elections* • *Digest of Educational Statistics* • *The Elusive Executive* • *The Gallup Poll* • *Handbook of Labor Statistics* • *Sourcebook of Criminal Justice Statistics* • *Uniform Crime Reports* • *Vital Statistics on American Politics* • *Vital Statistics of the United States*
State	• *Book of the States* • Various state manuals and statistical abstracts • *State and Metropolitan Area Databook*	• Various U.S. Bureau of the Census state census reports
Local	• *County and City Databook* • *Congressional District Databook* • *Municipal Yearbook* • *State and Metropolitan Area Databook*	• *County Business Patterns* • Various reports by state and local agencies, e.g., land use plans

Figure 6-12: *Statistical Abstract of the United States*, 110th edition, 1990

Washington, DC: Government Printing Office.

Abstract are collected from U.S. government agencies, but statistics reported from other reputable sources are also included.

Figure 6-12 shows an index page from the *Statistical Abstract* for 1990. The number listed under "Air transportation—Hijacking incidents" refers to Table 1066. (We tried "Air transportation" as an index heading after drawing a blank on both "Hijacking" and "Terrorism". When no headings or cross-references appear initially, you simply must be creative in trying synonymous or related words and phrases.) Note that this abstract's

Figure 6-13: *Statistical Abstract of the United States*, **110th edition, 1990**

No. 1066. Aircraft Accidents and Hijackings: 1975 to 1988

[For years ending December 31]

ITEM	Unit	1975	1980	1983	1984	1985	1986	1987	1988
Aircraft accidents: [1]									
General aviation [2]	Number	3,995	3,590	3,075	3,010	2,741	2,581	2,471	2,332
Fatal	Number	633	618	555	543	498	471	435	438
Rate per 100,000 aircraft hours flown	Rate	2.20	1.69	1.79	1.72	1.62	1.61	1.49	1.49
Fatalities	Number	1,252	1,239	1,064	1,039	950	961	830	782
Air carrier, all services [3]	Number	(NA)	19	24	16	22	23	38	30
Fatal	Number	(NA)	1	4	1	7	2	5	3
Rates	Rate	(x)	–	.001	–	.002	–	.001	–
Fatalities	Number	(NA)	1	15	4	526	4	232	285
Air carrier, scheduled services	Number	29	15	22	13	17	21	33	29
Fatal	Number	2	–	4	1	4	2	4	3
Rate per 1,000,000 aircraft miles flown	Rate	.001	–	.001	.003	.001	.002	.001	.001
Fatalities	Number	122	–	15	4	197	4	231	285
Commuter air carriers [4]	Number	48	38	17	22	21	15	34	20
Fatal	Number	12	8	2	7	7	2	12	2
Rate per 1,000,000 aircraft miles flown	Rate	.07	.04	.01	.02	.02	.01	.03	.01
Fatalities	Number	28	37	11	48	37	4	61	21
Air taxis [5]	Number	152	171	141	146	152	116	99	97
Fatal	Number	24	46	27	23	35	31	29	28
Rate per 100,000 aircraft hours flown	Rate	.95	1.27	1.05	.75	1.26	1.06	1.01	.97
Fatalities	Number	69	105	62	52	76	65	64	57
Hijacking incidents, worldwide	Number	25	40	33	22	35	12	15	16
U.S. registered aircraft	Number	12	21	18	3	4	4	4	(NA)
Successful [6]	Number	4	13	13	2	2	–	–	2
Foreign-registered aircraft	Number	13	18	15	21	31	8	11	(NA)
Successful [6]	Number	3	9	6	16	18	2	5	14
Bomb threats:									
U.S. airports	Number	449	268	188	139	256	238	376	153
Explosions	Number	4	1	1	–	–	–	–	–
U.S. worldwide and foreign aircraft in U.S.	Number	1,853	1,179	467	465	372	401	898	518
Explosions	Number	2	1	–	3	1	1	1	2

– Represents or rounds to zero.   NA Not available.   X Not applicable.   [1] Data from National Transportation Safety Board.   [2] See text, section 22.   [3] U.S. Air Carriers operating under 14 CFR 121.   [4] All scheduled service of U.S. Air Carriers operating under 14 CFR 135.   [5] All nonscheduled service of U.S. Air Carriers operating under 14 CFR 135.   [6] Hijacker controls flight and reaches destination or objective.

Source: U.S. Federal Aviation Administration, *FAA Statistical Handbook of Aviation*, annual; and unpublished data. Includes data from U.S. Department of Transportation, Research and Special Programs Administration.

No. 1067. Top 30 Airports—Traffic Summary: 1988

[In thousands, except percent change. For calendar year. Airports ranked by number of revenue passengers enplaned, 1988]

AIRPORT	Rank	AIRCRAFT DEPARTURES			REVENUE PASSENGERS ENPLANED		ENPLANED REVENUE TONS		
		Total [1]	Scheduled		Total	Percent change 1980–1988	Total [2]	Freight and express	U.S. mail
			Number	Completed					
All airports [3]	(x)	**6,724.4**	**6,827.3**	**6,661.9**	**456,026.4**	**53.6**	**7,577.8**	**5,860.0**	**1,701.2**
Atlanta, GA	2	275.8	280.9	274.8	21,824.1	9.2	256.6	142.8	113.8
Baltimore, MD	30	72.1	72.9	71.6	4,369.6	164.4	34.9	15.4	19.5
	10	115.2	116.3	113.2	10,141.3	48.2	148.2	117.9	30.2
		135.4	107.2	104.6	6,619.8	347.0	52.9	36.0	17.0
						28.3	456.8	312.1	144.7

Washington, DC: Government Printing Office.

index uses table numbers—not page numbers—to lead you to the information in the body of the abstract. It is a common mistake to confuse these table numbers with page numbers.

Table 1066 reports a great deal of information about "Aircraft Accidents and Hijackings" for selected years from 1975 to 1988 (see Figure 6-13). The section of the table for hijacking incidents shows a sharp decline in incidents worldwide in the 1980s. Hijacking incidents involving U.S.-registered aircraft declined from 18 in 1983 to 3 in 1984 and has held steady at 4 for the last three years reported. Knowing that aircraft hijacking was more prevalent in the 1970s, you may wish to examine earlier editions of *Statistical Abstract* to trace the long-term trend.

What caused this decline? Was it new laws enacted with more severe punishment for hijacking crimes? Or was the decline caused by more stringent security measures in airports? Or both? These are the questions which you might decide to carefully examine. If so, it would be helpful to see more detailed statistics or commentary which may have accompanied these figures when they were originally issued. The source for these statistics is listed as the *FAA Statistical Handbook of Aviation*, also published annually (see Figure 6-13). When a later yearbook is issued reporting the same statistics for 1988 or later, you can see if this trend continued.

Table 6-1 shows that, besides the *Statistical Abstract of the United States*, there are many other useful and commonly available statistical compendiums. In selecting which to use, you will often find it useful to consider what level of government and politics you are researching. For example, if you need statistical information at the international level, you may need to consult United Nations' publications, such as *Demographic Yearbook* or *Statistical Yearbook*. On the other hand, if your research is at the U.S. federal level, many specialized statistical compendiums are published by the U.S. government. A good example, given our sample topic, is *Uniform Crime Reports*. Moving down to the U.S. state level, commercial and government sources include *Book of the States* and the various individual state statistical abstracts. (In some states, the statistical abstract is commonly referred to as the state "bluebook".) At the level of local government and politics, you may need to consult *County and City Databook, Municipal Yearbook*, or sources produced locally. Finally, there are some publications that provide statistics on more than one level of government, including *State and Metropolitan Area Databook* and the various U.S. Bureau of the Census publications, such as *Census of Population, Census of Retail Trade*, and *Census of Agriculture*.

FINDING GENERAL FACTUAL INFORMATION: ALMANACS AND NEWS DIGESTS

As you conduct research in political science, you will often find that you need to locate a specific fact or small detail about your topic. Developing a familiarity with the content of almanacs and news digests often saves time in filling in these gaps.

Almanacs

Almanacs are hybrid, one-volume, reference sources containing some statistics, news summaries or chronologies, geographic and political information, biographies of famous persons, and sometimes even consumer information. Most are published annually. In deciding which year to use, check the title page, copyright date, table of contents, or introduction to determine whether the year given in the title of the almanac refers to the year of publication or the year for which it reports events. For example, the table of contents of *The World Almanac and Book of Facts 1991* lists various entries that show that this volume reports events occurring primarily in 1990, even though the contents

Figure 6-14: *Congressional Quarterly Almanac*, 1986, General Index

Agricultural exports
Agriculture Department post - 346
budget proposal - 532
Commerce Department post - 345
farm bill - 299-300
grain quality - 13, 306, 308
international bank loans - 350
market summary - 299-300, 340
Soviet wheat purchases - 12, 299-300, 347
targeted export assistance - 303, 345
trade adjustment aid - 351

67, 521
job training aid - 351, 583
pesticide control - 120, 124
railroad shipping contracts - 279, 280, 284, 569
SBA loans - 322-323
session summary - 11, 12-13, 299-300
South Africa sanctions - 359-373
tax reform - 501, 502, 515
Wright acceptance speech - 5
Agriculture Committee, House
jurisdiction - 157-158
Agriculture Department (USDA). *See also Commodity Credit Corporation; Farmers Home Administration; Food stamps; Forest Service*
appropriations - 153-154, 158, 159, 201-205, 220

budget proposal - 532
budget reconciliation, FY 1987 - 560-561
child nutrition programs - 248-250
elderly food programs - 273
farm law changes - 303-304
irrigation law reform - 62, 64
meat inspections - 575
nutrition monitoring - 263
pesticide control - 125, 126
price support cap - 308-310
rural development loan sales - 305
soil conservation - 502

Air traffic controllers
FAA staffing, research - 156
private aircraft procedures - 221
rehiring ban - 176, 178, 223
retirement plan - 316
Air transportation. *See also Air safety; Air traffic controllers; Aircraft; Federal Aviation Administration*
airline deregulation - 224
airport improvement funds - 556, 558
budget proposal - 526, 536
drug enforcement - 95, 100, 102
facilities financing - 500, 523
fringe benefits - 521, 556
handicapped discrimination - 291, 4A
Iran-contra scandal - 447
labor protection in mergers - 53, 294, 574

registration inspection - 94, 102
South Africa sanctions - 178, 359-373
terrorist attacks - 390, 441
Washington, D.C., airport transfers - 28, 176, 225, 293, 574
Airborne Warning and Control System (AWACS) planes
Saudi purchases - 374, 376
Aircraft. *See also Aircraft, military*
drug enforcement - 94, 95, 100, 167
liability insurance - 277, 289
Aircraft, military. *See also Bombers; Cargo planes; Fighter planes; Helicopters; Radar*

Alcohol, Tobacco and reau of
appropriations - 195
budget proposal - 535
gun control - 82, 83, 84
Alcoholic beverages
beer distributors antitrust - 193, 196, 223
drunken-driving - 28, 92, 100, 105-106
excise taxes - 568, 575
labels
health warning - 24, 103, 266-267
import purity - 193, 221
ingredients - 267
liability insurance - 287, 289
military base sales - 477, 481, 485
minimum drinking age - 294

Aldridge, Edward C. Jr. - 326-327
Alexander, Bill D-Ark. (1)
House leadership - 5
Alfonsin, Raul - 404
Aliens. *See Immigration*
Alkyl nitrites - 93, 103
Allen, Charles - 443, 449
Allen & Co. - 281
Alligators - 139
Alzheimer's disease
research authorization - 238, 241, 550
victims, family services - 251, 258, 567
America (carrier) - 392
American Airlines - 294
American Association of Retired Per-
alcohol sales on military, p
budget resolution - 548-550
Indian health care - 262
Nicaraguan contra aid - 411
Reagan campaign aid - 111
tax reform - 513
Angell, Wayne D. - 313
Angola
aid to rebels
intelligence agencies authorization - 383-388, 395
Stinger missile ban - 458
summary - 22, 358
Export-Import bank loans - 348, 349, 350
indirect aid ban - 165

header says "1991 Highlights". Specifically, the "Chronology of the Year's Events" in this volume covers 15 October 1989 to 31 October 1990.

Well-known examples of almanacs at the international and national level—in addition to *The World Almanac and Book of Facts*—are *Information Please Almanac*, *Political Handbook of the World*, and *Statesman's Year-Book*. Examples of more specialized almanacs at the U.S. federal and state level include *Almanac of American Politics*, *Congressional Quarterly Almanac*, and *Politics in America*. State almanacs are available in many cases. There are literally dozens of other general and specialized almanacs, some of which your library may have. A reference librarian can help you make selections from among the many you are likely to find.

The information given in *World Almanac* and *Information Please Almanac* relating to aircraft hijacking is listed in the chronology sections of each almanac. These sources list brief details of specific incidents, but do not add to our knowledge of prevention measures proposed or attempted to counter these events.

Turning to a more specialized almanac, *Congressional Quarterly Almanac*, for a year in which we know there was a lot of terrorist activity, 1986, we find some valuable information presented in a succinct style. Using *CQ Almanac* is rather like using a specialized encyclopedia, but the information relates to a single year of congressional activity instead of a time span of many years. The chapters of the *CQ Almanac* summarize major legislative activity in many different subject areas, such as environment/energy, health/education/welfare, and foreign policy. There is also an introductory chapter recounting internal events relating to the Congress, such as leadership developments and policy changes affecting Representatives and Senators. An

Figure 6-15: *Congressional Quarterly Almanac*, 1986, pp. 390 and 440

Libyan military targets in retaliation for that country's alleged backing of terrorism. Announcing the April 14 raid, Reagan said he would "do it again" if necessary.

Later in the year, it was reported that the administration had conducted a "disinformation" campaign aimed at destabilizing the Qaddafi regime by feeding false information to the press.

Economic Sanctions

The president Jan. 7 ordered a total ban on U.S. trade with Libya and directed all Americans there to leave — tightening several sanctions that he and President Carter had imposed since 1978.

The following day, in an effort to protect U.S. corporations in Libya against retaliation, Reagan ordered a freeze on all Libyan government assets located in the United States or held by U.S. banks. Officials said that the freeze affected several hundred million dollars, primarily in cash and other "liquid" assets; it did not affect Libyan assets held by foreign subsidiaries of U.S. banks or other companies. *(Texts of Reagan executive orders, p. 12-D)*

The president said he was holding Libya, especially its leader Muammar el-Qaddafi, responsible for simultaneous attacks Dec. 27 at check-in counters of the El Al Israeli airline at the Rome and Vienna airports. Nineteen persons, including five Americans, were killed and more than 100 persons were wounded in those incidents. Italian and Austrian officials traced the attacks to a renegade Palestinian ~~·····~~ summit meeting ~~·······~~

agreed to a drastic proposal of nuclear disarmament, apparently with little consideration of the consequences and without consulting allies and key military aides.

"I do not think it was an aberration. I think it goes deeper than that," said Sen. Nunn. "You can't have all these people running around town making foreign policy decisions on their own."

THE ARMS-FOR-HOSTAGES DEALINGS

The Tower panel traced the origin of U.S. arms sales to Iran to a White House effort late in 1984 to reassess overall policy toward Tehran. But, it said, intervention by Israel resulted in the policy developing faster than Washington had planned, and the initiative became inextricably linked with hostages rather than broader foreign policy objectives.

Laying fact upon fact, citing one internal White House memo after another, the commission report demolished Reagan's claims that he had not traded arms for hostages. The entire arrangement of U.S. and Israeli arms sales during a period of more than a year "was premised on ~~·····~~ ~~·····'ll release,"~~ the com-

Reagan's sanctions were the latest in a long series of actions the United States had taken against Qaddafi. Previous major steps included:

● In May 1978, Carter banned exports to Libya of military aircraft and tractors capable of hauling tanks.

● In September 1979, Carter designated Libya as a country that repeatedly supported terrorist acts. That action had the effect of banning exports of equipment with military uses.

● In October 1981, Reagan barred exports of aviation parts and equipment to Libya.

● In December 1981, during a scare about potential attacks on U.S. officials by Libyan "hit squads," Reagan invalidated the use of U.S. passports for travel to, in or through Libya, except for journalistic purposes. As a result, most of the several thousand Americans then in Libya left. By early 1985, some 1,000 to 1,500 Americans remained, most working for foreign firms, the Libyan national oil company or the Libyan government.

● In March 1982, Reagan barred imports of crude oil from Libya and restricted exports of oil and gas technology to that country. Importation of refined petroleum products from Libya was banned in November 1985.

In addition to those public sanctions, Reagan in 1985 reportedly signed an authorization for the CIA to conduct a covert operation to undermine the Qaddafi regime.

Gulf of Sidra Clash

Libyan attacks on U.S. naval forces in the Gulf of ~~·······~~ ~~·· U.S. military~~ actions against that nation ~~··an.~~

The Israeli response apparently came on July 3, when Kimche — director general of the Foreign Ministry — met with McFarlane in Washington. McFarlane testified that Kimche asked whether the United States was interested in talking to Iranians. To demonstrate their "bona fides," Kimche told McFarlane, the Iranians would try to win freedom for American hostages; the Iranians would need something in return, probably arms.

McFarlane said Reagan agreed to explore the proposal. The president's reaction, McFarlane testified Feb. 21, was "quite enthusiastic and perhaps excessively enthusiastic, given the many uncertainties involved."

McFarlane noted that Reagan's approval came shortly after the conclusion of a Middle East hostage crisis. Two Lebanese men on June 14 had hijacked a TWA airliner, killed an American sailor on board, and held 39 passengers hostage in Beirut. The hostages were released June 30 — possibly after the intervention of Iranian officials. Reagan, according to Muskie, became emotionally involved in that hostage crisis, especially on July 2, when he welcomed the hostages back to the United States and placed flowers on ~~·······~~ Navy diver who had

especially valuable part of the *CQ Almanac* is the "Roll-Call Charts" Appendix. This section gives individual members' chamber roll-call votes on major legislation, listed in chronological order.

Figure 6-16: *Congressional Quarterly Almanac*, 1986, Roll-Call Index

Roll Call Vote Index - 6

Individual Retirement Account - 6-C, 14-C, 23-S, 60-H
Medical deductions - 25-S
Passage - 27-S
Phillips Petroluem Company - 25-S
Small business - 26-S
Steel industry - 25-S
Tax rates - 23-S, 25-26-S
Tax shelters - 24-S
Three year recovery of pension plans - 25-S
Unocal, the Union Oil Company - 25-S
Unpaid taxes, punishment - 27-S
Windfall profits - 32-S
Technology export - 38-H
Teenagers - 51-52-S
Television coverage of Senate - 4-C, 14-C, 4-5-S, 31-S
Tennesee Valley Authority - 64-H
Terrorism - 4-S, 27-S, 44-S, 18-H
Textile Import Quotas - 10-C, 16-C, 76-H
Threshold test ban treaty - 34-S
Tobacco products - 33-S
Trade. *See also* Imports, Exports
Agricultural - 42-S, 40-H
Japan - 38-H
Oil and gas industry - 22-S
Presidential powers - 38-40-H
Romania - 68-H
Trade Bill - 38-40-H
U.S. Trade Representative - 38-H
With communist governments - 36-S

New York Metropolitan Transportation authority - 70-H
On Great Lakes - 90-H
Washington, D.C. mass transit rail - 70-H
Treasury Department appropriations - 74-78-H
Treaties
Convention on Wetlands of International Importance - 55-S
Genocide - 4-S
Inter-American Conventon on Letters Rogatory - 55-S
Patent Cooperation Treaty, 1985 - 55-S
Tax agreement with China - 30-S
United States-United Kingdom Extradition Treaty - 29-S
Trident II missiles - 84-H
Tropical Research Institute - 27-S
Truck licensing - 50-S
Turkey - 44-S

U.N. Convention on Contracts for the International Sale of Goods - 55-S
U.S. Coast Guard - 32-H, 70-H
U.S. Customs Service - 74-78-H, 96-H
U.S. Forest Service - 120-H

Veterans
Benefits for former prisoners of war - 76-H
Employment rights - 48-H
Health care amendments - 76-H
Home loan guarantees - 10-H, 38-H
Readjustment appointment authority - 48-H
Vietnam Veterans Memorial Fund - 44-H
Vietnam Veterans of America - 11-S
Veto. *See* President
Vietnam Veterans Memorial Fund - 44-H
Vietnam Veterans of America Charter - 11-S
VISTA - 48-H, 112-H
Vocational training - 16-S, 48-H, 112-H
Voting studies
Conservative coalition - 41-46-C
Party unity - 29-34-C
Presidential support - 21-27-C
Voting participation - 35-40-C

Washington, D.C. *See* District of Columbia
Water projects
Appropriations - 64-66-H
Authorization - 57-S, 126-H
Clean Water Act - 20-S, 56-S, 34-H, 122-H
Reclamation - 120-H
Resources development - 57-S
Welfare eligibility - 50-S

Although we can assume that aircraft hijacking will be included in the foreign policy section of *CQ Almanac*, the "General Index" tells us which specific pages relate to our topic. There are two page numbers listed under "Air transportation—terrorist attacks" (see Figure 6-14). (Again, drawing a blank when searching this index for "Hijacking", we next tried entries starting with the terms "Air", including "Air transportation" and "Aircraft".) The first page cited, page 390, reports President Reagan's imposition of economic sanctions against Libya in retaliation for the airport attacks at Rome and Vienna. Excerpts of President Reagan's speech announcing the sanctions are given, as well as a brief history of actions the U.S. government has taken against Qaddafi, dating back to 1978 (see Figure 6-15).

The other page referred to in the index, page 440, takes us to a review of the Iran-Contra Affair (see again Figure 6-15). It tells of testimony given to the Tower Commission by Robert McFarland in which he alleges the hostages of TWA Flight 847 were released because of intervention by Iranian officials. The accounts in these two references illustrate two methods of taking action against terrorists: economic sanctions and covert negotiations with terrorists' allies or leaders.

To find a record of votes taken in Congress on legislation relating to terrorism, look in the "Roll Call Vote Index", shown in Figure 6-16. Under "Terrorism" there are three pages cited in the Senate section of the voting charts and one in the House section. On page 18-H (see Figure 6-17) we learn in entry number 54 that the House of Representatives passed bill number HR 4151, a "...bill to authorize $4.4 billion to bolster security at U.S. diplomatic missions and adopt other provisions aimed at combatting international terrorism". The entry also tells us that the bill passed by a 389-7 margin;

Figure 6-17: *Congressional Quarterly Almanac*, 1986, Roll-Call Charts

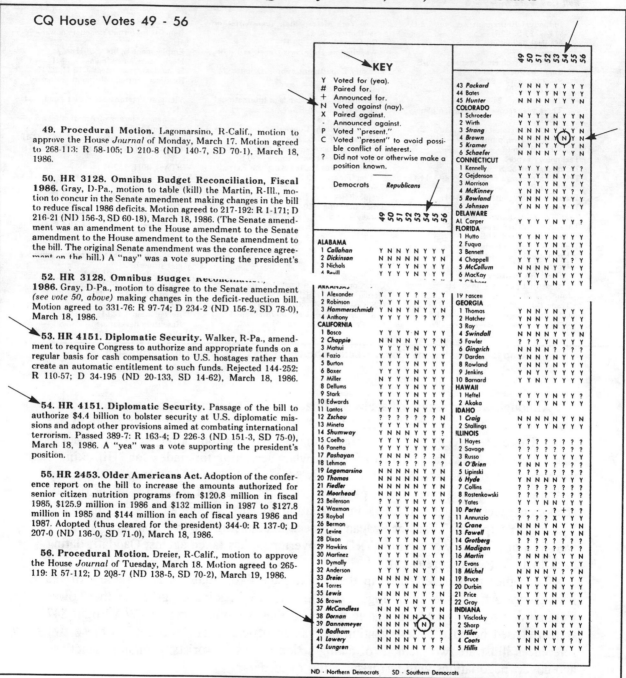

CQ House Votes 49 - 56

KEY

- Y Voted for (yea).
- \# Paired for.
- \+ Announced for.
- N Voted against (nay).
- X Paired against.
- \- Announced against.
- P Voted "present."
- C Voted "present" to avoid possible conflict of interest.
- ? Did not vote or otherwise make a position known.

Democrats *Republicans*

49. Procedural Motion. Lagomarsino, R-Calif., motion to approve the House *Journal* of Monday, March 17. Motion agreed to 268-113: R 58-105; D 210-8 (ND 140-7, SD 70-1), March 18, 1986.

50. HR 3128. Omnibus Budget Reconciliation, Fiscal 1986. Gray, D-Pa., motion to table (kill) the Martin, R-Ill., motion to concur in the Senate amendment making changes in the bill to reduce fiscal 1986 deficits. Motion agreed to 217-192: R 1-171; D 216-21 (ND 156-3, SD 60-18), March 18, 1986. (The Senate amendment was an amendment to the House amendment to the Senate amendment to the House amendment to the Senate amendment to the bill. The original Senate amendment was the conference agreement on the bill.) A "nay" was a vote supporting the president's

52. HR 3128. Omnibus Budget Reconciliation, 1986. Gray, D-Pa., motion to disagree to the Senate amendment *(see vote 50, above)* making changes in the deficit-reduction bill. Motion agreed to 331-76: R 97-74; D 234-2 (ND 156-2, SD 78-0), March 18, 1986.

53. HR 4151. Diplomatic Security. Walker, R-Pa., amendment to require Congress to authorize and appropriate funds on a regular basis for cash compensation to U.S. hostages rather than create an automatic entitlement to such funds. Rejected 144-252: R 110-57; D 34-195 (ND 20-133, SD 14-62), March 18, 1986.

54. HR 4151. Diplomatic Security. Passage of the bill to authorize $4.4 billion to bolster security at U.S. diplomatic missions and adopt other provisions aimed at combating international terrorism. Passed 389-7: R 163-4; D 226-3 (ND 151-3, SD 75-0), March 18, 1986. A "yea" was a vote supporting the president's position.

55. HR 2453. Older Americans Act. Adoption of the conference report on the bill to increase the amounts authorized for senior citizen nutrition programs from $120.8 million in fiscal 1985, $125.9 million in 1986 and $132 million in 1987 to $127.8 million in 1985 and $144 million in each of fiscal years 1986 and 1987. Adopted (thus cleared for the president) 344-0: R 137-0; D 207-0 (ND 136-0, SD 71-0), March 18, 1986.

56. Procedural Motion. Dreier, R-Calif., motion to approve the House *Journal* of Tuesday, March 18. Motion agreed to 265-119: R 57-112; D 208-7 (ND 138-5, SD 70-2), March 19, 1986.

	49	50	51	52	53	54	55	56
ALABAMA								
1 *Callahan*	Y	N	N	Y	N	Y	Y	Y
2 *Dickinson*	N	N	N	N	Y	Y	Y	N
3 Nichols	Y	Y	Y	Y	N	Y	Y	Y
4 *Bevill*	Y	Y	Y	Y	N	Y	Y	Y
ARKANSAS								
1 Alexander	Y	Y	Y	Y	?	?	?	Y
2 Robinson	Y	Y	Y	N	Y	Y	Y	Y
3 *Hammerschmidt*	Y	N	N	Y	N	Y	Y	N
4 Anthony	Y	Y	Y	Y	?	?	Y	?
CALIFORNIA								
1 Bosco	Y	Y	Y	Y	N	Y	Y	Y
2 *Chappie*	N	N	N	N	Y	Y	?	N
3 Matsui	Y	Y	Y	Y	N	Y	Y	Y
4 Fazio	Y	Y	Y	Y	Y	Y	Y	Y
5 Burton	Y	Y	Y	Y	N	Y	Y	Y
6 Boxer	Y	Y	Y	Y	N	Y	Y	Y
7 Miller	N	Y	Y	N	Y	Y	Y	Y
8 Dellums	Y	Y	Y	Y	N	Y	Y	Y
9 Stark	Y	Y	Y	Y	N	Y	Y	Y
10 Edwards	Y	Y	Y	N	Y	?	Y	Y
11 Lantos	Y	Y	Y	Y	N	Y	Y	Y
12 *Zschau*	?	?	?	?	?	?	?	N
13 Mineta	Y	Y	Y	Y	N	Y	Y	Y
14 *Shumway*	Y	N	N	Y	N	Y	Y	?
15 Coelho	Y	Y	Y	Y	N	Y	Y	Y
16 Panetta	Y	Y	Y	Y	N	Y	Y	Y
17 *Pashayan*	Y	N	N	?	?	?	N	
18 Lehman	?	?	?	?	?	?	?	?
19 *Lagomarsino*	N	N	N	N	Y	Y	Y	N
20 *Thomas*	N	N	N	N	Y	Y	Y	N
21 *Fiedler*	N	N	N	N	Y	Y	N	
22 *Moorhead*	N	N	N	N	Y	Y	Y	N
23 Beilenson	?	Y	Y	Y	N	Y	Y	Y
24 Waxman	Y	Y	Y	Y	N	Y	Y	Y
25 Roybal	Y	Y	Y	Y	N	Y	Y	Y
26 Berman	Y	Y	Y	Y	N	Y	Y	Y
27 Levine	Y	Y	Y	Y	N	Y	Y	Y
28 Dixon	Y	Y	Y	Y	N	Y	Y	Y
29 Hawkins	N	Y	Y	N	Y	Y	Y	Y
30 Martinez	Y	Y	Y	Y	N	Y	Y	Y
31 Dymally	Y	Y	Y	Y	N	Y	Y	Y
32 Anderson	Y	Y	Y	Y	N	Y	Y	Y
33 *Dreier*	N	N	N	N	Y	Y	N	
34 Torres	Y	Y	Y	Y	N	Y	Y	Y
35 *Lewis*	N	N	N	Y	Y	Y	?	N
36 Brown	Y	Y	Y	Y	N	Y	Y	Y
37 *McCandless*	N	N	N	Y	Y	Y	N	
38 *Dornan*	?	N	N	N	N	Y	N	
39 *Dannemeyer*	N	N	N	N	(N)	Y	N	
40 *Badham*	N	N	N	N	Y	Y	Y	
41 *Lowery*	N	N	N	N	Y	Y	?	
42 *Lungren*	N	N	N	N	Y	N	N	

	49	50	51	52	53	54	55	56
43 *Packard*	Y	N	N	Y	Y	Y	Y	Y
44 *Bates*	Y	Y	Y	Y	N	Y	Y	Y
45 *Hunter*	N	N	N	N	Y	Y	Y	N
COLORADO								
1 Schroeder	N	Y	Y	Y	N	Y	Y	N
2 Wirth	Y	Y	Y	Y	N	Y	Y	Y
3 *Strang*	N	N	N	N	Y	Y	Y	N
4 *Brown*	N	N	N	N	Y	(N)	Y	N
5 *Kramer*	N	Y	N	Y	Y	Y	Y	N
6 *Schaefer*	N	N	N	N	Y	Y	Y	N
CONNECTICUT								
1 Kennelly	Y	Y	Y	Y	N	Y	Y	?
2 Gejdenson	Y	Y	Y	Y	N	Y	Y	Y
3 Morrison	Y	Y	Y	Y	N	Y	Y	Y
4 *McKinney*	Y	N	N	Y	N	Y	?	?
5 *Rowland*	Y	N	N	Y	N	Y	Y	Y
6 *Johnson*	Y	N	N	Y	N	Y	Y	Y
DELAWARE								
AL Carper	Y	Y	Y	Y	N	Y	Y	?
FLORIDA								
1 Hutto	Y	Y	N	Y	N	Y	Y	Y
2 Fuqua	Y	Y	Y	Y	N	Y	Y	Y
3 Bennett	Y	Y	Y	Y	N	Y	Y	Y
4 Chappell	Y	Y	Y	Y	N	Y	?	Y
5 *McCollum*	N	N	N	N	Y	Y	Y	Y
6 MacKay	Y	Y	Y	Y	N	Y	Y	Y
7 *Gibbons*	Y	Y	Y	Y	N	Y	Y	Y
19 *Fascell*	.	.	.	.	.	.		
GEORGIA								
1 Thomas	Y	N	N	Y	N	Y	Y	Y
2 Hatcher	Y	N	N	Y	N	Y	Y	Y
3 Ray	Y	Y	Y	Y	N	Y	Y	Y
4 *Swindall*	N	N	N	Y	Y	Y	Y	N
5 Fowler	?	?	?	Y	N	Y	Y	Y
6 *Gingrich*	N	N	N	N	?	?	?	?
7 *Darden*	Y	N	N	Y	N	Y	Y	Y
8 Rowland	Y	N	N	Y	N	Y	Y	Y
9 Jenkins	Y	N	N	Y	Y	Y	Y	Y
10 Barnard	Y	N	Y	Y	N	Y	Y	Y
HAWAII								
1 Heftel	Y	Y	Y	Y	N	Y	Y	?
2 Akaka	Y	Y	Y	Y	N	Y	Y	Y
IDAHO								
1 *Craig*	N	N	N	N	Y	Y	Y	N
2 Stallings	Y	Y	Y	Y	N	Y	Y	Y
ILLINOIS								
1 Hayes	?	?	?	?	?	?	?	?
2 Savage	?	?	?	?	?	?	?	?
3 Russo	Y	Y	Y	Y	N	Y	Y	Y
4 *O'Brien*	Y	N	N	Y	?	?	?	Y
5 Lipinski	?	?	?	?	?	?	?	?
6 *Hyde*	Y	N	N	N	Y	Y	Y	Y
7 Collins	?	?	?	?	?	?	?	?
8 Rostenkowski	?	?	?	?	?	?	?	?
9 Yates	Y	Y	Y	N	Y	Y	Y	Y
10 *Porter*	?	-	-	-	?	+	?	?
11 Annunzio	?	?	?	X	Y	Y	Y	Y
12 *Crane*	N	N	N	N	Y	Y	N	
13 *Fawell*	N	N	N	N	Y	Y	Y	N
14 *Grotberg*	?	?	?	?	?	?	?	?
15 *Madigan*	?	?	?	?	?	?	?	?
16 *Martin*	?	N	N	N	Y	Y	Y	N
17 Evans	Y	Y	Y	Y	N	Y	Y	Y
18 *Michel*	N	N	N	N	Y	?	?	N
19 Bruce	Y	Y	Y	Y	N	Y	Y	Y
20 Durbin	N	Y	Y	Y	N	Y	Y	Y
21 Price	Y	Y	Y	Y	N	Y	Y	Y
22 Gray	Y	Y	Y	Y	N	Y	Y	Y
INDIANA								
1 Visclosky	Y	Y	Y	Y	N	Y	Y	Y
2 Sharp	Y	Y	Y	Y	N	Y	Y	Y
3 *Hiler*	N	N	N	N	N	N	Y	N
4 *Coats*	Y	N	N	Y	Y	Y	?	Y
5 Hillis	Y	N	Y	Y	N	Y	Y	Y

ND - Northern Democrats   SD - Southern Democrats

that a "yea" vote supported the position announced by the President; that the partisan division was 163-4 among Republicans and 226-3 among Democrats; and that the regional division among Democrats was 151-3 among northern Democrats and 75-0 among southern Democrats.

Notice that entry number 53 also relates to HR 4151, reporting that an amendment to the bill offered by Walker (R-Pa.) was rejected. It is not unusual for several votes to be taken on a particular bill—some votes might be on parliamentary motions (to table, to send back to committee); other votes might be to amend or for final passage. These votes may be on the same day or across days or weeks of a congressional session.

To determine the identity of the seven nay voters who opposed final passage of the Diplomatic Security bill, we first look at the "KEY" at the top of the Roll Call Vote Chart in order to find that "N" is the symbol used for nay votes. We can now look at the columns labelled "54" in the accompanying vote chart (see again Figure 6-17). Scanning the first page of this CQ roll call vote chart reveals the first two of the seven nay voters to be: Dannemeyer (R-CA, 39th) (i.e., Republican from California's 39th district) and Brown (R-CO, 4th).

News Digests

We discussed in Chapter 3, "Using Periodical and Newspaper Articles", how to find periodical and newspaper articles on aircraft hijacking. However, it is sometimes more convenient to use a news digest to get a brief overview of an incident and its conclusion or follow-up developments. Your library is most likely to have *Facts on File: World News Digest with Index*. It may also have available a similar British service, *Keesing's Record of World Events* (formerly, *Keesing's Contemporary Archives*).

Facts on File gives you a weekly summary of the world's events in international relations, U.S. affairs, other world events (internal affairs outside the U.S.), and other events in sports, entertainment, obituaries of notable persons, and so on. Indexes are issued semi-monthly and cumulate throughout the year. Cumulative indexes have also been issued at five-year intervals beginning with 1946. Index entries are arranged in chronological order within subject headings.

Using the *Facts on File* annual index for 1986, "Hijackings" refers us to "Aviation". Here we find a subdivision, "Hijackings & Bombings", which lists several dozen entries (see Figure 6-18). Looking at the index entry for "Canadian antiterror measures set", we are told the date of the event (10 March) and the page, margin letter, and column number of the news summary (234D2). This account tells of a special unit of the Royal Canadian Mounted Police newly created to combat terrorism (see again Figure 6-18). The news digest quotes a Canadian government official's description of his government's "...hard-line policy on terrorism. 'We won't make deals, pay ransoms, release prisoners or make other concessions that will encourage terrorists.'" Other index entries take you to news summaries of actions taken by aviation business and labor groups, as well as by individual travellers, in response to aircraft hijackings and bombings.

A CONCLUDING REMARK: CONSULT EXPERTS WHEN NECESSARY

Regardless of what type of biographical, statistical, or factual question you may have, there is probably a reference source that will provide the answer. However, because there are hundreds, if not thousands, of reference publications, you will often

Figure 6-18: *Facts On File*, 1986 Index and April 4, 1986 Issue

NYS sets reforms 6-24, 466A2
Catastrophic-illness plan unveiled 11-20,

Argentina metalworkers strike ends 7-21,
731G2
Canada W Coast ports closed
10-6—10-8, 756D3
S Africa GM workers strike 10-29, 826B3
GM sets 11 plant closings 11-6, 855E1
GM workers S Africa strike ends 11-18,
971F3
Toyota sets Ky plant pact 11-25, 905C2
Mergers & Acquisitions
UK ends Austin Rover/Ford sale talks,
confrms Unipart deal 1-6, 118C3
GM acquires Lotus 1-22, 100F3-101A1
Uniroyal, Goodrich set tire venture 1-28,
145C1
BL units sale fuels pol dispute
2-20—3-25, GM talks collapse 3-21,

Merrill Lynch sets Fruehauf deal,
Edelman bid 5-6—8-22, 723G3
Budget sale to mgmt group set 8-11,
641E2
Ex-Cell-O accepts Textron bid 8-19,
724B2
Libya sells Fiat stake 9-23, 708G1-E2
GM sets S Africa unit sale 10-20, reactn
10-21—11-6, 826B3, 827F1
Alfa Romeo OKs Fiat takeover, rejcts
Ford bid 11-6, 892B1
Natl Car Rental buyout set 12-23, 980D2
Obituaries
Kawamata, Katsuji 3-29, 240D3
Plant Issues—*See 'Labor & Plant Is-*
sues' above
Pollution Issues
Acid rain curbs introduced in House 4-10,
318A3

Driving habits surveyed 4-30, 355A2
Ford agrmt scored by GAO 6-10,
526G2-C3
NHTSA drops GM probe 8-15, 723D3
Speed limit rise passes Sen 9-24, 704B1
Speed limit rise dies in Cong 10-18,
813E3
Mass, Neb seat belt initiatives fail 11-4,
842A2
Ford, Chrysler set air bags for '90 12-11,
980D3
Audi recall asked 12-23, 980G2
NHTSA reopens GM probe 12-30, 980C3
Statistics (U.S.)
Producer price indexes described 5B3
Consumer credit data described 15D3

AVALOS, Col. Omar Napoleon
Exchng proposed 7-24, 662C1
AVEDIAN, Armen G.

AVIANCA Airlines
Sec chief finds drugs 8-30, slain 9-1,
994F2
AVIATION—*See also airline, aircraft com-*
pany names
Reagan budget proposals 2-5, 73D3
Packwood unveils tax plan 3-13, 168A3
Tax reform bill impact assessed 5-9,
351G1, A2
Communicatns satellite launch planned
5-12, 389C2
747s chosen as 'AF 1' 6-5, 565E1
Airlines ruled outside disability law by Sup
Ct 6-27, 527C1
Pan Am shuttle planned 7-9, 523D2
LTV files bankruptcy 7-17, 522A2
Airline smoking ban urged 8-13, 641B3

'87 space plane authrzn clears Cong
10-17, signed 10-18, 815F1
'87 space plane authrzn clears Cong
10-18, 815C1; vetoed 11-14, 872B1
Voyager circles world 12-14—12-23,
958C2
McDonnell Douglas plans MD-11 jet
12-30, 979A1
Accidents—*See ACCIDENTS—Avia-*
tion
Appointments & Resignations
Icahn named TWA chrmn 1-3, 191B2
Frontier exec shifts rptd 1-30, 88D2
Borman quits as Eastn chrmn/CEO 6-2,
443F2
Westn Air pres/COO named 8-5, 631F3
Lorenzo named Eastn Air chrmn 10-17,
824C1
Awards & Honors
Lindbergh given Order of Merit 2-12,

Fare Issues
Cross-country fares cut 1-2—1-8, 39D1
IATA scores Australia discounts 1-2,
Qantas slashes Eur fares 1-14, 98F1
Sr citizen 10% discount offered 1-15,
39B2
People cuts fares 30% 6-21, 523B2
Canada hike fuels July inflatn 8-22,
625G2
World halts scheduled svc 9-3, 655E1
EC deregulatn fails 11-11, 12-15, 944B3
Foreign Developments—*See also*
other subheads in this section
India-Pak pact signed 1-10, 32G2
UK plans airports flotatn 1-16, 235E3
Madrid airport security tightened 1-17,

Panama army cmdr implicated in money
laundering 6-12, 457B2
Iran frees Air France employee 6-25,
519E2
Commonwealth forms anti-apartheid
sanctns 8-2—8-5, 578E1
Libya gets embargoed jets 8-8—8-15,
651D2
S Africa sanctns OKd by US Sen 8-15,
594A2
BA ordrs 16 Boeing 747s 8-15, 620G1
Rolls-Royce wins BA bid 8-15, 624B1
W Ger sets refugee curbs 8-27, 658E2
Libya boycott sought by US 9-1—9-5,
651G1
Indonesia bars Australia AF 9-4, 732B3
UK, US sign 'Bermuda II' pact 9-11,
691A3
S Africa sanctns clear Cong 9-12,
Reagan vetoes 9-26, 697F1
CR airstrip closed 9-24, 789B1
US S Africa sanctns veto overridden
10-2, 765C2
UK bans Libya flights 10-27, 815B2
US tech trade gap seen 10-20, 817B1
EC deregulatn fails 11-11, 12-15, 944G2
US sets Syria sanctns 11-14, 867B1
Hijackings & Bombings
Rome airport raid retaliatn mulled
1-1—1-10, 1A1-3A1; for subsequent
developments, see ITALY—Rome
Airport Raid
Vienna airport raid retaliatn mulled
1-1—1-10, 1A1-3A1; for subsequent
developments, see AUSTRIA—Vienna
Airport Raid
'85 TWA, Egyptair med team alerts rptd
1-4, 224E3
Canada airports bomb alert 1-16—1-21,
hoax admitted 1-22, 42D2-C3
Pak convicts Sikhs in '81, '84 hijackings
1-20, 44B3
France gets Aerolinte jet bomb hoax, calls
for suspect's release
US chrgs Leb deal 3-13, 166F1
China sentncs Aeroflot '85 hijacker 3-4,
239B1
Canada antiterror measures set 3-10,
234D2
TWA Rome-Athens jet bomb kills 4
Amers 4-2, 271A1-F2; for subsequent
developments, see TRANS World
Airlines
US tourists avoid Eur 4-14—5-29; UK
issues plea 5-23, rebound seen
6-5—6-8, 447F3-448A1
TWA scraps Cairo-Rome-Athens route
4-14, 448D3
Pilots assn OKs antiterror boycotts 4-15,
448D3

Suriname rebels hijack jet 10-18, forgn
svc halted 11-5, 950G2
S Africa Airways, Air Malawi Zimbabwe
ofcs torched 10-21, 786B3
El Al bomb plot Israeli role hinted
10-25, 783A3
TWA employe drug test rule dropped 1-7,
Brit Caledonian sets job cuts 5-15,
381G2-B3, 448D1
BA sets job freeze 5-20, 448D2
Australia TWU bonus agrmt set 7-1,
airline pilots strike averted 7-8, 590F1,
B2
Argentina pilots strike 7-1—7-22, 731G2
Frontier shut 8-24, bankruptcy filed 8-28,
637D2
Eastn sets layoffs, cutbacks 9-2, 655A1
World sets firings 9-3, 655D1
BA pilot hiring rptd 9-19, 708D1
Air controllers plan new union 9-23,
858A1
UAL stewardess suit setld 10-7, 905D1
Boeing machinists OK pact 10-8,
773G3-773B1
Mergers & Acquisitions
Icahn/TWA purchase terms revised 1-3,
191B2
NWA to buy Republic 1-23, 81F1
Eastn OKs Tex Air bid 2-24, 131G2
TWA sets Ozark purchase 2-27, 191G1
UK delays Brit Airways sale 3-12, 235C3
DC airport leases, landing-slot sales bar
OKd by Sen 4-11, 353C1
NW, TWA set Pars deal 7-7, 523A3
Eastn, Tex Air terms set 7-9, 523C2
Frontier sale to UAL set 7-10, 523F1
TWA, Ozark merger opposed 7-15,
523E2-A3
Quebecair sale set 7-31, 590C3
Republic sale to NWA OKd 7-31, 725F1
Canadair sale to Bombardier set 8-18,
625F1
Ex-Cell-O accepts Textron bid 8-19,
Delta, Westn set merger 9-9, 724E2-F3
UK resets Brit Airways sale 9-11, 691G2
Tex Air sets People purchase 9-15, Eastn
merger OKd 9-18, 688F1-B3
Virgin Group flotatn set 10-19, 961E3
Goodyr unit sale planned 11-3, 887F3
Unisys sells aerospace unit to Honeywell
11-16, 939A2
Eastn clears Tex Air sale 11-25, 890E3
PWA sets CP Air purchase 12-2, 993C1
Canada sets Quebec airports merger
12-4, 948C2
USAir sets PSA purchase 12-8, 940A3
Lear Siegler buyout set 12-17, 980C1
UAL sets Hilton Intl purchase 12-23,
980F2
NWA/People merger completed 12-30,

---

minister, April 1 announced a C$400 million (US$288 million) program to aid the province's slumping oil industry.

About 90% of Canada's oil came from Alberta. With the sharp decline in world oil prices, Alberta crude had plunged to about C$17 (US$12) a barrel from C$33 (US$24) a barrel at the start of 1986. [See p. 219C3]

Zaozirny announced two measures to help producers, effective April 1.

One measure allowed producers to claim a credit of 50% of the cost of drilling exploratory wells on government-owned land in 1986 against royalties payable to the government after April 1, 1987. In effect, it permitted a producer to withhold C$500,000 (US$359,500) for each C$1 million (US$719 million) in royalty payments, up to an aggregate of C$300 million (US$216 million).

The second measure raised the existing royalty tax credit to 95% from 75%, to a maximum of C$3 million (US$2.1 million) a year, until Dec. 31, 1986. Zaozirny estimated that the measure could save Alberta's small producers and investors about C$100 million (US$72 million).

Alberta was also seeking an end to Ottawa's 10% tax on oil and natural gas revenues. Under the 1985 Western Accord, the tax was scheduled to be phased out in 1988.

Terrorist Hunted—Some

---

vacation March 31. His office issued a statement saying the government was "pleased" that the hunger strike was over. □

RCMP Forming Antiterror Unit. Federal Solicitor General Perrin Beatty March 10 announced that the Royal Canadian Mounted Police was creating a special unit to combat terrorism.

The unit, called the Special Emergency Response Team (SERT), was to be based near Ottawa and would be transported by the Canadian Forces to crisis spots in Canada.

Beatty did not say whether SERT would operate outside Canada if, for example, Canadians were taken hostage by terrorists in another country.

SERT was to be composed of two groups of about 24 Mounties each. The groups were to take turns on alert during alternate months.

Beatty explained that SERT members would undergo "constant training, constant drill and constant testing."

He estimated that it would cost about C$15.6 million (US$11 million) to create SERT.

Beatty said SERT's creation would underscore Canada's hard-line policy on terrorism. "We won't make deals, pay ransoms, release prisoners or make other concessions that will encourage terrorists."

April 1 and took Rahming hostage in her office. From that office, he telephoned local radio and television stations demanding aid for the homeless in Ontario in exchange for Rahming's release.

Clifford D. W. Maltby, 39, a convict on parole for a fraud offense, was arrested in the incident.

The Bahamian High Commission had been lightly guarded because it was not considered a "high risk" embassy. In the wake of the incident, the RCMP promised beefed-up security at foreign missions throughout the country.

In a further development, Solicitor General Perrin Beatty April 2 called for news organizations to join him in formulating voluntary guidelines on press coverage of hostage or terrorist situations. Beatty, who accused the gunman of being a publicity-seeker, noted that the assailant had a radio and was able to monitor police activity at the scene by listening to the on-the-spot news reports. □

Rail Safety Crackdown Ordered. Federal Transport Minister Donald Mazankowski Feb. 16 ordered a crackdown on railroad safety in the wake of 10 accidents since the start of 1986.

In the most recent mishaps:

■ A Via Rail Canada passenger train collided with a Canadian National Railways freight train near Hinton, Alberta Feb. 8, killing 23 people. [See p. 160E2]

Twenty-six people were killed by a

---

need to consult with the expert on reference sources: a reference librarian. Hopefully, studying this chapter has provided you the skills to locate such sources on your own. On the other hand, if an honest effort on your part fails to produce useful results, by all means ask for help. Asking a reference librarian for assistance is not an admission of ignorance as much as it is a sign of good judgment. To consult someone knowledgeable about library reference sources when you are not sure how to proceed will save much time and ease unnecessary frustration.

SUMMARY

1. When searching for biographical information—as with practically any type of research—the materials you need to examine are of two types: finding aids and actual sources.

2. Statistical information allows you to efficiently describe complex phenomena and to make valid inferences about their cause and effect. However, when comparing statistics, it is crucial to be sure that they were collected in the same manner and for the same subject population. Otherwise, you are likely to arrive at unwarranted conclusions about the nature, cause, and/or consequence of the phenomenon measured by your statistics.

3. Almanacs and news digests provide quick access to specific facts and chronologies concerning your topic.

CHAPTER 7

COMPUTER DATABASE SEARCHING

THE DEVELOPMENT OF THE DATABASE INDUSTRY

Many of the finding aids—catalogs and indexes—we have introduced throughout this book are also available in *machine-readable* format stored in computer files.[1] Such machine-readable files are usually referred to as databases.[2] These computer files are accessible through keyboard commands that allow you to search, view on a monitor, or print out a paper copy of the information in the file that you request.

Every finding aid—printed or machine-readable—is a compilation of *document descriptions* (or *records*) composed of parts or *fields*. In the simplest case, such as *Readers' Guide* or *Social Sciences Index*, the document description is limited to a bibliographic reference. In more complex indexes, such as the printed *United States Political Science Documents* (USPSD), the document description includes the bibliographic reference and an abstract.

Like many online finding aids, the online USPSD document descriptions add the subject headings (or descriptors) used to index that reference. The document descriptions in online finding aids may also contain author affiliation, publication language, document type (e.g., monograph, periodical article, or government document), and so on. Most of these document description fields are searchable online. A search of the online USPSD will be illustrated later in this chapter.

Although the databases we focus on in this chapter are bibliographic ones, there are also statistical and directory databases, and even databases providing the full text of articles. An example of an online statistical database is *CENDATA*, which contains selected statistical data issued by the U.S. Bureau of the Census. The *Encyclopedia of*

---

[1]Table 3-1, in Chapter 3, "Using Periodical and Newspaper Articles", lists those indexes most commonly used by undergraduate political science students and for each index tells which formats are available (print, CD-ROM, and online).

[2]In a broader sense, "database" is sometimes used generically to refer to any set of information, whether printed or machine-readable. In this chapter, when we refer to database, we mean a file of information stored in a computer.

Associations is a directory available in both print and online formats. A large volume of full-text online databases is available in the legal, medical, and business fields. Beyond those content areas, the undergraduate political science student may need to search full-text documents in two other areas—encyclopedias and daily news reports. An example of a full-text encyclopedia database is *Academic American Encyclopedia*. In the daily news category of full-text databases are wire services—such as United Press International and Reuters—many major metropolitan and national newspapers, and a weekly news digest—*Facts on File*.

The computer database industry's service to the general public essentially got started in the 1970s and experienced tremendous growth during the 1980s. The *Directory of Online Databases* listed 400 databases in their 1979/80 issue and 5026 databases in the July 1991 issue. Three interrelated changes in computer technology produced this revolution. First, during the 1970s most publishers replaced older technology with computers for typesetting and indexing their books and periodicals. Second, hardware and software innovations caused a significant reduction in data storage costs. These changes encouraged the production of a large and growing volume of machine-readable information. Third, computer terminals and microcomputers became available to the general public and academic users at an affordable cost. Hence, more people could now access that ever-expanding volume of machine-readable information. You may be one of the growing number of undergraduate students who owns or has access to a microcomputer or computer terminal. If so, you may already have some experience with online computer searching through *gateways* (EasyNet, CompuServe, etc.) or *end-user systems* (BRS After Dark, CompuServe, Knowledge Index, etc.)[3]

TWO TYPES OF DATABASE ACCESS IN LIBRARIES

Online Database Searching

Your library may offer online access to databases stored on a *main-frame computer* locally or hundreds of miles away.[4] In order to use such online information services, you will probably request the assistance of a librarian. The librarian will consult with you about your subject in order to choose the appropriate database(s) and the correct terminology to use in searching that database. The search is conducted using a computer

---

[3]A gateway is an intermediary computer service that provides an interface to other remote online services or databases with a common command language to aid in selecting and searching those databases. In contrast, an end-user service is provided by individual database vendors and offers simplified, menu-driven access to the databases resident on their in-house computers. CompuServe provides both a gateway to other remote online databases as well as end-user service to databases stored in its own computers.

[4]Until recently, mainframe computers were clearly distinguished from minicomputers and microcomputers on the bases of the mainframe's: 1) significantly larger computational and storage capacities and 2) ability to handle multiple, simultaneous users. Recent improvements in both minicomputers and microcomputers make these distinctions less valid, but people still use the term "mainframe" to denote a large computer with multi-user access.

terminal or microcomputer connected to the host computer of the online information service.

Three major remote database vendors (sometimes called host computer services) used by most university libraries are Dialog Information Services (Dialog), BRS Information Technologies (BRS), and FirstSearch on OCLC.[5] These companies contract with database producers, such as the publishers of *PAIS International in Print* (PAIS), to load a copy of the data into the vendor's computer. The vendors allow authorized users to search this and other databases using a common command language. The first two vendors charge users according to the time spent on the system, plus a charge for each record or citation printed out while FirstSearch charges a flat fee per search, regardless of time online and citations located. Ask your reference librarian about which bibliographic and full-text databases relevant to political science are available in your library.

CD-ROM Database Searching

Another form of computer database searching that your library may offer uses the compact disk read-only memory system, generally referred to as CD-ROM.[6] These microcomputer systems are so user-friendly that your library may have them set up for you to use on your own by simply following a set of menu-driven instructions. Some CD-ROM microcomputer systems offer the more sophisticated searching capabilities often found in online computer searching. Others are simpler, closer in search capabilities to their print counterparts. Some of the simpler ones are discussed in Chapter 3—namely, the Infotrac System (using databases such as *General Periodicals Index: Academic Library Edition*) and *NewsBank*. For our discussion in this chapter, we are interested in the more sophisticated CD-ROM indexes.

Besides the hardware differences between online and CD-ROM searching systems, the other major difference between the two concerns user charges. While remote database online searching systems typically involve connect-time charges that may or may not be passed on to you as the user, in contrast, CD-ROM searching systems are usually cost-free to the user.[7]

---

[5]There are many other database vendors whose services may be available at your library. The July 1991 issue of *Directory of Online Databases* lists 731 such vendors worldwide.

[6]You may already have a compact disk player for pre-recorded music. Other forms of information are also stored on CDs. Regardless of what is stored on them, most CDs now are read-only memory devices—that is, unlike magnetic tape on reels or cassettes, CD-ROMs cannot be erased and reused for recording new information. However, this laser technology is also changing rapidly. You may soon be able to buy CD recorders that work like tape decks capable of recording and re-recording music or information on the same CD.

[7]CD-ROM searching systems are, of course, not free of cost to your library. Like the books and periodicals that you use free of charge, CD-ROM databases must be purchased by the library and can be quite expensive.

At the beginning of Chapter 1, we discussed the importance of defining a manageable search topic. In moving on to searching the library catalog and print indexes, we showed the necessity of first identifying all the major concepts included in your topic and then further identifying other synonymous or related terms that also might be used by this or other finding aids to list sources that include information on your topic. In this section, we go beyond these two skills to additional search techniques useful in computer searching.

Boolean Logic

Boolean logic is a set of rules for linking concepts together into a descriptive profile. Such a profile can then be used to search a machine-readable finding aid for all document records that match the profile's particular combination of concepts. Each successful profile statement results in a set of records matching that profile.

Boolean logic was initially developed by George Boole (1815-1864). You may already have been introduced to this analytical method in an algebra or logic course. Boolean logic is often visually represented using Venn diagrams, developed by John Venn (1834-1923). Figures 7-1, 7-2, and 7-3 illustrate such Venn diagrams for each of the three Boolean operators.

Boolean logic uses the operators "and", "or", and "not" to link, combine, or exclude terms that describe concepts. There are some simple rules that govern the use of Boolean operators.

The "or" operator. One rule is that synonymous or closely related terms describing a single concept are linked by the "or" operator. Each additional link of terms using "or" potentially expands or increases the results of the search—in other words, enlarging the set of document records found.

For example, one basic concept in our sample topic is the seizure of commercial airlines, which is often described by the two synonymous terms, "hijacking" and "air piracy".[8] The search statement—HIJACKING or AIR PIRACY—can be used to retrieve all records from a database that includes either or both of these two character strings. Let us call this group of hijacking records "set one". It is illustrated by the Venn diagram in Figure 7-1. The shading indicates that all document records containing the word "hijacking" and all records containing the phrase "air piracy" are included in "set one". Hence, every time you use the "or" operator, you are expanding your search by linking terms inclusively.

The "and" operator. A second rule of Boolean logic is that terms describing different concepts are linked by the "and" operator. Each use of the "and" operator restricts the search and potentially reduces the number of document records retrieved as a set.

---

[8]A closely related term is "skyjacking". In an actual search, you would want to add it to this search statement. However, to keep our explanation and diagrams simple, we have omitted this (and other possible) search terms.

Figure 7-1: Venn Diagram Illustrating "OR" Operator

Set 1 =

HIJACKING OR AIR PIRACY

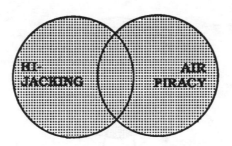

The 'OR' operator links two terms of similar meaning inclusively, hence, all records will be retrieved that contain either or both terms.

Using the 'OR' operator expands the search.

A second basic concept in our sample topic involves the prevention of aircraft hijacking. In order to limit "set one"—produced by the previous search statement profiling aircraft hijacking—to exclude all records that do not also deal with the prevention of aircraft hijacking, we use the following statement—SET ONE and PREVENTION.[9] The resulting group of records is "set two". It is illustrated by the Venn diagram in Figure 7-2. The shaded area portrays the records of "set one" that also contain the word "prevention". In contrast, the unshaded areas represent records that contain at least one term from "set one" or the word "prevention"—but not both. The benefit of limiting your search with the "and" operator is that it narrows the search to those records most relevant to your narrowed topic.

The "not" operator. A third rule of Boolean logic is that the operator "not" can be used to specifically exclude term(s). If you want to exclude document records dealing with the hijacking of the *Achille Lauro*, you can use the following statement— SET TWO not *ACHILLE LAURO*. The resulting groups of records is "set three". It is illustrated by the Venn diagram in Figure 7-3. The shaded area shows those records that contain the words "hijacking" or "air piracy" and "prevention" but not "*Achille Lauro*".

Special caution is needed when using the "not" operator. The "not" operator is included in this discussion because it exists. However, we strongly recommend that you

---

[9]Notice that Boolean operators can be used to link previously created sets of citations as well as terms defining concepts.

Figure 7-2: Venn Diagram Illustrating "AND" Operator

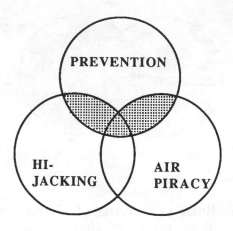

Set 2 =

Set 1 (HIJACKING OR AIR PIRACY) AND PREVENTION

The 'AND' operator links the intersection of two terms of dissimilar meaning, hence, only those records will be retrieved that contain both terms.

Using the 'AND' operator narrows the search.

use it only in rare circumstances—for example when your search retrieves an overwhelming number of records and you can afford to risk excluding some that may be relevant. The danger in using the "not" operator is that it often results in excluding relevant document records unintentionally. For instance, a reference that compares ship hijacking to aircraft hijacking might mention the *Achille Lauro* incident, and would therefore be excluded from "set three" in Figure 7-3.

Word Proximity

Linking search terms with the "and" operator can be thought of as a word-proximity search in which the computer searches for any occurrence of the "and"ed terms anywhere in a document description. Searching that looks for character strings in any part of a document description (as opposed to searching only certain fields, such as titles or subject descriptors) is known as *free-text searching*. In most cases, you can start and end with this type of search.

Figure 7-3: Venn Diagram Illustrating "NOT" Operator

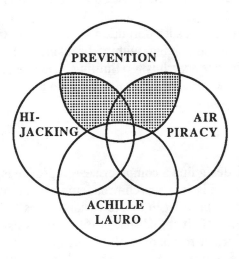

Set 3 =

Set 2 ((HIJACKING OR AIR PIRACY) AND (PREVENTION))
NOT ACHILLE LAURO

The 'NOT' operator eliminates unacceptable or irrelevant terms.

Using the 'NOT' operator narrows the search.

However, if too many or irrelevant records are retrieved by such a search profile, a more restrictive definition of word proximity may be necessary. Such situations require you to define how close together the search terms must be in the document description in order for that database entry to be included in the resulting search set. Three word-proximity patterns are commonly used: adjacent, same-sentence, and same-field proximity.

Adjacent-word proximity. For instance, when we search for "air piracy", we want the computer to search document descriptions for occurrences of these two words, in this order, with no intervening words. Depending upon which online service or CD-ROM system you are using, you may need to indicate this word proximity pattern with a special symbol. For example, in BRS this particular word proximity pattern would be expressed as "air adj piracy", while in Dialog it would be entered as "air(w)piracy", and in GPO on SilverPlatter (CD-ROM) the same word proximity pattern is indicated simply by "air piracy".

Same-sentence proximity. A somewhat broader definition of word proximity is to search for the occurrence of search terms appearing within the same sentence of a document description. For example, we may want to include in our search set any document description that includes both "hijacking" and "prevention" in the same sentence. The BRS command for this search is "hijacking with prevention", while the Dialog command is "hijacking(s)prevention". In any database that allows free-text searching, word order is irrelevant—using our example, the words "hijacking" and "prevention" can be entered in any order with the same results.

Same-field proximity. A broader definition of word proximity is to search for the occurrence of search terms appearing within the same field or part of a document description. If a same-sentence search is too limiting, you can always broaden to a same-field search. In BRS such a command is "hijacking same prevention", while in Dialog the command is "hijacking(f)prevention".

Truncation

A final technique for designing a computer search profile is to *truncate* (or shorten) terms—when appropriate. This is a search-broadening technique which searches for a word "stem" that you define in order to locate variant forms (e.g., singular or plural) or spellings (e.g., American or British) of that word. This is usually more efficient than "or"ing together all the variant forms or spellings of that word.

The simplest example is truncating at the end of the singular form of your term, so that your search will locate both singular and plural forms. For example, in BRS the command is "terrorist$" instead of "terrorist or terrorists". In Dialog the same command is "terrorist?".

In order to locate the many other variant forms or spellings of your search term, you may need to truncate before the end of that term. For example, in BRS the command "terroris$" would retrieve occurrences of "terrorism" in addition to "terrorist" or "terrorists".

However, too much truncating or shortening of a search term can lead to retrieving terms irrelevant to your search. For example, truncating "terrorist" to "terror$" or "terror?" (depending upon which retrieval service you use) could, in some databases, retrieve records dealing with many other forms of human terror (e.g., fear of heights).

A Comparison of Manual and Computer Searching

There are both advantages and disadvantages to searching a finding aid by computer instead of manually. When a catalog or index is available to you in both print and machine-readable form, there are certain judgments you need to make in order to decide whether to search that finding aid manually (in the print volumes) or use the computer-searching alternative. Such judgments entail discovering and measuring the relative limitations of each format. Since most of the information in the preceding chapters deals with manual searching, we now turn to the special characteristics (good and bad) of computer database searching. In discussing these general advantages and shortcomings, we are referring to either online or CD-ROM searching systems, unless we specify otherwise. Following these general comments, we take a closer look at selected online and CD-ROM searching systems.

Computer Searching Advantages

More access points. In manually searching the print-format finding aids, you are usually limited to author, title, and subject-heading access. In contrast, with computer searching, more access points are usually available. For example, you can often search for keywords or phrases found anywhere in the document description (or record). This free-text search capability is especially useful to locate terms or phrases not clearly defined by the finding aid's subject headings—such as is often the case with new jargon or catch-phrases, which if of enduring value will most likely be added to later subject-heading lists. You may also be able to search by such access points as author affiliation, language, publication date, document type, and others.

Boolean logic searching. The computer searching systems often allow you to use *Boolean logic* operators (and, or, not) to link several concepts together to give you just those articles which meet all the criteria you request. For example, if you wish to see articles dealing with prevention of aircraft hijacking, you are actually trying to search three topics: 1) prevention, 2) aircraft, and 3) hijacking. The computer can pinpoint which articles include all three of these topics, narrowing the number of articles you need to see for this precise subject.

Convenience. A computer search can be more convenient than manual searching of print-format finding aids for several reasons. First, it searches in minutes what could take you hours to do with print catalogs or indexes. Second, having a printout to make notes on, with complete document records, is an added convenience. Third, many computerized finding aids are very user-friendly (e.g., menu-driven) so you can search them with little or no training. Fourth, computerized finding aids will often automatically sort document records by publication date giving the most recent material first. Fifth, if you have a computer terminal or microcomputer with *communications software* and a *modem*,[10] you may be able to search a variety of online information services from your residence. For example, you can pay for access to a remote online-information service, such as Dialog, BRS, or FirstSearch. Or, you may be able to search your library's catalog if it is available in an online format and has a dial-up service.

Timeliness. The information in an online computer database is usually more current than the same information in its print counterpart.[11] Consider that the information for

---

[10]Communications software and modems are computer programs and equipment that allow two or more computers to communicate across telephone lines.

[11]The production and distribution of CD-ROM indexes may not be quicker than their print index counterparts. For example, while the paperbound issues of *Psychological Abstracts* are distributed monthly, the CD-ROM updates for PsycLit on SilverPlatter are issued quarterly. You might well need to search this finding aid for citations to articles on the psychological aspects of terrorism.

both print and computer-accessed finding aids is first loaded on a computer. To produce the print-format finding aid, the data are then sent to a printer, mailed, and processed by the library. These are time-consuming tasks. To provide online access to the same information, the vendor can more quickly load the database into its host computer.

Computer Searching Disadvantages

User charges. The most obvious disadvantage of online computer searching is its cost. Many libraries, unable to provide free access to online information services, charge the user a connect-time fee. Check with your library's reference department to get an estimate of the charges you must pay.[12] One of the major advantages of CD-ROM databases to the user is the elimination of connect-time charges. However, keep in mind that—like books and periodicals—acquiring CD-ROM sources is not cost-free for your library, so it is likely to purchase only those CD-ROM databases that will be heavily used.

Time-span. Many computer databases go back only a few years, to the time when the producer began using the computer to compile the finding aid. Most databases began in the late 1960s or early 1970s. At present, it is rare to find a database producer that has gone back and entered older records into its database. Hence, searches for information dating back two or more decades will require use of print-format finding aids.

Computers are extremely "picky". Misspelled words and improper use of search commands will not be corrected by the computer. Careless typographical errors can be costly if you are using a remote online search service. In any kind of computer searching, such errors will be time consuming, frustrating, and often produce confusing results. Illogical use of Boolean operators, improper truncation of terms, or lack of familiarity with the command syntax and functions that control searching in a particular database will cause you grief. These are all reasons why most libraries provide mediated searches in which the librarian designs and conducts the search. In addition, many libraries offer individual or group instruction in computer searching.

SAMPLE COMPUTER SEARCHES: USPSD ONLINE ON DIALOG AND PAO ON CD-ROM

To illustrate the general principles that we discussed above, we begin with an online search of USPSD. You will recall that a search of the print version of this index was illustrated in Chapter 3. Figure 7-4 shows the text of an online search of this same finding aid.

---

[12]There is considerable variation in library policies concerning online charges. Some libraries provide limited free access, others charge a flat rate per search, others simply pass along all connect-time costs. In any case, your library absorbs additional overhead costs for manuals, equipment, and personnel associated with online computer searching services.

Figure 7-4: An Online Search of USPSD Using Dialog Information Services

```
?Begin 93
...
    File 93:U S POLITICAL SCIENCE DOCUMENTS _ 75-90/ISS1

    Set    Items    Description

?select sets hijack? or highjack? or skyjack? or air(w)piracy
    S1     16       HIJACK?
    S2     13       HIGHJACK?
    S3     4        SKYJACK?
    S4     516      AIR
    S5     15       PIRACY
    S6     4        AIR(W)PIRACY
    S7     21       HIJACK? OR HIGHJACK? OR SKYJACK? OR AIR(W)PIRACY

?select sets (airplane? or aircraft or airline?) and terroris?
    S8     12       AIRPLANE?
    S9     155      AIRCRAFT
    S19    52       AIRLINE?
    S11    206      AIRPLANE? OR AIRCRAFT OR AIRLINE?
    S12    476      TERRORIS?
    S13    6        (AIRPLANE? OR AIRCRAFT OR AIRLINE?) AND TERRORIS?

?select s7 or s13
           21       S7
           6        S13
    S14    22       S7 OR S13

?select sets prevent? or anti(w)terroris? or antiterroris? or counter(w)terroris? or counterterroris?
    S15    1136     PREVENT?
    S16    1237     ANTI
    S17    476      TERRORIS?
    S18    15       ANTI(W)TERRORIS?
    S19    19       ANTITERRORIS?
    S20    410      COUNTER
    S21    476      TERRORIS?
    S22    6        COUNTER(W)TERRORIS?
    S23    39       COUNTERTERRORIS?
    S24    1197     PREVENT? OR ANTI(W)TERRORIS? OR ANTITERRORIS? OR
                    COUNTER(W)TERRORIS? OR COUNTERTERRORIS?

?select s14 and s24
           22       S14
           1197     S24
    S25    6        S14 AND S24

?type 25/5/1

25/5/1
8603206
 Cruise-Ship Terrorism and the Media.
 Quester, George H.
 Political Communication and Persuasion, Vol. No. 3, Iss. No. 4, (1986),
335-370.
 The difference between the hijacking of an airplane and a cruise ship are examined from the standpoint of the terrorist goal
of capturing media attention and from the anti-terrorist perspective of hostage rescue. The disadvantages of seizing a ship
instead of a plane are: 1) Numbers of hostages; 2) Vehicle endurance; 3) Disappearance into the unknown; 4) De facto torture;
5) Media visibility; and 6) Vehicle accessibility. The only advantage is the novelty. The 1985 "Achille Lauro" seizure—the basis
for these observations—revealed the lack of preparedness for such an occurrence. The possibility of attacks on other surface
vehicles is also covered. Media behavior reflects an irreconcilable conflict between the public's right to know and maximal
prevention of terrorism.
 DESCRIPTORS: *Mass Media Analysis; *News Coverage; *Highjacking; *Policy Conflict; *Air Piracy; *Western Bloc;
*Shipping Industry; +Strategy; *Terrorism; *Freedom of Information; +Public Safety Policy
 GEOGRAPHIC DESCRIPTORS: *United States of America; *Western Europe
 IDENTIFIERS: Achille Lauro Ship Seizure (1985)
```

Upon logging on to Dialog, the user is prompted for a command by a question mark. Our first step was to select the one or more files (databases) we wished to search. We chose file 93, USPSD.

At the second question-mark prompt, we used the "select sets" command to begin the search for records containing terms that are relevant to our first concept—aircraft hijacking. Hence, we started by searching for hijacking or its synonyms. Knowing that most finding aids use the "hijack" spelling but that USPSD uses the "highjack" spelling, we asked for either. "Skyjacking" and "air piracy" were related terms that had turned up in several finding aids, so they were added to make the search more comprehensive. Notice that the "or" operator is used here to link the search terms inclusively so that all records containing any of the terms are retrieved. Using the "or" operator will not exclude those records relating to the hijacking of trains, buses, ships, or other types of transportation.

Notice also that Dialog recognizes question marks within a search statement as a truncation symbol. Hence, "hijack?" retrieves "hijack", "hijacked", "hijacking", "hijacks", etc. As the "air(w)piracy" term illustrates, Dialog recognizes the "(w)" symbol as an adjacent-proximity command.

Dialog responded to our first search statement with a listing of the number of records retrieved for each term in our search statement, assigning a set number to each term. Any one set number can be used in subsequent search statements. Set seven tells us that 21 records were retrieved from USPSD that contained at least one of the four search terms.

At the third question-mark prompt, we continued the search for records containing other terms related to our first concept—aircraft hijacking. Here we used parentheses around two search terms, "(airplane? or airline?)". The parentheses tell Dialog to first perform the enclosed part of the search statement before linking that result with the remainder of that search statement. Hence, set thirteen tells us that 6 records were retrieved from USPSD that contained either "airplane? and terroris?" or "aircraft and terroris?" or "airline? and terroris?".

At the fourth question-mark prompt, we used the "or" operator to link sets seven and thirteen. Set seven contains 21 records. Set thirteen contains 6 records. By linking them with the "or" operator, we told Dialog to retrieve a new, combined set minus any duplicate records present in both sets. Hence, Dialog gave us set fourteen with 22 non-duplicate records out of the 27 possible. We can conclude that 5 of the records in set seven were also included in set thirteen.

At the fifth question-mark prompt, we searched for records containing terms related to our second search concept—prevention. Besides truncating prevention to "prevent?", we also searched for both hyphenated and un-hyphenated uses of the words anti-terrorism or counter-terrorism. This search statement retrieved 1197 records in set twenty-four.

At the sixth question-mark prompt, we used the "and" operator to narrow the search so that only those records were retrieved that contained terms relating to both search concepts—aircraft hijacking and prevention. The resulting set twenty-five contains 6 records that presumably all deal with prevention of aircraft hijacking.

At the seventh question-mark prompt, we used the Dialog command, "type 25/5/1", to request a printout of the first record in set twenty-five. The "5" is the designated format for printing a full record, which includes the citation, abstract, descriptors, geographic descriptors, identifiers,[13] and named people. We can see from the abstract that the article described in this first record of set twenty-five compares prevention of aircraft and cruise ship hijackings. Notice that, had we used the "not" operator to exclude records containing *Achille Lauro* (as we did in Figure 7-3), we would have missed retrieving this record.

In Chapter 3, we emphasized the importance of searching more than one periodical index in order to be thorough in locating all relevant sources. This general rule applies regardless of whether you are searching a print or computer-format finding aid. Our search of the online USPSD retrieved six highly relevant sources. However, as you can see in Figure 7-5, additional and important sources can be found by searching the CD-ROM index, *Periodical Abstracts Ondisc* (PAO).

As you will recall from the discussion in Chapter 3, PAO indexes over 450 "high-demand" magazines and journals published since 1986. In Figure 7-5, we replicated the online search in USPSD. Such a search in PAO involves three basic steps: 1) typing in the search terms linked by Boolean operators and then viewing the item counts that resulted, 2) viewing the first line of the periodical article titles in the last search set, and 3) viewing and printing (or downloading to a microcomputer disk) the document records selected. These steps are illustrated in the three computer screens reproduced in Figure 7-5.

GETTING HELP WITH COMPUTER SEARCHING

Computer searching is a rapidly expanding and not yet standardized form of library research. However, many types of help are available in most libraries to assist your mastery of these new resources. First, ask a reference librarian which computer search systems are available to you. Second, find out what kinds of training aids are offered—printed guides, group or individual instruction with a librarian, or computer-based tutorials. Third, budget time to investigate these options.

---

[13]Identifiers are used to provide additional subject terms that are not descriptors because they are generally proper names that are too numerous and specific to be included in the controlled vocabulary. For example, in USPSD, identifiers are notable events (the *Achille Lauro* Ship Seizure [1985]), organizations (Interpol), acts of legislation (Act for the Prevention and Punishment of the Crime of Hostage-Taking), or ethnic groups (Palestinians).

Figure 7-5: A CD-ROM Database Search of *Periodical Abstracts Ondisc*, January 1989 - June 1991

```
ProQuest              Periodical Abstracts           Jan 1989 -- Jun 1991
_____

        Previous Activities
[ 1]  hijack? or highjack? or skyjack? or air piracy              39
[ 2]  (airplane? or aircraft or airline?) and terroris?           89
[ 3]  prevent? or counter-terroris? or counterterroris?         2712
[ 4]  [3] or anti-terroris? or antiterroris?                     2725
[ 5]  [1] or [2]                                                  124
[ 6]  [5] and [4]                                          ----->  11

Search term(s):

_____

To Search:  Enter key work or phrases, press <--.

                                                   F1=Help   F2=Commands
=============================================================================
ProQuest              Periodical Abstracts           Jan 1989 -- Jun 1991
                    Item 1 of 11 in the Search
_____

Lockerbie Official Says System for Matching Bags with Passengers Might...

Lockerbie Panel Urges Major Security Reform

Pan Am 103:  The German Connection

FAA Orders U. S. Airlines to Install Bomb Detectors

It's a Bomb All Right

Technology VS. Terror

ICAO Upgrades Security Unit as Part of Antiterrorist Effort

Six-Million-Dollar Man

Airport Security:  Patchy

Increased Government Role Requested to Prevent Terrorism Against Aircraft
_____
89007492
Title:      Airport Security:  Patchy
Authors:    Anonymous
Journal:    Economist  Vol: 310  Iss: 7585  Date: Jan 14, 1989  pp: 42
            Jrnl Code: ECT  ISSN: 0013-0613  Jrnl Group: News; Business
Abstract:   The biggest problem with airport security is that it is geared to
            prevent the hijackings of the 1970s rather than the bombings of
            the 1980s.  Security depends in equal parts on governments,
            airlines and airports.  Photograph
Subjects:   Aircraft accidents & safety; Airports; Airlines; Terrorism;
            Security systems
Type:       Feature
Length:     Medium (10-30 col inches)
```

Copyright © 1992 by UMI. Reprinted by permission.

166   CHAPTER 7: DATABASE SEARCHING

SUMMARY

1. There are two basic types of computer searching systems—online and CD-ROM. Although online databases are more up-to-date, CD-ROM database searching is usually cost-free to the user.

2. Computer search advantages over manual searching of print-format finding aids include: more access points, Boolean logic searching, convenience, and timeliness.Computer search disadvantages include: user charges, shorter time-span of databases, and complexity of command language rules.

3. There are three techniques unique to defining computer search profiles—Boolean operators, word proximity symbols, and truncation symbols.

4. Ask a reference librarian about the computer database search services available at your library. You may need to make an appointment for a search. Your library may have equipment and provide training to allow you to do your own searching. The librarian can advise you about the suitability of your topic for a computer search, and will explain the library's fee policy.

APPENDIX I: BIBLIOGRAPHY OF SOURCES AND FINDING AIDS

CHAPTER 1: GETTING STARTED ON A TERM PROJECT

Political Science Dictionaries

Ali, Sheikh R. 1989. *The Peace and Nuclear War Dictionary*. Santa Barbara, CA: ABC-Clio.

Ali, Sheikh R. 1991. *The International Organizations and World Order Dictionary*. Santa Barbara, CA: ABC-Clio.

Bledsoe, Robert L., and Boleslaw A. Boczek. 1987. *The International Law Dictionary*. Santa Barbara, CA: ABC-Clio.

Chandler, Ralph C., Richard A. Enslen, and Peter G. Renstrom. 1985. *The Constitutional Law Dictionary, Volume 1: Individual Rights*. Santa Barbara, CA: ABC-Clio.

Chandler, Ralph C., Richard A. Enslen, and Peter G. Renstrom. 1987. *The Constitutional Law Dictionary, Volume 1: Individual Rights, Supplement 1*. Santa Barbara, CA: ABC-Clio.

Chandler, Ralph C., Richard A. Enslen, and Peter G. Renstrom. 1991. *The Constitutional Law Dictionary, Volume 1: Individual Rights, Supplement 2*. Santa Barbara, CA: ABC-Clio.

Chandler, Ralph C., Richard A. Enslen, and Peter G. Renstrom. 1987. *The Constitutional Law Dictionary, Volume 2: Governmental Powers*. Santa Barbara, CA: ABC-Clio.

Chandler, Ralph C., and Jack C. Plano. 1988. *The Public Administration Dictionary*. 2nd ed. Santa Barbara, CA: ABC-Clio.

Dunner, Joseph, ed. *Dictionary of Political Science*. 1964. New York: Philosophical Library.

Elliot, Jeffrey M., and Robert Reginald. 1989. *The Arms Control, Disarmament, and Military Security Dictionary*. Santa Barbara, CA: ABC-Clio.

Elliot, Jeffrey M., and Sheikh R. Ali. 1984. *The Presidential-Congressional Dictionary*. Santa Barbara, CA: ABC-Clio.

Elliot, Jeffrey M., and Sheikh R. Ali. 1988. *The State and Local Government Political Dictionary*. Santa Barbara, CA: ABC-Clio.

Fry, Gerald W., and Galen R. Martin. 1991. *The International Development Dictionary*. Santa Barbara, CA: ABC-Clio.

Heimanson, Rudolph. 1967. *Dictionary of Political Science and Law*. Dobbs Ferry, NY: Oceana Publications.

Kruschke, Earl R., and Byron M. Jackson. 1987. *The Public Policy Dictionary*. Santa Barbara, CA: ABC-Clio.

McCarthy, Eugene J. 1968. *Dictionary of American Politics*. New York: Macmillan.

McCrea, Barbara P., and Jack C. Plano. 1992. *The Soviet and East European Political Dictionary*. 2nd ed. Santa Barbara, CA: ABC-Clio.

Phillips, Claude S. 1984. *The African Political Dictionary*. Santa Barbara, CA: ABC-Clio.

Plano, Jack C., and Milton Greenberg. 1989. *The American Political Dictionary*. 8th ed. New York: Holt, Rinehart and Winston.

Plano, Jack C., Robert E. Riggs, and Helenan S. Robin. 1982. *The Dictionary of Political Analysis*. 2nd ed. Santa Barbara, CA: ABC-Clio.

Plano, Jack C., and Roy Olton. 1988. *The International Relations Dictionary*. 4th ed. Santa Barbara, CA: ABC-Clio.

Raymond, Walter John. 1978. *Dictionary of Politics: Selected American and Foreign Political and Legal Terms*. 6th ed. Lawrenceville, VA: Brunswick Publishing Company.

Renstrom, Peter G. 1989. *The Electoral Politics Dictionary*. Santa Barbara, CA: ABC-Clio.

Renstrom, Peter G. 1991. *The American Law Dictionary*. Santa Barbara, CA: ABC-Clio.

Rossi, Ernest E., and Barbara P. McCrea. 1985. *The European Political Dictionary*. Santa Barbara, CA: ABC-Clio.

Rossi, Ernest E., and Jack C. Plano. 1992. *The Latin American Political Dictionary*. 2nd ed. Santa Barbara, CA: ABC-Clio.

Safire, William. 1978. *Safire's Political Dictionary: An Enlarged, Up-to-date Edition of the New Language of Politics*. 3rd ed. New York: Random House.

Simpson, J.A., and E.S.C. Weiner, eds. 1989. *The Oxford English Dictionary*. 2nd ed. Oxford, UK: Clarendon Press; New York: Oxford University Press.

Smith, John W., and John S. Klemanski. 1990. *The Urban Politics Dictionary*. Santa Barbara, CA: ABC-Clio.

Sperber, Hans, and Travis Trittschuh. 1962. *American Political Terms: An Historical Dictionary*. Detroit: Wayne State University Press.

Tallman, Marjorie. 1953. *Dictionary of Civics and Government*. New York: Philosophical Library.

Ziring, Lawrence. 1991. *The Middle East Political Dictionary*. 2nd ed. Santa Barbara, CA: ABC-Clio.

Ziring, Lawrence, and C.I. Eugene Kim. 1985. *The Asian Political Dictionary*. Santa Barbara, CA: ABC-Clio.

Social and Political Science Encyclopedias

Bogdanor, Vernon, ed. 1987. *The Blackwell Encyclopaedia of Political Institutions*. Oxford, UK; New York: Blackwell Reference.

Borgatta, Edgar F., and Marie L. Borgatta, eds. 1992. *Encyclopedia of Sociology*. New York: Macmillan.

Greene, Jack P., ed. 1984. *Encyclopedia of American Political History*. New York: Scribner.

Kuper, Adam, and Jessica Kuper, eds. 1985. *The Social Science Encyclopedia*. London: Routledge & Kegan Paul.

Miller, David, ed. 1987. *The Blackwell Encyclopaedia of Political Thought*. Oxford, UK; New York: Blackwell Reference.

Seligman, Edwin R.A., and Alvin Johnson, eds. 1930-35. *Encyclopaedia of the Social Sciences*. Reprint. New York: The Macmillan Company, 1950.

Sills, David L., ed. 1968. *International Encyclopedia of the Social Sciences*. New York: Macmillan.

Thackrah, John Richard. 1987. *Encyclopedia of Terrorism and Political Violence*. London: Routledge & Kegan Paul.

Guides to the Literature of Political Science

Goehlert, Robert. 1982. *Political Science Research Guide*. Monticello, IL: Vance Bibliographies.

Harman, Robert B. 1974. *Political Science: A Bibliographical Guide to the Literature*. Third Supplement. Metuchen, NJ: Scarecrow Press, Second Supplement, 1972; First Supplement, 1968; Original Edition, 1965.

Holler, Frederick L. 1986. *Information Sources of Political Science*. 4th ed. Santa Barbara, CA: ABC-Clio.

International Political Science Association. 1953-. *International Bibliography of Political Science*. London: Lavistock Publications; Chicago: Aldine Publishing Company.

York, Henry E. 1990. *Political Science: A Guide to Reference and Information Sources*. Englewood, CO: Libraries Unlimited.

Subject Bibliographies on Political Terrorism

H.W. Wilson Company. 1937- [three issues a year, third issue is annual cumulation]. *Bibliographic Index: A Cumulative Bibliography of Bibliographies*. New York: H.W. Wilson Company.

Janke, Peter, and Richard Sim. 1983. *Guerrilla and Terrorist Organizations: A World Directory and Bibliography*. New York: Macmillan.

Lakos, Amos. 1986. *International Terrorism: A Bibliography*. Boulder: Westview Press.

Norton, Augustus R., and Martin H. Greenberg. 1980. *International Terrorism: An Annotated Bibliography and Research Guide*. Boulder: Westview Press.

Ontiveros, Suzanne R., ed. 1986. *Global Terrorism: A Historical Bibliography*. Santa Barbara, CA: ABC-Clio Information Systems.

CHAPTER 2: LOCATING BOOKS

Using the Right Words

Library of Congress, Office for Subject Cataloging Policy. 1991. *Library of Congress Subject Headings*. 14th ed. Washington, DC: Cataloging Distribution Service, Library of Congress.

Evaluating Books

Gale Research. 1965- [bimonthly with annual cumulation]. *Book Review Index*. Detroit: Gale Research.

H.W. Wilson Company. 1905- [monthly except February and July with quarterly and annual cumulation]. *Book Review Digest*. New York: H.W. Wilson Company.

Locating Parts of Books

H.W. Wilson Company. 1900- [semi-annual with annual and five-year cumulation]. *Essay and General Literature Index*. New York: H.W. Wilson Company.

CHAPTER 3: USING PERIODICAL AND NEWSPAPER ARTICLES

Four Basic Periodical Indexes

H.W. Wilson Company. 1974- [quarterly with annual cumulation]. *Social Sciences Index*. New York: H.W. Wilson Company. [Continues *Social Sciences and Humanities Index*, 1965-74, *International Index*, 1916-65 and *Readers' Guide to Periodical Literature Supplement*, 1907-1915.]

Information Access Company. 1980- [cumulates monthly, CD-ROM]. *General Periodicals Index - Academic Library Edition*. Foster City, CA: Information Access Company.

Public Affairs Information Service. 1991- [monthly with annual cumulation]. *PAIS International in Print*. New York: Public Affairs Information Service. [Continues *PAIS Bulletin*, 1915-1990 and *PAIS Foreign Language Index* 1976-.]

University Microfilms International. 1986- [monthly cumulation, CD-ROM]. *Periodical Abstracts Ondisc*. Ann Arbor, MI: University Microfilms International.

Abstracts

ABC-Clio. 1964- [four per year with annual index]. *America: History and Life*. Santa Barbara, CA: ABC-Clio.

American Psychological Association. 1927- [monthly with annual cumulative indexes]. *Psychological Abstracts*. Washington, DC: American Psychological Association.

H.W. Wilson Company. 1986- [eight per year in microfiche]; 1988- [ten per year in print]. *Readers' Guide Abstracts*. New York: H.W. Wilson Company.

IFI Plenum Company. 1967- [annual]. *Political Science Abstracts*. New York: IFI Plenum. [Continues Universal Reference System: Political Science, Government, and Public Policy Series.]

International Political Science Association. 1951- [bimonthly with annual cumulative indexes]. *International Political Science Abstracts*. Paris: International Political Science Association.

National Council on Crime and Delinquency. 1977 [quarterly with annual cumulative indexes]. *Criminal Justice Abstracts*. Monsey, NY: Willow Tree Press. [Continues *Crime and Delinquency Literature*. 1970-.]

Peace Research Institute. 1964- [monthly]. *Peace Research Abstracts Journal*. Dundas, Ontario: Peace Research Institute.

Sage Publications. 1978- [bimonthly with annual index]. *Communication Abstracts*. Newbury Park, CA: Sage Publications.

Sociological Abstracts, Inc. 1953- [5 issues a year]. *Sociological Abstracts*. San Diego: Sociological Abstracts, Inc.

University of Pittsburgh, University Center for International Studies. 1975- [annual]. *United States Political Science Documents*. Pittsburgh: University Center for International Studies, University of Pittsburgh.

Citation Indexes

Institute for Scientific Information. 1972- [three per year with annual cumulation]. *Social Sciences Citation Index*. Philadelphia: Institute for Scientific Information.

An Index to Mass-Audience Periodicals

H.W. Wilson Company. 1900- [thirteen per year with quarterly and annual cumulation]. *Readers' Guide to Periodical Literature*. New York: H.W. Wilson Company.

Newspaper Indexes

Information Access Company. 1979- [online]. *National Newspaper Index*. Foster City, CA: Information Access Company.

New York Times Company. 1913- [semi-monthly with quarterly and annual cumulation]. *New York Times Index*. New York: New York Times Company. [See also, *New York Times Index: Prior Series*, 1851-1912, New York: R.R. Bowker.]

NewsBank. 1981- [monthly with quarterly and annual cumulation]. *NewsBank Index*. New Canaan, CT: NewsBank.

CHAPTER 4: LOCATING U.S. GOVERNMENT DOCUMENTS

The Federal Government's Basic Documents' Index

U.S. Superintendent of Documents. 1951- [monthly with semi-annual and annual cumulative indexes]. *Monthly Catalog of United States Government Publications*. Washington, DC: U.S. Government Printing Office. [Continues *United States Government Publications: Monthly Catalog* 1940-1950; *Monthly Catalog, United States Public Documents* 1907-1939; *Catalogue of the United States Public Documents* 1895-1907.]

Other Approaches to Locating Documents: Commercially Produced Indexes

Congressional Information Service. 1970- [annual with five-year cumulation]. *CIS/Index to Publications of the Congressional Information Service*. Washington, DC: Congressional Information Service.

Infordata International. 1970- [quarterly with annual cumulation]. *Index to U.S. Government Periodicals*. Chicago: Infordata International.

Information Access Company. 1976- [monthly cumulation, CD-ROM]. *Government Publications Index*. Foster City, CA: Information Access Company.

NewsBank. 1971- [monthly in eight geographic-area editions with annual cumulation for each]. *Index to the Foreign Broadcast Information Service Daily Reports*. New Canaan, CT: NewsBank.

University Microfilms International. 1975- [monthly with annual microform cumulation]. *Transdex Index*. Ann Arbor, MI: University Microfilms International. [Variant title: *Bell & Howell Transdex Index*.]

CHAPTER 5: LEGAL RESEARCH[1]

Citation Format for Primary Legal Sources

American Political Science Association. 1988. *Style Manual for Political Science*. Washington, DC: American Political Science Association.

Harvard Law Review Association. 1981. *A Uniform System of Citation*. 13th ed. Cambridge, MA: Harvard Law Review Association.

---

[1]The legal references with an asterisk by the date cite the beginning date of coverage provided. The other legal references cite the year of publication.

Statute Law: Chronological Primary Sources

U.S. Congress. 1789*-. [issued first as Slip Laws which are cumulated by session of Congress]. *United States Statutes at Large*. Washington, DC: U.S. Government Printing Office.

West Publishing Company. 1939- [semi-monthly when Congress is in session, otherwise monthly]. *U.S. Code Congressional and Administrative News*. St. Paul: West Publishing Company.

Statute Law: Codified Primary Sources

Lawyers' Cooperative. 1972- [monthly advance pamphlets, cumulative annual pocket parts, volumes replaced irregularly]. *United States Code Service*. Rochester, NY: Lawyers' Cooperative. [Continues *Federal Code Annotated*, 1937-1970.]

U.S. Congress. 1988 [cumulative editions published every six years since 1934 with annual supplements]. *United States Code*. 11th ed. Washington, DC: U.S. Government Printing Office.

West Publishing Company. 1927- [cumulative annual pocket parts, volumes replaced irregularly]. *United States Code Annotated*. St. Paul: West Publishing Company.

Statute Law: Secondary Sources

Congressional Quarterly Service. 1948- [annual]. *Congressional Quarterly Almanac*. Washington, DC: Congressional Quarterly Inc. [Continues *Congressional Quarterly*.]

Congressional Quarterly Service. 1945- [beginning with volume 2 (1964-1968), each volume covers one presidential term]. *Congressional Quarterly Congress and the Nation*. Washington, DC: Congressional Quarterly Inc.

Congressional Quarterly Service. 1946- [weekly with quarterly indexes that cumulate annually]. *Congressional Quarterly Weekly Reports*. Washington, DC: Congressional Quarterly Inc.

Administrative Law: Chronological Primary Sources

U.S. General Services Administration, National Archives and Records Service, Office of the Federal Register. 1936- [daily with monthly, quarterly, and annual indexes]. *Federal Register*. Washington, DC: U.S. Government Printing Office.

U.S. General Services Administration, National Archives and Records Service, Office of the Federal Register. 1965- [weekly with quarterly, semiannual, and annual indexes]. *Weekly Compilation of Presidential Documents*. Washington, DC: U.S. Government Printing Office.

Administrative Law: Codified Primary Sources

U.S. General Services Administration, National Archives and Records Service, Office of the Federal Register. 1949- [annual]. 2nd ed. *Code of Federal Regulations*. Washington, DC: U.S. Government Printing Office. [Supersedes *Code of Federal Regulations* 1st ed., 1938-.]

U.S. General Services Administration, National Archives and Records Service, Office of the Federal Register. 1961/77- [irregular]. *Codification of Presidential Proclamations and Executive Orders*. Washington, DC: U.S. Government Printing Office.

Administrative Law: Secondary Sources

Congressional Quarterly Service. 1979/80- [every four years]. *Federal Regulatory Directory*. Washington, DC: Congressional Quarterly Inc.

National Journal. 1986- [semi-annual]. *The Capital Source: The Who's Who, What, Where in Washington*. Washington, DC: National Journal.

National Journal. 1969- [weekly with semi-annual index]. *National Journal*. Washington, DC: National Journal.

U.S. General Services Administration, National Archives and Records Service, Office of the Federal Register. 1935- [annual]. *The United States Government Manual*. Washington, DC: U.S. Government Printing Office.

Whitnah, Donald R., ed. 1983. *Government Agencies*. Westport, CT: Greenwood Press.

Case Law: Chronological Primary Sources

Lawyers' Cooperative Publishing Company. October term 1790*- [biweekly advance sheets during the Court's term cumulate annually, the latter with pocket supplements]. *United States Supreme Court Reports, Lawyers Edition*. Rochester, NY: Lawyers' Cooperative Publishing Company.

U.S. Supreme Court. September 1754*- [initially issued separately as "slip opinions" and subsequently published in advance sheets ("preliminary prints") that are replaced by bound volumes for each term]. *United States Reports: Cases Adjudged in the Supreme Court*. Washington, DC: U.S. Government Printing Office.

West Publishing Company. October term 1882*- [biweekly advance sheets during the Court's term cumulate annually]. *The Supreme Court Reporter*. St. Paul: West Publishing Company.

Case Law: Secondary Sources

American Bar Association, Public Education Division. 1963-1973; 1982- [fourteen issues per Court term]. *Preview of U.S. Supreme Court Cases*. Chicago: American Bar Association.

Lawyers' Cooperative. October term 1790*- [cumulative annual pocket parts, volumes replaced irregularly]. *United States Supreme Court Reports Digest, Lawyers Edition*. Rochester, NY: Lawyers' Cooperative.

Guenther, Nancy Anderman. 1983. *United States Supreme Court Decisions: An Index to Excerpts, Reprints, and Discussions*. 2nd ed. Metuchen, NJ: Scarecrow Press.

Kurland, Philip B., and Gerhard Casper, eds. 1975- [supplement volumes for each Court term]. *Landmark Briefs and Arguments of the Supreme Court of the United States*. Washington, DC: University Publications of America.

Lawyers' Cooperative Publishing Company. 1962- [cumulative annual pocket parts, volumes replaced irregularly]. *American Jurisprudence: A Modern Comprehensive Text Statement of American Law, State and Federal*. 2nd ed. Rochester, NY: Lawyers' Cooperative Publishing Company.

West Publishing Company. 1936- [cumulative annual pocket parts, volumes replaced irregularly]. *Corpus Juris Secundum: A Complete Restatement of the Entire American Law as Developed by All Reported Cases 1658 to Date*. St. Paul: West Publishing Company.

West Publishing Company. 1754*- [cumulative annual pocket parts, volumes replaced irregularly]. *United States Supreme Court Digest, 1754 to Date*. St. Paul: West Publishing Company.

International Law: Chronological Primary Sources

U.S. Department of State. 1950- [initially issued separately as "slip treaties" (known as *Treaties and Other International Acts Series* {TIAS}) that are replaced irregularly by bound volumes]. *United States Treaties and Other International Agreements*. Washington, DC: U.S. Government Printing Office. [Continues Charles I. Bevans, ed., *Treaties and Other International Agreements of the United States of America, 1776-1949*, Washington, DC: U.S. Government Printing Office.]

International Law: Secondary Sources

U.S. Department of State. 1956- [annual]. *American Foreign Policy Current Documents*. Washington, DC: U.S. Government Printing Office. [Continues *American Foreign Policy Basic Documents*, 1950-.]

U.S. Department of State, Office of the Legal Adviser. 1973- [annual]. *Digest of United States Practice in International Law*. Washington, DC: U.S. Government Printing Office.

W.S. Hein Company. 1982- [annual]. *A Guide to the United States Treaties in Force*. Buffalo, NY: W.S. Hein Company.

CHAPTER 6: LOCATING GENERAL INFORMATION
FINDING BIOGRAPHICAL INFORMATION

Three Finding Aids: Indexes to Biographical Material

Gale Research Company. 1975- [annual with five-year cumulation]. *Biography and Genealogy Master Index*. Detroit: Gale Research Company. [The online version is *Biography Master Index* and the microfiche version is *Biobase*.]

Gale Research Company. 1981- [irregular]. *Biography Almanac*. Detroit: Gale Research Company.

H.W. Wilson Company. 1946- [quarterly with semi-annual, annual, and three-year cumulations]. *Biography Index*. New York: H.W. Wilson Company.

Two Styles of Biographical Reference Sources:
Encyclopedic Narrative and Abbreviated Abstract

American Council of Learned Societies. 1928- [five-year supplements]. *Dictionary of American Biography*. New York: Scribner.

Europa Publications Limited. 1935- [annual]. *The International Who's Who*. London: Europa Publications Ltd.

H.W. Wilson Company. 1940- [monthly with annual cumulation]. *Current Biography*. New York: H.W. Wilson Company.

Marquis. 1899- [biennial with an annual supplement]. *Who's Who in America*. Chicago: Marquis.

R.R. Bowker. 1967- [biennial]. *Who's Who in American Politics*. New York: R.R. Bowker.

U.S. Congress, Joint Committee on Printing. 1857- [biennial for each Congress]. *Official Congressional Directory*. Washington, DC: U.S. Government Printing Office.

FINDING STATISTICAL INFORMATION

Four Finding Aids: Indexes to Statistical Material

Congressional Information Service. 1974- [monthly with quarterly and annual cumulations]. *American Statistics Index: A Comprehensive Guide to the Statistical Publications of the U.S. Government*. Washington, DC: Congressional Information Service.

Congressional Information Service. 1983- [monthly with quarterly and annual cumulations]. *Index to International Statistics*. Washington, DC: Congressional Information Service.

Congressional Information Service. 1980- [monthly with quarterly and annual cumulations]. *Statistical Reference Index*. Washington, DC: Congressional Information Service.

Ondrasik, Allison, ed. 1983-1990 [annual]. *DataMap: Index of Published Tables of Statistical Data*. Phoenix: Oryx Press [published by Longman, 1983-1984.].

Statistical Sources: Compilations of Statistical Information

American Institute of Public Opinion. 1978- [annual]. *The Gallup Poll*. Wilmington, DE: Scholarly Resources. [Continues *The Gallup Poll: Public Opinion, 1935-1971* and *The Gallup Poll: Public Opinion, 1972-1977*.]

Congressional Quarterly Service. 1985. *Congressional Quarterly's Guide to U.S. Elections*. 2nd ed. Washington, DC: Congressional Quarterly Inc.

Council of State Governments. 1935- [biennial]. *Book of the States*. Chicago: Council of State Governments.

Elections Research Center (Governmental Affairs Institute). 1956- [biennial]. *America Votes*. Washington, DC: Elections Research Center (Governmental Affairs Institute), Congressional Quarterly Inc.

Gilbert, D.A. 1983- [annual]. *American Public Opinion Index*. Boston: Opinion Research Service.

Hastings, Elizabeth Hann, and Philip K. Hastings. 1980- [annual]. *Index to International Public Opinion*. Westport, CT: Greenwood Press.

International City Management Association. 1934- [annual]. *The Municipal Year Book*. Washington, DC: International City Management Association. [Continues *City Manager Yearbook*.]

King, Gary, and Lyn Ragsdale. 1988. *The Elusive Executive: Discovering Statistical Patterns in the Presidency*. Washington, DC: Congressional Quarterly Press.

Mackie, Thomas T., and Richard Rose. 1982. *International Almanac of Electoral History*. 2nd ed. London: Macmillan.

Mitchell, Brian R. 1980. *European Historical Statistics, 1750-1975*. 2nd ed. New York: Facts on File.

Scammon, Richard M., ed. 1965. *America at the Polls: A Handbook of American Presidential Elections Statistics, 1920-1964*. Pittsburgh: University of Pittsburgh Press.

Scammon, Richard M., and Alice V. McGillivray, eds. 1988. *America at the Polls 2: A Handbook of American Presidential Election Statistics, 1968-1984*. Washington, DC: Elections Research Center, Congressional Quarterly Inc.

Sivard, Ruth Leger, et al., eds. 1974- [annual]. *World Military and Social Expenditures*. Washington, DC: World Priorities.

Stanley, Harold W. 1992. *Vital Statistics on American Politics*. 3rd ed. Washington, DC: Congressional Quarterly Press.

Stanley, Harold W., and Richard G. Niemi. 1988. *Vital Statistics on American Politics*. Washington, DC: Congressional Quarterly Press.

U.N. Department of Economic Affairs, Statistical Office. 1948- [annual]. *Demographic Yearbook*. New York: United Nations.

U.N. Educational, Scientific and Cultural Organization. 1963- [annual]. *Statistical Yearbook*. Paris: UNESCO. [Continues *Basic Facts and Figures*.]

U.S. Department of Commerce, Bureau of the Census. 1790- [decennial]. *Census of Population*. Washington, DC: U.S. Government Printing Office.

U.S. Department of Commerce, Bureau of the Census. 1961- [irregular]. *Congressional District Databook*. Washington, DC: U.S. Government Printing.

U.S. Department of Commerce, Bureau of the Census. 1949- [irregular]. *County and City Databook*. Washington, DC: U.S. Government Printing Office. [Continues *Statistical Abstract of the United States: Cities Supplement, 1940* and *County Data Book, 1947*.]

U.S. Department of Commerce, Bureau of the Census. 1975. *Historical Statistics of the United States, Colonial Times to 1970*. Washington, DC: U.S. Government Printing Office.

U.S. Department of Commerce, Bureau of the Census. 1979- [annual]. *State and Metropolitan Area Data Book*. Washington, DC: U.S. Government Printing Office.

U.S. Department of Commerce, Bureau of the Census. 1878- [annual]. *Statistical Abstract of the United States*. Washington, DC: U.S. Government Printing Office.

U.S. Department of Education. 1962- [annual]. *Digest of Educational Statistics*. Washington, DC: U.S. Government Printing Office.

U.S. Department of Labor, Bureau of Labor Statistics. 1927- [biennial since 1982]. *Handbook of Labor Statistics, 1924/26-*. Washington, DC: U.S. Government Printing Office.

U.S. Department of Justice, Bureau of Justice Statistics. 1973- [annual]. *Sourcebook of Criminal Justice Statistics*. Washington, DC: U.S. Government Printing Office.

U.S. Department of Justice, Federal Bureau of Investigation. 1930- [annual since 1958]. *Uniform Crime Reports for the United States*. Washington, DC: U.S. Government Printing Office.

FINDING GENERAL FACTUAL INFORMATION

Council on Foreign Relations. 1975- [annual]. *Political Handbook of the World*. New York: Simon and Schuster. [Continues *Political Handbook and Atlas of the World* 1963-1974 and *Political Handbook of the World* 1927-1962.]

Facts on File. 1940- [weekly with semiannual and annual indexes]. *Facts on File*. New York: Facts on File.

Longman. 1987- [monthly]. *Keesing's Record of World Events*. London: Longman. [Continues *Keesing's Contemporary Archives*, 1931-1986.]

Pharos Books. 1923- [annual]. *The World Almanac & Book of Facts*. New York: Pharos Books. [Continues *World Almanac and Encyclopedia* 1868-1876, 1886-1922.]

St. Martin's Press. 1864- [annual]. *The Statesman's Year-book*. New York: St. Martin's Press.

APPENDIX II: STYLE MANUAL FOR POLITICAL SCIENCE

The *Style Manual for Political Science*, reprinted below, is written for authors submitting manuscripts for publication in political science journals. Therefore, some of the instructions at the beginning of the *Style Manual* may not be relevant to students preparing papers to fulfill course requirements. For example, the *Style Manual* instructs the reader to submit four copies of the manuscript. Other typing instructions, such as to double-space table contents, may conflict with your course instructor's directions.

The APSA's *Style Manual* is intended to be the authoritative style guide for political science publications. However, in some books and articles on political topics, you will find that the publisher, for aesthetic purposes, may vary from the *Style Manual*'s detailed specifications.

This reprint of the 1988 revision of the *Style Manual* includes a few corrections to examples given in the References section. These corrections have been approved by the publisher, the American Political Science Association, and will be incorporated in their next revision.

CONTENTS

The more care you—as an author—take with both editorial and literary style, the less your work will be subject to the well-meaning "improvements" of copy editors who do not know your field, the more control you will have over your own prose, and the more professional will be the final form of your published work. On the other hand, if you fail to make your meaning sufficiently clear, the copy editor may have to take a chance and commit to one of a number of possible meanings. A successful outcome, in this case, will depend partly on luck.

You do not have time to learn the stylistic peculiarities of every journal you might publish in. For that reason APSA follows the thirteenth edition of the *Chicago Manual of Style (CMS)* as currently the most universal standard. Much of what follows essentially summarizes, amplifies, and reformulates the contents of *CMS* in application to political science texts. Numerical references are to chapters and sections of that manual.

In general aim for the cleanest and most compact presentation possible. For instance, *Martinez 1988* is cleaner than *Martinez, 1988* because it saves a comma.

Webster's Ninth New Collegiate Dictionary is our first standard for spelling, capitalization, and hyphenation—then the older, unabridged edition, *Webster's Third New International Dictionary*. In addition the English-German volume (volume 1) of Wolfgang J. Koschnick's *Standard Dictionary of the Social Sciences* happens to be an exhaustive and invaluable reference for spelling, capitalization, and hyphenation of social science terms.

The APSA has the ambition to achieve the highest standard of prose style. Avoid the Socialsciencese habit of piling up nouns to make unwieldy if not incomprehensible adjectival phrases, as in *states welfare medicine policy decisions*. Even *medicine policy decisions* is excessive. Again and again we find that the never-failing touchstone is the spoken language. What makes good speech makes good writing. Similarly, what makes bad speech makes bad writing. Punctuation and hyphenation, for instance, are really little more than guides to intonation. Listen to how you would *say* a sentence and punctuate accordingly. Such a habit, leavened with a healthy distaste for the superfluous, is a surer guide to good writing than any knowledge of the mere rules.

Submission Form

Please do not submit your manuscript to two or more journals simultaneously. Submit four copies of your manuscript, with your name and affiliation on the title page of one copy only. (To ensure the integrity of the referee process, this is the only place where your name and affiliation should appear.) Copies cannot be returned. Your manuscript should be typed on one side of the page only and double-spaced (even the tables), allowing 1 1/2-inch margins on all sides. Do not justify the right margin.

Title and Abstract

The title should be descriptive and short (12 words maximum, preferably fewer). A subtitle should not be necessary. On a separate sheet of paper include an abstract of no more than 150 words (roughly 15 lines) describing succinctly what research problem you investigated, how you tackled the problem, and what findings or conclusions you present. The abstract should summarize, not introduce, your article.

Length

Many journals, including the *American Political Science Review*, cannot consider a manuscript that exceeds 50 double-spaced pages, including title page, abstract, appendixes, notes, references, figures, and tables. Papers published in political science journals are usually 20 to 30 manuscript pages long.

Order of Contents

All parts of a manuscript should be double-spaced and should appear in the following order, each on a new, sequentially numbered page:

> title page, with author's name and affiliation on one copy only
> abstract (with article title at top)
> text
> appendix, if necessary
> notes, if necessary
> references
> tables, titled and numbered, each on a separate page
> figures, titled and numbered, each on a separate page

Headings

Use three orders of headings, in both upper- and lowercase letters:

Primary Heading

Secondary Heading

Tertiary heading. Text follows immediately.

Center primary headings; place secondary heads flush left; tertiary heads should be underlined and flush left, with sentence-style capitalization and a period at the end.

Text Style

That or Which?

In choosing between the relative pronouns *that* and *which* (in absence of a preposition), use *that* whenever your ear tells you there is no preceding comma:

> Influences that disturb partisan ties affect voters differentially.

Possessives

All one-syllable singular names and common nouns ending in an *s* or *z* sound form possessives with *'s* (sauce's, fox's, Zeus's). All those of three or more syllables form possessives with *'* alone (*existence', Goldilocks', Achilles'*). Those of two syllables take *'s* as a rule but take *'* alone if *'s* would result in three *s, sh, z,* or *zh* sounds in a row in unstressed syllables (*disease's, index's, Congress's* but *thesis', Xerxes', Bridges'*).

Compound Words

A compound word consists of two (or more) words in any combination of nouns and adjectives (and some adverbs that look like adjectives) that *together* form either a noun or an adjective. Hyphenation draws the elements of a compound word closer together. A compound functioning as a noun and not found in the dictionary should be spelled open unless it falls into the category of one of the exceptions found in *CMS* (pp. 176-77). A compound serving as an adjective and not found in the dictionary should be hyphenated when

1. the first element is an adverb not ending in *-ly (ill-conceived, never-failing, much-touted, now-famous)*—but not in predicative position (after a form of *to be*, expressed or understood)

2. it expresses ranking or measurement (*third-world, nineteenth-century, high-income, long-term, aggregate-level*)

3. the first element stands in object relation to the second, with or without an understood preposition (*role-specific, value-free, theory-guided, vote-maximizing, all-encompassing, self-fulfilling*)

4. the first element is an adjective modifying a noun hidden in the second element (*hard-headed, large-sized, one-sided, primary-preventive*)

5. two elements stand in a mutual relationship (*agree-disagree, male-female, city-state*)

6. it is a complex phrase (*agreed-on, none-too-keen, not-to-be-gainsaid, equal-to-equal, rank-and-file*)

More examples can be found in *CMS* (pp. 178-79).

Don't use a / to make a compound. *And/or* may instead be rendered *one or the other or both* if it is absolutely necessary to convey all three alternatives; but more often than not *and* or *or* alone suffices.

Roman, Italics, or Quotation Marks?

Roman, italics, and quotation marks have distinctive uses. For instance, democracy means everything we associate with that word, "democracy" means what is (rightly or wrongly) called by that word, and *democracy* means the spoken or written word itself (6.65-66, 68).

Use italics for unnaturalized foreign words (those not found in the dictionary) (6.54). Most Latin expressions are considered naturalized and are therefore not italicized. Use italics, with restraint, for emphasis (6.53). Use italics for letters representing mathematical quantities.

Use quotation marks for words used in a qualified, nonstandard, or ironical sense or else taken from a general context the reader is expected to recognize.

Verb Tense

In surveys of literature *Ripley showed* or *has shown* or *Ripley's study shows* are all correct uses of tense. Avoid jumping back and forth between the author as subject (acting in the past) and the work as subject (acting in the present). In contexts where chronology is not the focus, *Ripley shows* is correct. Use past tense to describe your own procedures and results (*the respondents indicated*) but present tense to present findings (*the data indicate*). Consider the following example:

> Hart *was* clearly not *associated* with the black wing of the party, and we *would* therefore *expect to see* Hart's vote share *diminish* rapidly as the proportion of black votes in a state *rises*.

Here *vote share* and *proportion of black votes* refer to items in a model.

Titles and Terms

Individual titles attached to a name are capitalized (*President Reagan, Congressman Jones*); otherwise they are lowercased (*U.S. president Reagan, ex-president Reagan, the emperor Huang-ti, the pope John Paul II*) (7.15).

Use *United States, U.S., U.S. citizen,* or *citizen* in preference to *America(n)* when the country is meant; use *America(n)* for one or both continents *only*. Because the use of *America* for the United States is ethnocentric, we discourage its use in article text or titles.

Gender-neutral Language

Avoid inappropriately gender-specific language, including gender-specific terms for groups of people or the characterization of groups as male or female.

The following are some ways to avoid the most common sexist language trap, the use of *he, him,* or *his* as the default pronoun:

1. Replace the pronoun with *the* or *a* or delete the pronoun.

2. Replace the pronoun with its referent or a synonym (and delete the original referent).

3. Replace the personal pronoun with a relative pronoun (*who, whose,* or *whom*).

4. Replace *he* with *he or she*, and so on (with discretion). Do not alternate *he* and *she*.

5. Convert the sentence to the plural (with discretion).

6. Convert the sentence to the passive voice (with great discretion).

The secret of editing to avoid sexist language is *variety*—usually a mix of the first four tactics. Consider the following sentence:

> The *congressman's* staff is itself intimately involved in *his* committee participation, keeping *him* briefed on committee activities, looking out for *his* interests, and often acting on *his* behalf. Information it provides *him* is often an important basis for *his* perception of a bill.

Edited it becomes

> The staff is intimately involved in *the* committee participation *of its representative, whom* it keeps briefed on committee activities. It looks out for *the member's* interests and often acts on *his or her* behalf. Information it provides is thus often an important basis for *the representative's* perception of a bill.

I or *We*?

Don't be afraid to call yourself *I*. *We* is appropriate only for joint authors. Self-effacement by means of the third person (*this author*) or the passive voice are also unnatural.

Acronyms and Abbreviations

Acronyms should be in parentheses at the first reference, following the spelled-out full form. In later references the letters are sufficient. Two-letter acronyms for the 50 states may be used in "tight matter," that is, tables, figures, notes, and references. Names of countries should be spelled out in the text and abbreviated in tight matter. An exception is the acronym *USSR*, which may be used even in the text (14.19). Also, *U.S.* is acceptable as an adjective, but as a noun *United States* is preferable. Avoid computer acronyms when explaining results of multivariate analysis.

Very common abbreviations like *dept.* and scholarly abbreviations like *e.g.* and *i.e.*—in roman, not italic, type—are acceptable in parentheses and tight matter.

Spelling Out Numbers

Spell out *one* through *nine* and spell out even hundreds, thousands, millions, and billions. (This means that only part of some numbers will be spelled out, e.g., *10 thousand*. See *CMS*, p. 232n.) Spell out all ordinal numbers through *hundredth* (*seventh deciles, nineteenth century*) (8.3). Use arabic figures for other numbers (8.3). Percentages are expressed as figures followed by % even if the numeral is less than 10 (8.18). Always write out a number if it begins a sentence.

Inclusive Numbers

Inclusive numbers are written according to how they are spoken. Do not divide digit pairs that are expressed as single words (i.e., 11-99). Thus forms like *11-6; 23-8; 13,998-4,001*, and so on are unacceptable because they divide such digit pairs. (The numbers 1,100-9,999 are assumed to be spoken "eleven hundred" and so on, so that *1,495-500* is also unacceptable.)

To write inclusive numbers, omit the initial unchanged digits of the second number as long as they are not part of an unbreakable pair (*3-10; 71-72; 105-6; 321-25; 415-532; 1,200-1,300; 1,496-1,504; 11,564-68*). If the first number should be an even hundred, carry the second number at least to the hundreds place (*100-104, 600-613, 1,100-1,123*) (8.67).

Inclusive years can normally be treated in the same way (the word *years* being understood) unless *from* or *between* precedes the dates (5.92, 8.68):

the years 1944-47, war of 1914-18, during 1878-85, the 1878-1910 period

but

from 1914 to 1918, between 1879 and 1902

Tables

Tables are used to display trends, findings, or relationships; tables merely providing information or data—"storage" tables—should be relegated to an appendix if they must be included at all. Do not use a table to duplicate what is already in the text. Do not let the information in one table overlap that of another. Often two tables sharing the same row or column headings can be combined into one. Also, plan tables to avoid extreme width, as wide tables are difficult both to typeset and to read.

Tables should stand on their own; they should be understandable to the reader who has not yet consulted the text. Thus all columns and rows should be clearly labeled (with only the most common abbreviations). The exact meaning of numbers should be explained. Are they percentages, frequencies, or something else? Indicate the number of cases on which percentages are calculated and whether they are column, row, or table percentages. Spell out the phrase *Number of cases*; however, N is acceptable in parentheses within the text of the manuscript. Do not carry a number beyond two decimal places unless absolutely necessary.

Each table should have an arabic numeral and a title (centered, with headline-style capitalization) and should be typed on a single sheet of paper and inserted in sequence at the end of the manuscript. Indicate the preferred placement of each table in the text (e.g., *Tables about here*), which should follow the first text reference to it. Column heads take headline capitalization and should be centered above the column, with the numbers below precisely aligned. (With numbers of grossly different magnitudes that are not being compared, align commas with decimal points.) The units used in a column may be added in parentheses just beneath the head. Place single horizontal rules above and below the column heads and at the foot of the table. Do not use vertical rules. Stub heads should be flush left and take headline capitalization. Items in the stub take only sentence capitalization; if such items have subheads, indent them three spaces. (See Table 1.)

The table title should bear no note. Any general note should be placed at the foot of the table, with the heading *Note*: (or *Source*:—a source note must be given for all previously published tables). Other notes should be keyed by superior, italicized, lowercase letters both in the table and where the note appears. Probability levels should be keyed by *, **, and *** in order of decreasing probability. For more details on tables with numerous examples see *CMS* (chapter 12).

Table 1: Coefficient Estimates for Gubernatorial Election Outcomes, 1940-82

Variable	Model with National Economic Conditions		Model with National and State Economic Conditions	
	Coefficient	t-score	Coefficient	t-score
Constant[a]	4.51	.43	2.64	.24
Prior % Democratic, governor[b]	.91	4.24*	.94	4.44*
Gubernatorial incumbency	-.59	.52	-.73	.63
% Democratic, president	.01	.15	.01	.16
Presidential election year	-.12	.03	-.11	.03
% Democratic, Senate	.12	2.49*	.12	2.26*
Senatorial election year	-6.36	2.39*	-5.86	2.12*
Surge or decline	.00	2.60*	.009	2.70*
Presidential responsibility for change in national income growth[c]	.32	3.75*	.32	3.68*
Gubernatorial responsibility for change in state income growth[d]			.07	1.79**
Number of cases	666		666	
R^2	.65		.64	
Adjusted R^2	.61		.61	

Source: John E. Chubb, "Institutions, the Economy, and the Dynamics of State Elections," *American Political Science Review* 82:148.

Note: The dependent variable is the Democratic percentage of the gubernatorial vote by state.

[a]The variable list excludes dummies that were included for 34 states.

[b]The instrumental variables used to estimate this model include all exogenous variables and their two-year lags.

[c]Annual change in the percentage-point growth of national real per capita disposable income.

[d]Annual change in the percentage-point growth of real per capita personal income by state.

*$p \leq .05$, two-tailed test.

**$p \leq .10$, two-tailed test.

Figures

Titles and sources for figures should follow the same format as for tables. Figures should be placed after any tables at the end of the manuscript, with preferred placement indicated in the text. Each figure, too, should be self-explanatory, with all parts clearly labeled using headline-style capitalization (*not* block capitals). Letters representing number quantities take italics. A separate sheet should be used for each figure, and copies—not originals—should accompany the manuscript.

If your manuscript is accepted, photomechanical transfers (PMTs) will be required. These PMTs should be professionally drawn (both figure and lettering) in black india ink on high-quality, bright white photostat paper. For the *American Political Science Review*, the figure should be large enough to be clear and attractive when reduced to one-column size (about 2 1/2 inches in width).

Citations

General Principles

Citations are brief notes on sources and appear in the text. They are designed to provide immediate source information without interrupting the flow of argument. A citation usually requires only the last name of the author(s), year of publication (*n.d.* if it is forthcoming), and (sometimes) page or chapter numbers. The page or chapter numbers must appear unless the reference is really to the entire work as a whole.

The simple author-date citation is an abbreviated way of referring to the work itself. You might think of it as a kind of short title. No comma separates the two elements:

"the transmogrifying of mayoral power" (Bailey 1987)

For a lucid assessment, see Ripley 1988.

In the second example, the "short title" is grammatically part of the sentence, hence it is not set off by parentheses. If the sentence were about the author rather than, as here, about the work—we are not directed to see Ripley himself—the date alone would be set off by parentheses to indicate the work:

Trish (1988) sharply disagrees.

If there are two or three authors, cite all names each time (15.14):

(Kelly, Colter, and Lane 1980)

If there are four or more authors, *et al.* (in roman type) should follow the first author's name, even in the first reference (15.17):

(Angel et al. 1986)

When more than one study is cited, arrange the references in alphabetical order and separate them with semicolons (15.24):

(Confucius 1951; Gurdjieff 1950; Wanisaburo 1926)

If two or more authors have the same last name, a first initial should be used to distinguish between them:

(B. Ripley 1988; R. Ripley 1964)

Use commas to separate two works by the same author (15.25):

(Barbarosa 1973, 1975)

If works by the same author are also published in the same year, add lowercase letters to the dates of publication and repeat these in the reference section (15.25):

(Frankly 1957a, 1957b)

Pages, chapters, and so forth follow the date, preceded by a comma; *p.* and *pp.* are omitted (15.10):

Beaute (1975, 121-25)

(Rex et al. 1985, chaps. 6, 7)

Older Works

For reprints, both original and reprint dates should be given (15.27):

(Marx and Engels [1933] 1964, 25)

For new editions only the date of the edition used should be specified.

Classics may be cited in either of two ways. The first is to use the author-date system with the date of a particular edition and page numbers. The second commonly includes the author's name, title of the work, and a series of numbers representing decreasing subdivisions of the work:

(*Thucydides Peloponnesian War* 2.40.2-3)

In this case the numbers happen to refer to book, section, and sentence (17.69-70). Citations to chapters and verses of the Bible or to numbers of the *Federalist Papers* would be of the same type. Since the subdivisions are the same for all editions, no edition need be specified and the reference entry may be omitted. If you wish to specify an edition, add it to the references and insert the year in [] following the number series.

Government Documents

Government documents may be cited in the normal author-date form. However, many have corporate authors whose names are too long to write out each time in the text. In this case include a short form or acronym in parentheses (or in brackets in parentheses) immediately after the first reference and use the acronym thereafter. For example, a first reference might be *U.S. International Trade Commission (1980, 12; hereafter USITC)*, and the second *USITC (1980, 16)*.

Legal citations. An in-text citation to a statute or court case should include the name of the statute or case (in italics except for *v.*) and the year:

(Budget and Impoundment Act 1975)

(*Baker* v. *Carr* 1962)

References

Citations direct attention to the more detailed references, which provide complete source information to aid further research. Include no reference that is not actually cited.

The examples that follow show proper forms for common kinds of references. All references are listed alphabetically by author (15.87). Give the full first name instead of an initial unless the author is widely known by the first initials. All lines are double-spaced and all after the first in an entry are indented. When there are several works by the same author, place them in chronological order, with the earliest publication first, repeating the name of the author with each new entry. This differs slightly from *CMS* 15.90.

Books

One author

Kessel, John H. 1968. *The Goldwater Coalition: Republican Strategies in 1964*. Indianapolis: Bobbs-Merrill.

The author's name and date—the bits of information in the citation—appear first, followed by the book title, place of publication, and publisher (16.5). If the city is well known, there is no need to identify the state (or DC) (16.70-71). Use postal acronyms for states (*MA, OH*). Chapter and page numbers should be in the citations, not the references.

Two authors (16.15)

Sorauf, Frank J., and Paul Allen Beck. 1988. *Party Politics in America*. 6th ed. Glenview, IL: Scott, Foresman.

The surname comes first for the initial author only, and a comma separates the names.

Edited collection (16.24)

> Ball, Terence, James Farr, and Russell L. Hanson, eds. 1988. *Political Innovation and Conceptual Change.* New York: Cambridge University Press.

Chapter in multiauthor collection (16.53)

> Hermann, Margaret G. 1984. "Personality and Foreign Policy Decision Making: A Study of Fifty-Three Heads of Government." In *Foreign Policy Decision Making*, ed. Donald A. Sylvan and Steve Chan. New York: Praeger.

The chapter title takes headline capitalization and quotation marks. No page numbers for the chapter are necessary. If the author and the editor are the same person, repeat the name:

> Crotty, William J. 1968. "The Party Organization and Its Activists." In *Approaches to the Study of Party Organization*, ed. William J. Crotty. Boston: Allyn & Bacon.

Do not use a form analogous to this one for a chapter in a single-author book. Rather, indicate the whole book and specify the chapter in the citation.

Multivolume work (16.41-43)

> Foucault, Michel. 1980. *The History of Sexuality.* 2 vols. Trans. Robert Hurley. New York: Vintage Books.

> Foucault, Michel. 1980. *The Use of Pleasure.* Vol. 2 of *The History of Sexuality.* Trans. Robert Hurley. New York: Vintage Books.

If a cited work consists of more than one volume, give the number of volumes after the title. If the cited work is just one volume in a set, give its volume number after the title, followed by the more general title.

Publisher's names (16.76-77). *The* and *Inc.* may be omitted from publisher names as may *Press* (except for *University Press*), *Publisher*, and *Company*.

Journal Articles

Journal with continuous pagination for each volume

> Aldrich, John H. 1980. "A Dynamic Model of Presidential Nomination Campaigns." *American Political Science Review* 74:651-69.

The article title takes headline capitalization regardless of how it was handled in the actual journal. Allow no space between the colon and the page numbers (16.107).

Journal in which pagination begins anew with each issue (infrequent) (16.105)

> Bronfenbrenner, Martin. 1985. "Early American Leaders—Institutional and Critical Traditions." *American Economic Review* 75(6): 13-27.

Put the issue number in parentheses and allow one space between the colon and the pages.

Forthcoming work (16.95)

> Jacoby, William G. N.d. "Ideology and Popular Culture." *American Political Science Review*. Forthcoming.

Unpublished Works

Should any unpublished work have a sewn or glued binding, the title should take italics, like a book; otherwise, quotes.

Dissertation or thesis (16.128-29)

> Munger, Frank James. 1955. "Two-Party Politics in the State of Indiana." Ph.D. diss. [or *Masters thesis*.] Harvard University.

Paper presented at a meeting (16.130)

> Mefford, Dwain, and Brian Ripley. 1987. "The Cognitive Foundation of Regime Theory." Presented at the annual meeting of the American Political Science Association, Chicago.

Manuscript in author's possession (16.131)

> Banks, Jeffrey S., and George Bordes. 1987. "Voting Games, Indifference, and Consistent Sequential Choice Rules." University of Rochester. Typescript.

Identify the material form that you used (*typescript, mimeo, photocopy*, etc.) and the institution (e.g., university) with which the author is affiliated.

Older Works (16.55-58)

Reprint editions. Both the original date (in []) and the reprint date should be given; then publication information for the reprint should follow, with the word *Reprint* included:

> Marx, Karl, and Friedrich Engels. [1933] 1964. *The Communist Manifesto*. Reprint. New York: Monthly Review Press.

Modern editions of classics

> Burke, Edmund. 1987. *Reflections on the Revolution in France*. Ed. J.G.A. Pocock. Indianapolis: Hackett.

> Madison, James, Alexander Hamilton, and John Jay. 1966. *Federalist Papers*. Ed. Roy P. Fairfield. Garden City, NY: Anchor Books.

No reference is necessary if you prefer not to specify a particular edition, provided the work has short, numbered sections to replace page numbers in the citation.

Government Documents

The method of referring to government documents varies but some of the more common in political science follow. For more information see, first, *CMS* 16.141-75, then Kate L. Turabian, *A Manual for Writers of Term Papers, Theses, and Dissertations*, 5th ed. (Chicago: University of Chicago Press, 1987), 12.1-21.

Congressional reports and documents. In general, congressional reports and documents require the corporate author, date, committee (if known), title, Congress, session, and document or report number.

> U.S. Congress. 1941. *Declarations of a State of War with Japan, Germany, and Italy*. 77th Cong., 1st sess. S. Doc. 148.

Congressional debates. Use *Congressional Record*, date, Congress, session, volume, and part. The publisher (Government Printing Office) need not be named.

> *Congressional Record*. 1966. 89th Cong., 2d sess. Vol. 112, pt. 16.

Executive department documents. Supply corporate author, date, title, serial number, and publisher.

> U.S. International Trade Commission. 1978. *The History and Current Status of Multifiber Arrangement*. Document no. 850. Washington: USITC, January.

If the author and publisher are the same, repeat the name or use an acronym.

Statutes

> National Environmental Policy Act of 1969, Pub. L. No. 91-190, sec. 102, 83 Stat. 852 (1970).

Legal references. List full bibliographic information for court cases in the references. (This differs from *CMS*.) Give the case, year, volume, source, page on which the case begins, and (in parentheses) district of any lower federal court. If possible use *U.S.*

Reports for Supreme Court decisions rather than *Lawyer's Edition* or *Supreme Court Reporter*.

> *Baker* v. *Carr*. 1961. 369 U.S. 86.

> *Lessard* v. *Schmidt*. 1972. 349 F. Supp. 1078 (E.D. Wisc.).

Early in the Supreme Court's history, cases were identified by the recording clerk's name rather than a source title:

> *Marbury* v. *Madison*. 1803. 1 Cranch 137.

English Translations

> Duverger, Maurice. 1954. *Political Parties*. Trans. Barbara and Robert North. New York: Wiley.

Sources in Foreign Languages

Translate titles of books and articles in [] after the foreign title; if only the English translation is given, identify the original language in [] after the title. Do not translate the names of periodicals. For foreign language titles capitalize only the first word and any proper nouns occurring in it, except for German, in which all common nouns are also capitalized:

> Miyamoto, Yoshio. 1942. *Hoso to kokka* [Broadcasting and the national defense state]. Tokyo: Nihon hoso shuppan kyokai.

> Miyamoto, Yoshio. 1942. *Broadcasting and the National Defense State* [in Japanese]. Tokyo: Nihon hoso shuppan kyokai.

(For more information on foreign language sources, see *CMS* 9.1-138, 16.38-40, 16.121-23, and 17.22.)

Magazine Articles

References to popular magazines require only the author, year, article title, magazine title, month, and day (for a weekly or bimonthly) (16.124-25).

> Prufer, Olaf. 1964. "The Hopewell Cult." *Scientific American*, December, 90-102.

Television and Radio Programs

Material presented in news broadcasts or documentaries should be referenced by broadcaster's name, year, title of show, and date:

> National Public Radio. 1984. "All Things Considered," 10 September.

NOTES

Notes are for presenting explanatory material and should be used sparingly.

All notes should be double-spaced consecutively at the end of the article (2.21). An acknowledgment note, without an asterisk or number, may be placed above the first numbered note (15.71). Please do not thank anonymous reviewers or the journal editor.

The corresponding note numbers in the text should be typed in superscript, preferably at the end of a sentence and at least at the end of a clause (15.40). The note number should follow end punctuation (except a dash) and be placed outside a closing parenthesis (15.39).

Information on citations of newspaper articles, interviews, and personal communications should be included in the notes, not the references.

Interviews and Personal Communications

These are usually best indicated in the text or in a note. Give the name of the person, the means of communication (*telephone conversation, personal correspondence, interview*, etc.), and the date and place (if appropriate) (17.61).

Newspaper Articles

Include the author's name (unless anonymous), title of article, title of paper, day, month, year, and section if relevant. Do not give page numbers unless you also give the edition (e.g., *eastern edition*) (17.57-58).

> Daniel F. Cuff, "Forging a New Shape for Steel," *New York Times*, 26 May 1985, sec. F.

Appendixes

If your article draws on data not documented in standard sources or in the text of the article, an appendix describing these data may be necessary. For example, with respect to survey data, you might wish to include such things as a description of the sample, including a definition of the geographical area and details about how the sample was drawn to permit replication; the response rate (for quota designs, the number of refusals); and the exact wording of survey questions.

This revision of the *American Political Science Association Style Manual* was prepared by Jean P. Kelly, Michael K. Lane, and Susan C. Angel.

Additional copies of the manual can be obtained through the American Political Science Association, 1527 New Hampshire Avenue NW, Washington, DC 20036.